AA004027

COGNTIVE 2023

The Fifteenth International Conference on Advanced Cognitive Technologies and Applications

June 26 - 30, 2023

Nice, France

COGNITIVE 2023 Editors

Ricardo Ron-Angevin, University of Málaga, Spain

Printed from e-media with permission by:

Curran Associates, Inc.
57 Morehouse Lane
Red Hook, NY 12571

CURRAN ASSOCIATES INC.
proceedings.com

Some format issues inherent in the e-media version may also appear in this print version.

International Academy, Research, and Industry Association (IARIA)
412 Derby Way
Wilmington, DE 19810

Phone: (408) 893-6407
Fax: (408) 527-6351

petre@iaria.org

Additional copies of this publication are available from:

Curran Associates, Inc.
57 Morehouse Lane
Red Hook, NY 12571 USA
Phone: 845-758-0400
Fax: 845-758-2633
Email: curran@proceedings.com
Web: www.proceedings.com

Table of Contents

COGNITIVE 2023

Forward

The Fifteenth International Conference on Advanced Cognitive Technologies and Applications (COGNITIVE 2023), held on June 26 - 30, 2023, targeted advanced concepts, solutions and applications of artificial intelligence, knowledge processing, agents, as key-players, and autonomy as manifestation of self-organized entities and systems. The advances in applying ontology and semantics concepts, web-oriented agents, ambient intelligence, and coordination between autonomous entities led to different solutions on knowledge discovery, learning, and social solutions.

The conference had the following tracks:

- Brain information processing and informatics
- Artificial intelligence and cognition
- Agent-based adaptive systems
- Applications
- Autonomous systems and autonomy-oriented computing
- Hot topics on cognitive science

Similar to the previous edition, this event attracted excellent contributions and active participation from all over the world. We were very pleased to receive top quality contributions.

We take here the opportunity to warmly thank all the members of the COGNITIVE 2023 technical program committee, as well as the numerous reviewers. The creation of such a high quality conference program would not have been possible without their involvement. We also kindly thank all the authors that dedicated much of their time and effort to contribute to COGNITIVE 2023. We truly believe that, thanks to all these efforts, the final conference program consisted of top quality contributions.

Also, this event could not have been a reality without the support of many individuals, organizations and sponsors. We also gratefully thank the members of the COGNITIVE 2023 organizing committee for their help in handling the logistics and for their work that made this professional meeting a success.

We hope COGNITIVE 2023 was a successful international forum for the exchange of ideas and results between academia and industry and to promote further progress in the area of cognitive technologies and applications. We also hope that Nice provided a pleasant environment during the conference and everyone saved some time to enjoy enjoy this beautiful city.

COGNITIVE 2023 General Chair

Jaime Lloret Mauri, Universitat Politecnica de Valencia, Spain

COGNITIVE 2023 Steering Committee

Charlotte Sennersten, CSIRO Mineral Resources, Australia
Jayfus Tucker Doswell, The Juxtopia Group, Inc., USA
Roberto Saracco, IEEE New Initiative Committee Chair, Italy
Thomas Ågotnes, University of Bergen, Norway
Muneo Kitajima, Nagaoka University of Technology (Emeritus), Japan

COGNITIVE 2023 Publicity Chair

José Miguel Jiménez, Universitat Politecnica de Valencia, Spain
Sandra Viciano Tudela, Universitat Politecnica de Valencia, Spain

COGNITIVE 2023

Committee

COGNITIVE 2023 General Chair

Jaime Lloret Mauri, Universitat Politecnica de Valencia, Spain

COGNITIVE 2023 Steering Committee

Charlotte Sennersten, CSIRO Mineral Resources, Australia
Jayfus Tucker Doswell, The Juxtopia Group, Inc., USA
Roberto Saracco, IEEE New Initiative Committee Chair, Italy
Thomas Ågotnes, University of Bergen, Norway
Muneo Kitajima, Nagaoka University of Technology (Emeritus), Japan

COGNITIVE 2023 Publicity Chair

José Miguel Jiménez, Universitat Politecnica de Valencia, Spain
Sandra Viciano Tudela, Universitat Politecnica de Valencia, Spain

COGNITIVE 2023 Technical Program Committee

Witold Abramowicz, University of Economics and Business, Poland
Thomas Agotnes, University of Bergen, Norway
Vered Aharonson, University of the Witwatersrand, Johannesburg, South Africa
Thangarajah Akilan, Lakehead University, Canada
Luis Alfredo Moctezuma, Norwegian University of Science and Technology, Trondheim, Norway
Piotr Artiemjew, University of Warmia and Masuria in Olsztyn, Poland
Divya B, SSNCE, India
Petr Berka, University of Economics, Prague, Czech Republic
Ateet Bhalla, Independent Consultant, India
Mahdi Bidar, University of Regina, Canada
Guy Andre Boy, CentraleSupélec, LGI, Paris Saclay University / ESTIA Institute of Technology, France
Dilyana Budakova, Technical University of Sofia - Branch Plovdiv, Bulgaria
Valerie Camps, Paul Sabatier University - IRIT, Toulouse, France
Yaser Chaaban, Leibniz University of Hanover, Germany
Olga Chernavskaya, P. N. Lebeved Physical Institute, Moscow, Russia
Helder Coelho, Universidade de Lisboa, Portugal
Igor Val Danilov, Academic Center for Coherent Intelligence, Latvia
Angel P. del Pobil, Jaume I University, Spain
Soumyabrata Dev, University College Dublin, Ireland
Jerome Dinet, University of Lorraine, France
Serena Doria, Università degli Studi G. d'Annunzio Chieti e Pescara, Italy

Piero Dominici, University of Perugia, Italy
Jayfus Tucker Doswell, The Juxtopia Group, Inc., USA
António Dourado, University of Coimbra, Portugal
Birgitta Dresp-Langley, Centre National de la Recherche Scientifique (CNRS) | ICube Lab, CNRS - University of Strasbourg, France
Mounîm A. El Yacoubi, Telecom SudParis, France
Fernanda M. Eliott, Noyce Science Center - Grinnell College, USA
Mauro Gaggero, National Research Council of Italy, Italy
Foteini Grivokostopoulou, University of Patras, Greece
Grace Grothaus, University of California San Diego, USA
António Guilherme Correia, INESC TEC / University of Trás-os-Montes e Alto Douro, Vila Real, Portugal
Fikret Gürgen, Bogazici University, Turkey
Ioannis Hatzilygeroudis, University of Patras, Greece
Hironori Hiaishi, Ashikaga University, Japan
Michitaka Hirose, RCAST (Research Center for Advanced Science and Technology) - University of Tokyo, Japan
Tzung-Pei Hong, National University of Kaohsiung, Taiwan
Gahangir Hossain, West Texas A&M University, USA
Md. Sirajul Islam, Visva-Bharati University, Santiniketan, India
Makoto Itoh, University of Tsukuba, Japan
Xinghua Jia, ULC Robotics, USA
Yasushi Kambayashi. Nippon Institute of Technology, Japan
Ryotaro Kamimura, Tokai University, Japan
Fakhri Karray, University of Waterloo, Canada
Jozef Kelemen, Silesian University, Czech Republic
Muneo Kitajima, Nagaoka University of Technology, Japan
Joao E. Kogler Jr., Polytechnic School of Engineering of University of Sao Paulo, Brazil
Damir Krstinić, University of Split, Croatia
Miroslav Kulich, Czech Technical University in Prague, Czech Republic
Leonardo Lana de Carvalho, Universidade Federal dos Vales do Jequitinhonha e Mucuri - UFVJM, Brazil
Nathan Lau, Virginia Tech, USA
Hakim Lounis, UQAM, Canada
Prabhat Mahanti, University of New Brunswick, Canada
Wajahat Mahmood Qazi, COMSATS University Islamabad, Lahore, Pakistan
Giuseppe Mangioni, DIEEI - University of Catania, Italy
Ardavan S. Nobandegani, McGill University, Montreal, Canada
Yoshimasa Ohmoto, Shizuoka University, Japan
Andrew J. Parkes, University of Nottingham, UK
Elaheh Pourabbas, National Research Council of Italy (CNR), Italy
J. Javier Rainer Granados, Universidad Internacional de la Rioja, Spain
Om Prakash Rishi, University of Kota, India
Paul Rosero, Universidad de Salamanca, Spain / Universidad Técnica del Norte, Ecuador
Alexandr Ryjov, Lomonosov Moscow State University | Russian Presidential Academy of National Economy and Public Administration, Russia
José Santos Reyes, University of A Coruña, Spain
Abdel-Badeeh M. Salem, Ain Shams University, Cairo, Egypt
Roberto Saracco, IEEE New Initiative Committee, Italy
Razieh Saremi, Stevens Institute of Technology, USA

Copyright Information

Art and Brain with Kazuo Takiguchi

– Revealing the Meme Structure from the Process of Creating Traditional Crafts –

Muneo Kitajima
Nagaoka University of Technology
Nagaoka, Niigata, Japan
Email: mkitajima@kjs.nagaokaut.ac.jp

Makoto Toyota
T-Method
Chiba, Japan
Email: pubmtoyota@mac.com

Jérôme Dinet
Université de Lorraine
Nancy, France
Email: jerome.dinet@univ-lorraine.fr

***Abstract*— What factors make traditional art what it is? This paper attempts to answer this question through an analysis from the cognitive science perspective. The subject of the study is Japanese traditional crafts. We believe that the process of artwork production is formed as a result of the interaction between the individual behavioral ecology of the artist and the collective behavioral ecology surrounding them, and attempt to analyze it using a functional brain model. This study aims to elucidate memes that interface the Perceptual, Cognitive, and Motor (PCM) processes that artists employ while creating artworks with the individual and collective behavioral ecologies that are used in these processes. This study focuses on the artwork production process of Kazuo Takiguchi, a leading Japanese ceramic artist. In elucidating the processes, Model Human Processor with Realtime Constraints (MHP/RT), cognitive architecture that can simulate human behavioral processes by means of PCM processes and Multi-Dimensional Memory Frames (MDMFs) that represent memes, and Cognitive Chrono-Ethnography (CCE), a survey method to understand the characteristics of behaviors expressed on the basis of these processes are employed. The CCE results revealed that the collective behavioral ecology, which contains the individual production experience of each artist folded into the individual behavioral ecology of the artist, and the skill acquisition of the production area formed over a long time, enables the artist to unconsciously imagine and meditate on the production process results, working on the production itself and on the firing and glazing process that bring irreversible changes to the production, to predict with accuracy, and to consciously evaluate the actual results.**

Keywords—Traditional arts; Inheritance; CCE; MHP/RT; Meme.

I. Introduction

A. Objective: A Meme Perspective on Traditional Arts

In the modern era, information worldwide is interconnected, and modern educational systems are widespread. Historically, such a situation was unusual. In fact, in the past, each region had its own unique collective behavioral ecology, formed over a long period of time while adapting to the local climate. The generated collective behavioral ecology formed region-specific memes, which have become the basis for individual behavioral ecologies today. In other words, the natural and spiritual climates are reflected in the collective behavioral ecology, which in turn is reflected in the individual behavioral ecology through memes.

This paper focuses on traditional arts, which are creative activities rooted in the local community and developed as traditions in a collective behavioral ecology, and describe the process by which they were established and the environmental conditions that enabled them to continue. An individual's artistic disposition belongs to their individual behavioral ecology and is expressed through a structured meme that is formed on the brain's parallel distributed memory structure [1] and the activities that utilize them [2][3]. Therefore, the focus of this study will be to answer the following research questions:

RQ-1 What does the structured meme look like?
RQ-2 How is it formed?
RQ-3 What are the environmental conditions that allow its formation to continue?
RQ-4 How are the artistic activities performed on it?

B. Subject: Japanese Traditional Crafts "Ceramics"

Some of the Japanese traditional crafts have been handed down to recent times. This study focuses on Japanese ceramics, a traditional art form with a strong regional flavor, as the subject of study. The basis of the modern Japanese cultural genealogy is represented by the expression "wabi and sabi," which was systematized around the tea ceremony from the Azuchi-Momoyama period (1568 – 1598 or 1600) to the early Edo period (after 1603) (see e.g., [4][5]). During the next 300 years of the stable Edo period (1603 – 1868), ceramics became firmly established as the foundation of Japanese culture.

From the cognitive science perspective, the behavior of ceramic artists in creating ceramics can be captured in the four bands of Newell's time scale of human action [6, Fig. 3-3]. The four bands are biological (B-band), cognitive (C-band), rational(R-band), and social bands (S-band), corresponding to human activities in the time rages of $10^{-4} \sim 10^{-2}$, $10^{-1} \sim 10^{1}$, $10^{2} \sim 10^{4}$, and $10^{5} \sim 10^{7}$ in seconds, respectively. The actions in each of these bands are continuously passed down through generations in the environment in which the artwork is created. However, unpredictable changes in the environment, trigger discontinuous leaps, and the continuously inheritable behavior survives in a different form.

Major ceramic production centers are scattered throughout Japan. It is one of them. Kyoto is the center of a culture represented by the tea ceremony, and a strong creative orientation has long existed here. The purpose of this study is to understand the characteristics of inheritance in Japanese traditional arts, focusing on the RQs mentioned above.

C. Organization of This Paper

This paper is organized as follows. In Section II, we will give an overview of traditional art activities and look at the brain functions that make them possible. Then, the six steps of CCE, a method for understanding collective and individual behavioral ecology involved in artistic activities, are presented. In Section III, we apply the CCE explained in the previous section to a famous Japanese ceramic artist, Kazuo Takiguchi, and attempt to understand the activity of ceramic art from a cognitive science perspective. In Section IV, we conclude the paper by presenting the core of inherited ceramic activities.

II. Traditional Art Activities and Memes

A. Imagination, Meditation, and Memes in Ceramics

Artifacts for daily use in each region are made from materials available there. The materials reflect the constraints of the *natural climate* unique to the region. As production activities continue in that environment, the techniques for making artifacts progress, and production methods and works suited to the natural climate are established. Technological progress in the production of daily necessities is supported by the ability to imagine the "desired state" and the path to it. Imagination can be paraphrased as the ability to design and imagine how one would like things to be. The source of imagination is the parallel and distributed memory in the brain [1], which makes it possible to imagine a variety of desired states and explore a vast amount of pathways from the current state to that state.

The same process of using one's imagination to create everyday objects can be used to "explore beauty." The *spiritual climate* has a great influence on this process. The ceramics initially existed as an aminist craft of Shinto shrines, but its artistry was further enhanced by the influence of the tea ceremony, a representative of traditional Japanese arts that formed the basis of the Japanese aesthetic system under the strong influence of Zen Buddhism. The influence of the spiritual climate on ceramics is evident here. In the activity of "exploring beauty," the "desired state" is much more abstract compared to the case of producing daily necessities. Therefore, the activity of searching for a quasi-stable activation pattern by spreading activation inside the memory network through "meditation," in which the target state does not exist, and "imagination," in which the target state does exist, requires a long time. Not only that, it also requires a lot of experience to form a memory network for imagining and meditating, which is a necessary condition for performing such activities.

The memory network is developed in the form of a Multi-dimensional Memory Frame (MDMF) [7, Fig. 3] by projecting Newell's human behavioral bandwidth [6, Fig. 3-3]. MDMF has the function of providing the foundation for the execution of $M \otimes N$ mapping, a cognitive process that maps M-dimensional perceptual information input to humans from the environment via sensory organs to N-dimensional motor information output to the environment via effectors.

The memes that exist between the individual and the collective behavioral ecologies and interface between the two play a major role in how the behaviors in the respective time bands are generated. There exist three types of memes: action-level, behavior-level, and culture-level memes. All of them are acquired through imitation, and their complexity increases in this order. The B- and C-bands are for the activities using action-level memes, the R-band is for the activities using behavior-level memes, and the S-band is for the activities using culture-level memes [2, Fig. 5].

The "exploration of beauty" process that the ceramic artist performs can be seen as the processes of "imagination and/or meditation" practiced through $M \otimes N$ mapping, using memes that interface the collective and individual behavioral ecology.

B. Cognitive Chrono-Ethnography (CCE)

This study attempts to understand the individual behavioral ecology of artists by addressing the aforementioned RQs. In doing so, we will apply CCE [8], a method for investigating and analyzing behavioral ecology. In CCE, we first identify behaviors of interest that occur in the target domain. Second, we perform brain simulations for those behaviors based on a cognitive architecture that can handle perceptual, cognitive, motor, and memory processes in a unified manner. We use the Model Human Processor with Realtime Constraints (MHP/RT) [8][9][10] for this purpose. Finally we identify the parameters that characterize the behavior and clarify the relationship between the values taken by the parameters and the behavior expressed.

CCE consists of six steps. Below is a brief overview of each step of the CCE and how each step relates to the RQs.

1) CCE-Step 1 – Phenomenological Observations for Dealing with RQ-2 and RQ-3: In traditional art activities, the individual behavioral ecology is an imaginative and meditative activity for drawing a path to a desired state expressed in abstract form, while the collective behavioral ecology encompasses the individual behavioral ecology over several generations. The collective behavioral ecology contains an "education and training system" constrained by the existence of the natural and spiritual climate of the region. In ancient times, education conducted within a professional group was incorporated into the collective behavioral ecology as a form of family inheritance or apprenticeship. The RQs can be addressed by clarifying the educational constraint's parameters and educational content parameters to understand how the practice and inheritance of characteristic techniques in specific traditional arts are carried out in the field through field observations and documents reporting on them. More details on this are given in Section III-A.

This study focuses on ceramics as a specific traditional art form, this study will focus on. In this study, based on the idea that a unique person recognized as a ceramic artist should be an instance of a combination of values of characteristic parameters, we will observe the activities of such an artist and interview him to understand how the practice and inheritance of characteristic techniques in ceramic art are carried out. More details on this are given in Section III-B.

2) CCE-Step 2 – Matching with Brain Properties: For an art form to be called "traditional," it must have inherited techniques essential to the creative practice of that art form (e.g., ceramics) through generations. The inheritance of techniques in traditional Japanese arts is done through the practice of "watching and stealing work." The results obtained by "watching and stealing work" appear as imaginative and meditative activities that are concretely put into practice. These activities are simulated by the cognitive architecture MHP/RT. More details on this are given in Section III-C.

3) CCE-Step 3 – Structural Modeling: The performance of imagination and meditation activities can be characterized as the "variety" and "coverage" of $M \otimes N$ mappings from perception to motion. For these practices to take place, "what is stolen" must be present in the visible range. Since traditions are unique to a region, it is a prerequisite that the people who maintain them have been born and raised in the region. The availability of information, the diversity and coverage of $M \otimes N$ mappings, and the relationship between feedforward and feedback processes become the set of parameters that characterize an individual's behavioral ecology. More details on this are given in Section III-D.

4) CCE-Step 4 – Formulation of the CCE Survey Methodology: In a typical CCE survey, screening is conducted using a questionnaire that includes the values of a set of parameters in the questions for selecting an elite sample. In the ceramic survey conducted in this study, we found "Kazuo Takiguchi" as a subject that can be called a super elite sample with the characteristics of traditional art bearers and with whom we can see the entire sample in one example when we assume the parameter space set by CCE-Step one through three.

5) CCE-Step 5 – Conduct CCE Survey: Therefore, focusing on Kazuo Takiguchi, we attempted to clarify the individual behavioral ecology, collective behavioral ecology, and memes.

6) CCE-Step 6 – Match against Characteristics for Dealing with RQ-1 and RQ-4: By observing the activities of Kazuo Takiguchi, specific examples of imaginative and meditative activities can be obtained when a person, represented by the parameter value combinations, performs creative activities using memes at the site. This will validate the model constructed in CCE-Step 3.

III. Elucidating Memes with CCE

A. CCE-Step 1-1: Field Observation

1) Collective Behavioral Ecology as a Foundation for Traditional Arts: Emmanuel Todd [11] lists the following as inherited collective memes: 1) Group form, 2) The nature of authority to choose the group's behavior, and 3) The implicitly practiced action selection rules as a method for the inheritance of the group. These are inherited as collective memes, and groups are managed and developed accordingly. Here, what and how is taught, RQ-2, in the form of inherited, RQ-3, is encapsulated. Therefore, different collective memes develop in different ways.

The culture of a group is part of the collective memes. Therefore, in culture, each group possesses its own distinctive way of passing on its manufacturing methods and techniques that are unique to the group and distinguishable from those of other groups. Behind this is the existence of evaluation criteria for cultural products that are unique to that culture.

The collective memes that have been nurtured as a Japanese tradition has become effective in the acquisition of individual skills. The reality of this effectiveness can be characterized as follows. The collective and individual behavioral ecology develop by influencing each other in an interdependent relationship in which the individual, as a member of the group, influences the formation of the collective behavioral ecology and thus, influences the formation of the individual memes. This interdependence determines the forms that make it possible to maintain, develop, and inherit traditions – RQ-3.

Individual behavioral ecology can be viewed as action-level, behavior-level, and cultural-level memes. The development of perception and movement leads to the development of the action and behavior level memes. The development process is unique to each individual's developmental environment and is often acquired through trial and error based on "imitation."

The acquired memes are incorporated into the collective behavioral ecology of the group to which they belong. This is effective for the next creative activity within the group. The incorporation of diverse experiences through trial and error into the collective behavioral ecology gives individuals in the group the opportunity to "imitate" them and become the source of new innovations. In the traditional arts, memes are acquired and utilized in the creative activities of the entire field, functioning as a cyclical system of inheritance and continuity. This defines the characteristics of the collective behavioral ecology of the group – RQ-2 and RQ-3.

2) Japanese Traditional Art, "Ceramic Art": In this study, "ceramics" is taken up as a traditional Japanese art form. It is the art of making ceramics by molding clay and firing it at high temperatures. In ceramics, the process consists of imaging the desired form of the object, molding the clay base into the desired form, applying a glassy coating, heating it in a kiln to increase strength, hardening, and fixing the form. It is the activity to be imitated (individual behavioral ecology) that is handed down, and the environment in which imitation is practiced (collective behavioral ecology) enables the inheritance of the imitated activity. The ceramic art process is described below.

a) Master Planning: The first step in ceramic art is to solidify the image of the form.

b) Modeling: It is necessary to remove air from the clay. This process is called "degassing," and is done either by using a vacuum kneader or by hand. After the clay has been degassed and kneaded, it is dried in preparation for firing. There are several stages of drying. At the stage where the clay has a moisture content of approximately 15%, the clay is very firm and not very plastic. Cutting, attaching handles, etc. are often done at this stage. When the moisture content is nearly 0%, the clay is very brittle and easily broken. Before the clay is formed, something can be kneaded into it to create the desired effect in the ware.

TABLE I. STEPS IN THE PRODUCTION OF ARTWORKS OF YUDAI AND MUDAI. THE STEPS INDICATED IN ∗ ARE THE STEPS COMMON TO BOTH WORKS

	YUDAI	MUDAI
Artwork	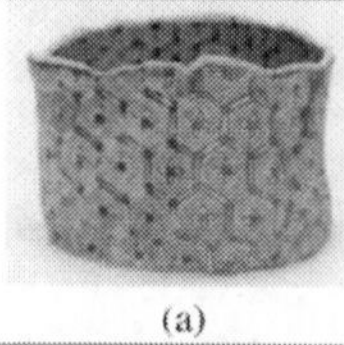 (a)	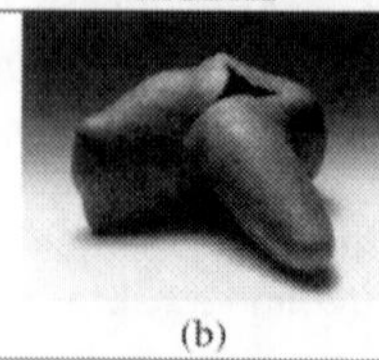 (b)
Work Step	For YUDAI	For MUDAI
Master-Planning	∗ Decide on the rough image of the work • Decide on the specific title of the work • Decide on the image of the work that adequately represents the title • Decide on the number of parts that comprise the work ∗ Decide on the material / Decide on the size	∗ Decide on the rough image of the work ∗ Decide on the material / Decide on the size
Natural-Modeling		• Form the overall shape of a plate-like material by effectively utilizing the gravity field
Modeling	• Create the model you have in mind (if the modeling consists of multiple parts, make that number of parts) with the consideration that it will not break during unglazed-firing ∗ Consider a plan for unglazed-firing	• Modify the overall shape of the foundation according to one's own inspiration to create the final form ∗ Consider a plan for unglazed-firing
Unglazed-Firing	∗ Fire in a kiln according to the unglazed firing plan	∗ Fire in a kiln according to the unglazed firing plan
⇒ End		
Coloring *repeat*	• Select a glaze that matches the finished image of the work • Glaze it • Considering glazed firing plan .	
Glazed-Firing	• Fire in kiln according to glaze firing plan	
⇒ End		
Glazing *repeat*	∗ Choose a glaze that is matched to the surface texture of the piece ∗ Glaze ∗ Consider a firing plan that suits the glaze	∗ Choose a glaze that is matched to the surface texture of the piece ∗ Glaze ∗ Consider a firing plan that suits the glaze
Main-Firing	∗ Fire based on the firing plan	∗ Fire based on the firing plan
⇒ End		

c) Unglazed-Firing: Firing brings about irreversible changes in the clay. Only after firing does the work become ceramic ware. In low-temperature firing, a change called sintering occurs, in which the coarse powders in the clay fuse with each other contact. For porcelain, where different materials are used and fired at higher temperatures, significant changes occur in the physical, chemical, and mineral properties of the constituents. In both cases, the purpose of firing is to permanently harden the ceramics. The firing method must be consistent with the materials used.

d) Glazing: Glaze is the glassy coating of a ceramic ware. Its main purpose is to decorate and protect. Glaze is applied by sprinkling solids or by spraying, dipping, pouring, or brushing on dilute mixtures of glaze and water. The color of the glaze can be very different before and after firing.

e) Main-Firing: The environmental air of the kiln during firing can affect the appearance of the finished product. An oxidizing environment causes oxidation reactions between the clay and glaze. A reducing environment deprives the clay and glaze surfaces of oxygen. This affects the appearance of the finished piece. By adjusting the kiln environment, complex effects can be produced in glazes.

B. CCE-Step 1-2: Observation of the Super Elite Sample

The second part of CCE-Step 1 takes the ceramics artist as a super elite sample, a singularity in the individual behavioral ecology of ceramics activity, and summarizes his ceramics activity as a structure of individual behavioral ecology. The super elite sample is the ceramic artist "Kazuo Takiguchi," who has been creating ceramics mainly in Kyoto, the center of traditional Japanese art, for a long time, sublimating imagination and meditation activities in ceramic production, and practicing perceptual and motor $M \otimes N$ mapping at a level that cannot be reached by ordinary people. We observed and interviewed him during the process of ceramic production. The results are shown in Table I.

1) Craft Artist "Kazuo Takiguchi": He is one of the leading contemporary ceramic artists in Japan, born in 1953 as the son of a tableware wholesaler in Gojozaka, a traditional ceramic production area in Kyoto. He studied briefly under Rokubei Kiyomizu VI (1901–1980) followed by a brief time under Kazuo Yagi (1918–1979). It was Yagi's aesthetic and focus on non-traditional, sculptural forms that made a lasting impact on him. Years later, he studied at the Royal College of Arts, London and graduated in 1992. Living overseas made him realize the important role the Japanese language played in his life and how it impacted his artwork. Since then, he has focused on words as a source of inspiration. He emphasizes that just as he is free to use language according to his own desires and needs, he endeavors to give each work a presence unique to itself. It is important to him that his works touch the viewers' hearts outside the context of functionality.

2) Description of Kazuo Takiguchi's Production Process: Kazuo Takiguchi has produced two very different groups of works, YUDAI and MUDAI, both extremely different in appearance. Examples of each of these works are shown in Table I. Table I also shows the working process of YUDAI and MUDAI according to the work processes described in Section III-A2.

The most important perception in making clay and creating works of art, especially MUDAI, is the tactile sense of the palm. The palm of the hand can be used to judge a wide variety of conditions, such as dampness/dryness, hardness, the state of the clay joints, and the resistance of the clay to breakage during drying and firing. Kazuo's sculpturing process is both complicated and highly creative. Using pulleys, he first flattens a slab of thinly pounded clay between 1/8-1/4 inches of thick and lays it in a canvas sheet. As shown in Figure 1, with the use of pulleys, he then hoists it and suspends it in the air, molding it into the amoebic form he wishes. After the clay body is dry enough to maintain its shape, he tears open a hole at the top. His ambitiously abstract forms have made him one of the standard-bearers of contemporary Japanese ceramics.

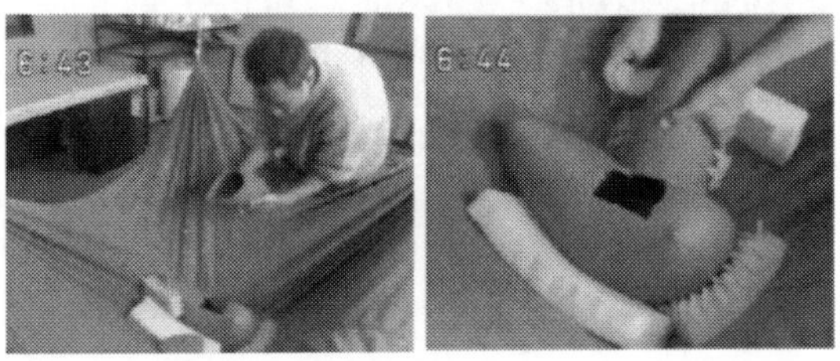

Figure 1. Natural modeling using a canvas sheet.

C. CCE-Step 2: Matching with Brain Properties

In this step, the results of the CCE-Step 1 survey are reviewed from the perspective of individual behavioral ecology. We will perform brain simulations assuming the action-level, behavior-level, and culture-level memes on the cognitive architecture to identify the way the brain works, in a way that best explains the results of the survey. That is, we identify critical parameters that characterize the behavioral ecology of individuals. Brain simulations are based on the cognitive architecture MHP/RT [8][9][10]. In the following, we will give an overview of MHP/RT, focusing on the part related to the identification of critical parameters.

1) Outline of MHP/RT: MHP/RT consists of two components. Figure 2 provides an overview of each component.

a) Perceptual-Cognitive-Motor (PCM) Processes: The first component comprises cyclic PCM processes (Figure 2, left). They execute a series of events in synchronous with changes in the external environment. The parallel distributed processing [1] for realizing these PCM processes is implemented as hierarchically organized bands introduced by Newell [6, Figure 3-3]. These bands are characterized by characteristic operation times, as mentioned in Section I, which are defined by associating relative times with individual PCM processes. Events occur by connecting what happens in a band to what happens in its adjacent band *non-linearly*. A mechanism is required to connect the events; MHP/RT suggests that this connection is provided by *the resonance mechanism* via the MDMFs.

b) Multi-dimensional Memory Frame (MDMF): The second component is the autonomous memory system consisting of five MDMFs, which are perception, motion, behavior, relation, and word MDMFs (Figure 2, right). The MDMFs store information associated with the corresponding autonomous processes defined in the PCM processes. The MDMFs are subservient to the PCM processes because they do not exist unless the PCM processes do.

A copy of MDMFs is shown in Figure 2. This indicates that the memory that has been constructed up to that point is used in the PCM processes. Since both the memory system and the PCM processes are autonomous systems, there is no relationship in which one system subordinates the other. Any active states in the autonomous memory can be used by other autonomous systems through "resonance." This is indicated by the symbol "•—•" in Figure 2.

c) Four Operation Modes: Humans interact with the external environment and select appropriate actions to achieve behavioral goals through a cycle of PCM processes. In MHP/RT, the action selection process is controlled by System 1 and System 2 of Two Minds [12]. These systems cooperate to link perception and movement, and the degree of cooperation depends on the state of the external environment with which the MHP/RT interacts. Table II shows the Four

TABLE II. FOUR OPERATION MODES OF MHP/RT AND THEIR RELATIONSHIP WITH THE FOUR BANDS IN THE TIME SCALE OF NEWELL'S HUMAN ACTION [6, FIGURE 3-3]

Synchronous Modes	
Mode 1:	System 1 driven mode *A single set of perceptual stimuli initiate feedforward processes at the B- and C-bands to act with occasional feedback from an upper band, i.e., C-, R-, or S-bands.*
Mode 2:	System 2 driven mode *A single set of perceptual stimuli initiate a feedback process at the C-band, and upon completion of the conscious action selection, the unconscious automatic feedforward process is activated at the B- and C-bands for action.*
Asynchronous Modes	
Mode 3:	In-phase autonomous activity mode *A set of perceptual stimuli initiate feedforward processes at the B- and C-bands with one and another intertwined occasional feedback processes from an upper band, i.e., C-, R-, or S-bands.*
Mode 4:	Heterophasic autonomous activity mode *Multiple threads of perceptual stimuli initiate respective feedforward processes at the B- and C-bands, some with no feedback and others with feedback from the upper bands, i.e., C-, R-, or S-bands.*

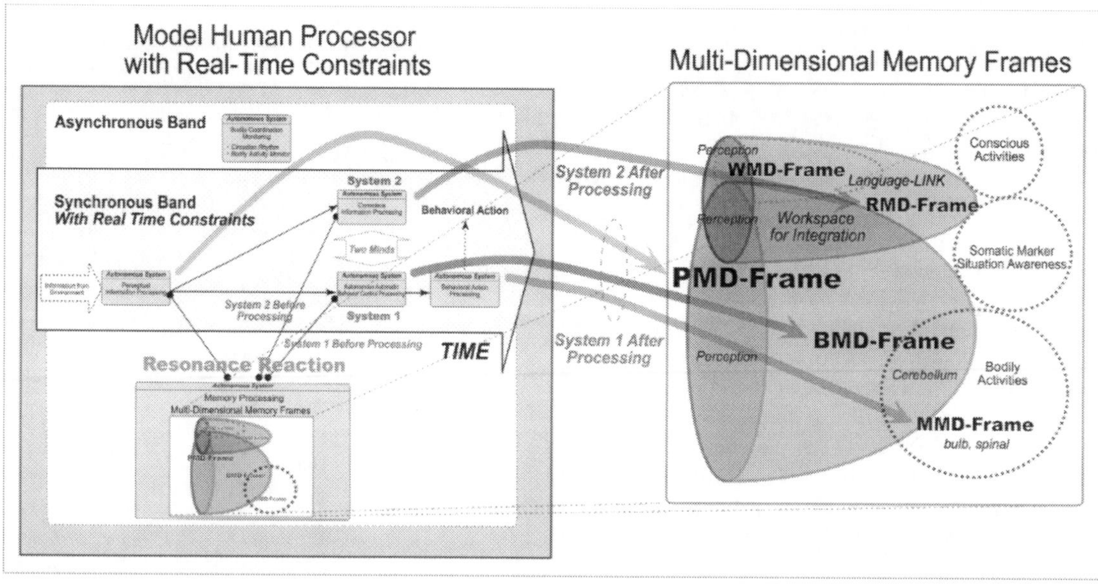

Figure 2. MHP/RT and Multi-dimensional Memory Frame [7, Figure 2].

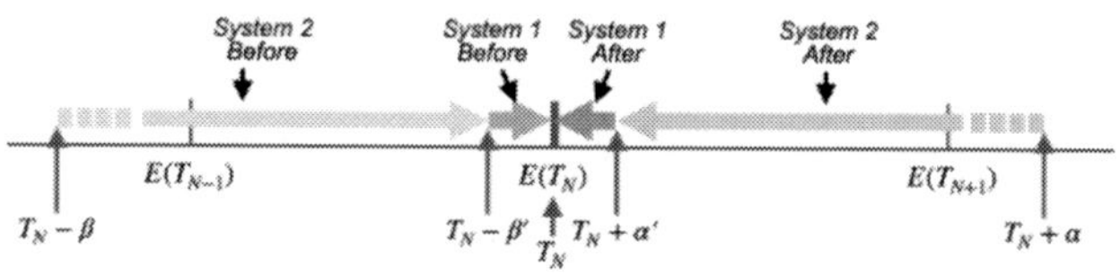

Figure 3. Four processing modes of MHP/RT.

Operation Modes characterized by the relationship between System 1 and System 2. There are synchronous and asynchronous modes. The ceramic work is performed primarily in the synchronous mode.

d) Four Processing Modes: The experience associated with an individual's activity is characterized by a series of events that are consciously recognized serially. Let $E(T_N)$ denote the event that occurred at time T_N. The experience is then defined as a series of events along the timeline as follows:

$$\cdots \rightarrow E(T_{N-1}) \rightarrow E(T_N) \rightarrow E(T_{N+1}) \rightarrow \cdots$$

Considering the way System 1 and System 2 are involved in individual events, four processing modes can be defined as shown in Figure 3.

Before the Event ($T < T_N$)

The event $E(T_N)$ that occurs at time T_N reflects the result of the resonance between MDMFs and the perceptual and cognitive systems during the time before T_N. The part of the system that resonates is indicated by •—• in the left diagram of Figure 2. $E(T_N)$ is generated by the activities of System 1 and System 2 in the time period before T_N. The different time bands of processing activities result in two processing modes before the event:

- **System-2-Before-Event-Mode:** In the time range of $T - \beta \le t < T - \beta'$, MHP/RT plans for future events to occur. There is enough time to think carefully.
- **System-1-Before-Event-Mode:** In the time range of $T - \beta' \le t < T$, the action selections smoothly generate the immediate event.

The minimum value of β' is $\sim$ 150msec, and β ranges from seconds to hours and months. In these two modes, the part of MDMFs activated through resonance in response to perceptual processing could resonate with System 1 and System 2 processing (Figure 2, left).

After the Event ($T > T_N$)

When event $E(T_N)$ occurs at time T_N, the result is stored. Actions occur by integrating the resonances that emerge through interacting with the environment prior to the event, and after the actions are taken, they are bundled and collected. The existing MDMFs are updated to reflect the results of $E(T_N)$ by the activities of System 1 and System 2 during the time period after T_N. This process is indicated by the arrows from each element of the PCM cycle shown in the upper left of Figure 2 to the MDMFs in the upper right. The different time bands of processing activities result in two processing modes after the event:

- **System-1-After-Event-Mode:** In the time range of $T < t \le T + \alpha'$, to perform better for the same event that may be encountered in the future, the connection between the incoming perceptual information and the output motor content is adjusted unconsciously.
- **System-2-After-Event-Mode:** In the time range of $T + \alpha' < t \le T + \alpha$, the event is reviewed and reflected upon. The results are stored and used in the next System-2-Before-Event-Mode before a similar event occurs.

The minimum value of α' is $\sim$ 150msec, and α ranges from seconds to months. In these two modes, action selection results for the event at T_N would be reflected in the network connections of the respective MDMFs (Figure 2, right).

2) MHP/RT Simulation of Each Ceramic Process: In this section, we present an MHP/RT simulation of the ceramic process shown in Table I, which is a summary derived from intensive interviews with Kazuo Takiguchi and observations of his work processes. We explain which of the four operation modes MHP/RT operates in, and what kind of processing is carried out regarding the four processing modes with a focus on the memory use represented by the MDMFs. Brief discussions for some work processes concerning the implication of the contents of simulated processes for the individual behavioral ecology of ceramic process follow.

a) Master-Planning: This work process consists of the following steps as shown in Table I.

1) Decide on the rough image of the work.
   – In the case of YUDAI, this step is accompanied by the following steps.
   a) Decide on the specific title of the work.
   b) Decide on the image of the work that adequately represents the title.
   c) Decide on the number of parts that comprise the work.
2) Decide on the material.
3) Decide on the size.

Steps 1, 2, and 3 for MUDAI and YUDAI, and a, b, c for YUDAI, is carried out in Mode 2 of MHP/RT shown in Table II. Each step is essentially a conscious decision-making process for accomplishing the purpose of that step, i.e., forming the rough image of the work, selecting the material, selecting the size, and so on. It starts with an initial idea followed by an evaluation-update cycle of the idea. It terminates when an idea is evaluated satisfactory for the purpose established.

The chart below will be used to schematically illustrate what is happening in each step in terms of the characteristic moments of the four processing modes, i.e., β, β', $*$, α', and α. At β, a conscious activity starts for the future event to be carried out at $*$ as a consciously recognizable event. At α, the event is consciously reflected. During the period of (β', α'), unconscious activities related with the event are carried out.

Each Step of Master-Planning in Mode 2

$$(\beta —— \beta' -*- \alpha' —— \alpha) \quad \textit{Repeat}$$

β: Consciously clarify the policy for updating the current idea.
β': Spread activation in the MDMFs.
$*$: Decide on an update for the current idea.
α': Organize activation in the MDMFs.
α: Consciously evaluate the updated idea.

Each step starts at β for performing conscious reasoning to elaborate the current idea, which could be the initial idea for the step or the updated idea of the previous evaluate-update cycle. The spreading activation within the MDMFs proceeds through a series of divergences starting at β', followed by the moment of decision on the updated idea at $*$, and the period for convergences terminating at α'. Afterward, the decision is evaluated at α. The events correspond to the moments when decisions on the rough image of the work, material, size, specific title, and so on, are obtained. This process is repeated until a satisfactory evaluation for the current idea is obtained. The result is "master plan of the work," which consists of a series of images that should appear in the P-MDMF as the results to be achieved in subsequent steps.

The content of the master plan of the work is affected by the extent to which activity is propagated within the MDMFs during the period leading up to it. The individual behavioral ecology of this work process is characterized by the richness of the MDMFs. These steps are carried out by initially placing seeds that represent the initial idea *consciously* in the P-MDMF that ultimately lead to a final decision by means of spreading activation in the MDMFs, which has been constructed through extensive $M \otimes N$ mapping experience; the updated ideas are obtained as activated patterns of the network in the MDMFs centered on P-MDMF. When accompanied by title setting as in the case of YUDAI, the center of *conscious* activity appears in the W-MDMF as well.

b) Natural-Modeling for MUDAI: In this process, the shape is created by modifying the material. The overall shape is formed by effectively utilizing the gravitational field operating on the plate-like material. The reasons for conforming to the gravitational field is to make it resistant during firing and to make maintaining the balance of the overall shape easy. Figure 1 are the photos from the process of natural modeling. The ceramic clay is placed on the suspended cloth to form the shape by utilizing the gravitational field (Figure 1, left). A cone-like piece is attached to the base while maintaining the overall balance (Figure 1, right). It takes a certain amount of time for the materials formed to reach equilibrium in the gravitational field. During that time, the laws of nature govern the change in shape. The Natural-Modeling for MUDAI is carried out solely by hand.

In this process, the state of the material is perceived primarily by sight and touch, and the material is formed into the final model defined by the master plan, by moving one's hands and fingers. Therefore, this process is simulated by MHP/RT's Mode 1, where action selections are carried out mainly by System 1 with timely interventions of System 2.

Natural-Modeling for MUDAI in Mode 1′

$$\beta - \beta' -*- \alpha' ———// ——— \alpha$$

β: Clarify the final modeling of the plate-like material and a candidate is placed in the P-MDMF.
β': Spread activation in the MDMFs.
$*$: Make a decision with the modeling and carry it out.
α': Organize activation in the MDMFs.
α: Evaluate the decision consciously.

At β, the final modeling is consciously clarified in the MDMFs. Then, a modeling candidate is placed in the P-MDMF for each piece of the work, followed by $M \otimes N$ mapping from there into the MDMFs to have the M-MDMF get activated, which specifies hands' movements for modeling. Unconscious $M \otimes N$ mapping is carried out during the period of $(\beta', *)$ for making decisions on the modeling and accomplishing it at $*$. After completion of modeling at $*$, the form changes according to the laws of nature.

After a certain amount of period shown by —//— , the result of the work will be evaluated at α by System 2. During the period $(*, \alpha)$, two things happen before the shape of the material is established at α as its equilibrium. The shape of material changes in the gravitational field due to the weight of the self, and simultaneously, the moisture content of the material gradually decreases and the material becomes harder and less deformable. There might exist discrepancies between the final modeling imagined at β and the resultant modeling obtained at α. By integrating the traces of spreading activation from β to $*$ for modeling and the evaluation result at α, the MDMFs, which can be used in the $M \otimes N$ mapping for the future Natural Modeling step, is updated. The four processing mode characterized by this pattern will be called Mode $1'$.

c) Modeling: The purpose of this step is to create the modeling manually that will not break in the next process, Unglazed-Firing. For MUDAI, the result of Natural Modeling is finalized. For YUDAI, the pieces are assembled together to accomplish the plan. At β, a candidate of modeling is placed consciously in the P-MDMF. Then, $M \otimes N$ mapping is carried out during the period of $(\beta', *)$ to obtain a candidate movement of hands in the M-MDMF at $*$ for creating the model defined in the master plan. During the period of $(*, \alpha')$, the result of candidate movement, which is virtual, plays the role of a seed in the P-MDMF to spread activation in the MDMFs, to make a judgement at α whether the final modeling defined in the master plan of the work would be obtained after the next step, Unglazed-Firing. This updating process is repeated until a satisfactory one is obtained. The satisfactory one is carried out at $*$, followed by conscious reflection of the work at α including what will be obtained after the next step, Unglazed-Firing. The satisfactory modeling is carried out at $*$ according to the active M-MDMF. The four processing mode characterized by this pattern will be called Mode $1''$.

Modeling in Mode $1''$

(β – β' ——//——*——//—— α'– α) *Repeat*

- β: Consciously think of the finished form of modeling.
- β': Spread activation in the MDMFs.
- $*$: Create a form as a candidate for the finished form of modeling.
- α': Organize activation in the MDMFs.
- α: Imagine the results of unglazed firing for the finished form of modeling.

d) Unglazed-Firing: Upon completion of Modeling, the result of the expected Unglazed-Firing process is activated in the P-MDMF. From there, the MDMFs involved in the Unglazed-Firing are also activated. The Unglazed-Firing plan appears as an activity pattern in the W-MDMF, R-MDMF, and B-MDMF. In these MDMFs, the activation patterns come from the P-MDMF that resonates with the results of Modeling, providing the basis for conscious reasoning by System 2. Firing is a process in which heating the clay causes irreversible changes in the physical, chemical, and mineralogical properties of the constituents, just as gravity works in Natural-Modeling. The firing plan, carried over from Modeling, activates the M-MDMF within the MDMFs to perform Unglazed-Firing. It takes time to obtain the results of Unglazed-Firing. The process is similar to Natural-Modeling carried out in Mode $1'$.

e) Coloring for YUDAI: This step is executed only in the case of YUDAI production. The process is carried out in Mode $1''$ similar to Modeling. The subject of Modeling is to form the shape while considering the next step, Unglazed-Firing; the subject of Coloring for YUDAI is to put color with the consideration of the next step, Glazed-Firing.

f) Glazed-Firing for YUDAI: This step is executed only in the case of YUDAI production. Its process is similar to that of Unglazed-Firing. The process is carried out in Mode $1'$.

g) Glazing: This step consists of the following sub-steps: choosing a glaze that is matched to the surface texture of the piece, glazing, and considering a plan for Main-Firing that suits the glaze. The process is carried out in Mode $1''$.

h) Main-Firing: The firing plan that has been activated in Glazing is executed. Whether the kiln air environment during firing is oxidizing or reducing causes irreversible changes in the appearance of the fired piece. It takes time to obtain the results of the firing according to the firing plan. The process is carried out in Mode $1'$.

D. CCE-Step 3: Structural Modeling

Based on the considerations in CCE-Step 1 and 2, we can construct *a simplified individual behavioral ecological model of the surveyed space* that explains the differences among people acting in the collective behavioral ecology of that space. The results of the simulation by MHP/RT for each of the ceramic steps shown in CCE-Step 2, we can see that the unconscious spreading activation in the MDMFs by System 1 affects the performance of each process. Except for Master-Planning, MHP/RT operates in Mode 1. The following patterns characterize the way of operation.

Operation patterns

Mode $1''$
A: (β – β' ——//——*——//—— α'– α) *Repeat*

Mode $1'$
B: β – β' –*– α' ————//———— α

Similarity between the patterns is the upcoming event $*$ is consciously processed by System 2 and the event that has occurred is consciously evaluated by System 2. In doing so, the part of the $M \otimes N$ mapping that was active during the period of $(\beta,\ \alpha)$ is made consciously available for future processing by System 2 at α. The contents of the MDMFs to be integrated at α will differ depending on where the event $*$ is located in relation to β, β', α' and α. Nevertheless, the contents that diverged during $(\beta,\ *)$ converge during $(*,\ \alpha)$, and the whole is organically related and integrated.

The characteristics of the way of operation can be summarized as follows. In Pattern A, processing by System 1 is performed for a long time before and after the event. In Pattern B, processing by System 2 is performed after a long time after the event. In Pattern A, System 1 executes imaginative and meditative activities by activating a variety of possible pathways of $M \otimes N$ mappings within the MDMFs, constructed through years of experience. How divergence and convergence are executed over time influences the ceramic activity.

E. CCE-Steps 4 and 5: Super Elite Sample

Unlike the usual CCE survey, in this study, Kazuo Takiguchi, a ceramic artist, practicing an inherited traditional art form, was identified as a super elite sample, and a field survey through observation and interviews were already conducted as the CCE-Step 1-2. The results are presented in Table I.

F. CCE-Step 6: Match against Characteristics

Two operating patterns, Patterns A and B, were identified in CCE-Step 3. They characterize how the MDMFs should be used in the respective steps. By checking that these patterns match the actually observed ceramic activity of Kazuo Takiguchi, RQ-1 and RQ-4 will be addressed.

1) Hierarchical Mapping Structure: Based on the results of the observations and interviews of Kazuo Takiguchi, the production process is summarized in the lower part of Table I. In each step, it was evident that the appropriate timings for starting, change in condition, and ending were applied; these were acquired empirically through repeated production activities. It was possible to identify the actually applied work conditions that should produce the desired results by memorizing the points indicating the changes within the perceivable range and their superficial changes through observation of the process of work, and comparing what has been memorized with the results after the work.

This is shown schematically in Figure 4(a). The left side of the figure shows the manipulated object, **O**, and the right side shows the artist, **A**, which is Kazuo Takiguchi. **A** executes the following processes:

1) Observe **O** under consciousness (OBJECT-Cognition-2), and 1) become aware of the timing to start the execution of work, 2) become aware of the conditions for changing and updating the work content that has been started, and 3) become aware of the conditions for ending the work. This is executed by System 2.
2) Execute the contents that have been made conscious by activating the work sequences that have been acquired through training. Execution is done by perceiving the state of **O** with the five senses (OBJECT-Cognition-1) and applying the appropriate exercise to **O**. This is done by System 1.

The work is stored as an experience of System 1 and System 2, and influences future work.

The way in which each work step is carried out is well

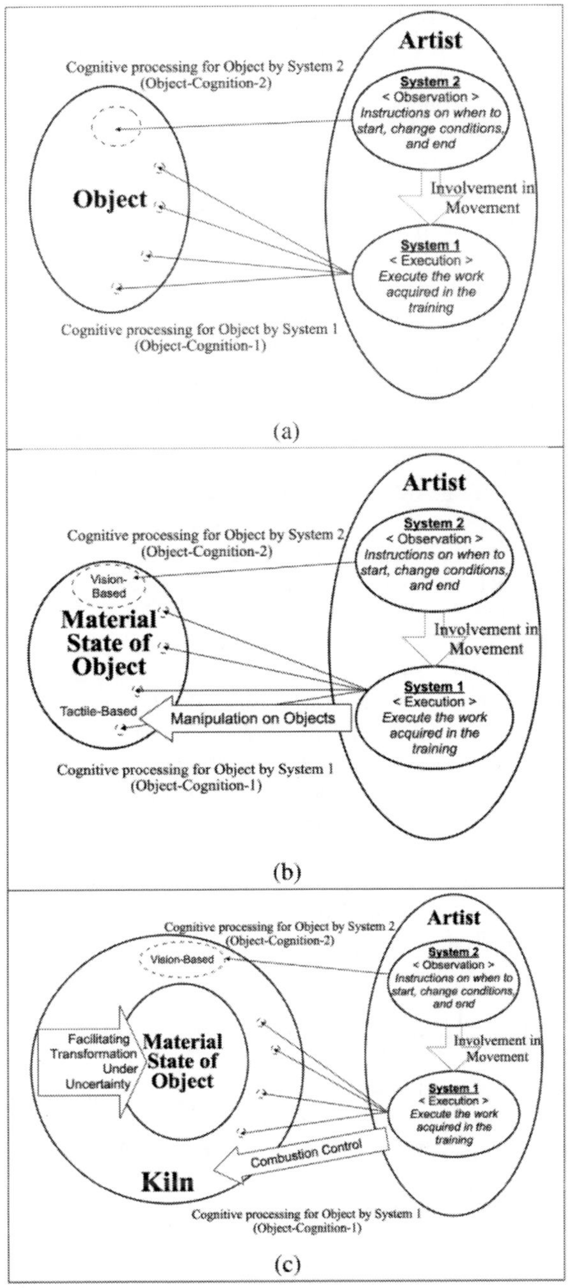

Figure 4. (a) hierarchical mapping structure characterized by $M \otimes N$ mapping; (b) changes in material state due to object manipulation in Modeling, Coloring, and Glazing; (c) changes in material state due to environmental manipulation in Natural-Modeling and Unglazed-, Glazed-, and Main-Firing.

aligned with the four processing modes of the MHP/RT, each of which is carried out during the periods of $[\beta,\ \beta')$, $[\beta',\ *)$, $(*,\ \alpha']$, and $(\alpha',\ \alpha]$. Considering the activities performed in the respective four periods, they are represented by the following two hierarchical mapping structures.

2) Hierarchical Mapping Structure of Transformation caused by OBJECT Manipulation: When an operation is applied to **O**, it changes according to its contents. This is related to the steps of Modeling, Coloring, and Glazing shown in Table I. What is happening in these steps is shown schematically in Figure 4(b). The current state of **O** is mainly perceived visually (with the help of tactile sense), and the immediate aim is to reach the final goal and the contents of operations to reach it are selected and decided by System 2 through the experience accumulated thus far (OBJECT-Cognition-2). Based on this decision, **A** perceives the state of **O** mainly through the tactile sense and perceives the progress of the operation by System 1 (OBJECT-Cognition-1) while moving his limbs to interact with **O** to change it. Once the immediate goal is achieved, the next goal is set and this process is repeated until the final goal is achieved. The way these work processes proceed is well matched to Pattern A.

3) Hierarchical Mapping Structure of Transformation caused by Environmental Change: In the steps to perform the firing in Table I, Natural-Modeling and Unglazed-, Glazed, and Main-Firing, the objects created due to the direct transformation of the objects in the preceding steps are irreversibly transformed and fixed by the application of gravitational field or firing environment in the kiln. What is happening in this process is shown schematically in Figure 4(c). The following provides an explanation for the firing process, which can be applied to Natural-Modeling as well. The current state of **O** is perceived visually, and the firing parameters that realize the firing environment in the kiln to reach the final goal are selected and determined by System 2 using the experience accumulated (OBJECT-Cognition-2). Based on this decision, the kiln is adjusted for firing and firing is started. Firing is an unpredictable and uncertain process. During firing, the state of the kiln is recognized by System 1 via all five senses (OBJECT-Cognition-1) and integrated with previous experiences as a new experience. This way of proceeding with the work process is well matched with Pattern B.

IV. CONCLUSIONS

This study focused on ceramics, a traditional Japanese craft, and investigated the memes that make it a traditional craft by conducting a CCE survey with a ceramist as a super-elite monitor. In ceramics, the manipulation of objects that are malleable and whose properties change with time and the setting of firing conditions that produce irreversible physical and chemical changes in the clay and glaze, are performed. In both cases, the initial image is placed in the P-MDMF and the activity is propagated in the MDMFs, which are constructed with extensive experience as memes, to simulate whether or not a work that matches the final image is obtained. When time constraints are strong, the richness of the MDMFs related to System 1 can be an effective help. The quality of the memory is important for the experiential content during the training period. Tradition can be understood as a generic term referring to the results of improving the content quality of one's training over a long period of time.

In the West, there is a strong emphasis on logical thinking by System 2, seeking eternity and finding laws in nature. Based on this way of thinking, they have discovered objectivity, the golden ratio, perspective, and so on, and have applied them to their creations. In modern times, this attitude can be seen in the cubism of Picasso, for example. On the other hand, in Japan, as revealed in this study, there is a tendency to devise pseudo-expressive methods to express what one truly wants to express, based on the experiential perception obtained from interacting with the natural world. This can be seen in ink paintings and ukiyoe.

ACKNOWLEDGEMENT

In this study, Kazuo Takiguchi kindly agreed to be interviewed about the inner aspects of the ceramic process, which could be observed superficially, and provided us with valuable information. He confirmed the results of the application of CCE. Without his cooperation, this study would not have been possible. We would like to express our deepest gratitude to him. This work was supported by JSPS KAKENHI Grant Number 20H04290. The authors would like to thank Editage (www.editage.com) for the English language editing.

REFERENCES

[1] J. L. McClelland and D. E. Rumelhart, Parallel Distributed Processing: Explorations in the Microstructure of Cognition : Psychological and Biological Models. The MIT Press, 6 1986.

[2] M. Kitajima, M. Toyota, and J. Dinet, "How Resonance Works for Development and Propagation of Memes," International Journal on Advances in Systems and Measurements, vol. 14, 2021, pp. 148–161.

[3] M. Kitajima, M. Toyota, and J. Dinet, "The Role of Resonance in the Development and Propagation of Memes," in COGNITIVE 2021 : The Thirteenth International Conference on Advanced Cognitive Technologies and Applications, 2021, pp. 28–36.

[4] A. Juniper, Wabi Sabi: The Japanese Art of Impermanence. Tuttle Publishing, 11 2003.

[5] A. L. Sadler, The Japanese Tea Ceremony: Cha-no-Yu and the Zen Art of Mindfulness, paperback ed. Tuttle Publishing, 4 2019.

[6] A. Newell, Unified Theories of Cognition (The William James Lectures, 1987). Cambridge, MA: Harvard University Press, 1990.

[7] M. Kitajima et al., "Language and Image in Behavioral Ecology," in COGNITIVE 2022 : The Fourteenth International Conference on Advanced Cognitive Technologies and Applications, 2022, pp. 1–10.

[8] M. Kitajima, "Cognitive Chrono-Ethnography (CCE): A Behavioral Study Methodology Underpinned by the Cognitive Architecture, MHP/RT," in Proceedings of the 41st Annual Conference of the Cognitive Science Society. Cognitive Science Society, 2019, pp. 55–56.

[9] M. Kitajima and M. Toyota, "Simulating navigation behaviour based on the architecture model Model Human Processor with Real-Time Constraints (MHP/RT)," Behaviour & Information Technology, vol. 31, no. 1, 2012, pp. 41–58.

[10] M. Kitajima and M. Toyota, "Decision-making and action selection in Two Minds: An analysis based on Model Human Processor with Realtime Constraints (MHP/RT)," Biologically Inspired Cognitive Architectures, vol. 5, 2013, pp. 82–93.

[11] E. Todd, The Diversity of the World: Family and Modernity (La Diversité du monde. Famille et modernité), paperback ed. SEUIL, 3 1999.

[12] D. Kahneman, Thinking, Fast and Slow. New York, NY: Farrar, Straus and Giroux, 2011.

A Multi-Agent Control and Automation Architecture with Integrated Flexible User Communication Agents

Ahmed Kamel
Offutt School of Business
Concordia College
Moorhead, Minnesota, USA
Email: kamel@cord.edu

Abstract—**In this paper, we present a flexible integrated multi-agent automation and control architecture. The architecture relies on a knowledge-based module. This module is custom designed to every application and is thus open to personalization to other domains requiring a similar control scheme. It, thus, provides an important level of adaptability. The architecture also provides a flexible communication agent that can communicate with a user using a variety of communication media to meet the user's needs at any given point in time.**

Keywords-multi-agents; decision-support system;knowedge-based system; human-computer collaboration.

I. INTRODUCTION

While every control system is unique in terms of its needs, many control systems share a common characteristic; They need to gather input from a user, manage a situation based on the user's needs, monitor their environment to update the control plans as needed, and communicate with the user to inform them of any changes and update the plans based on the user's preferences.

While several general purpose agent architectures exist, in the work developed here, we custom-designed an agent architecture that balances our need for efficient execution and flexibility to customize

In Section II, we present the current state of multiagent architectures, in Section III, we present the basic architecture we developed for control systems, and in Section IV, we present two different applications we developed using our architecture. These applications include an agricultural management system with weather monitoring [1] and a call routing system for a teachnical support center [2]. A general conclusionis provided in Section V.

II. STATE OF MULTI-AGENT ARCHITECTURES

Multiagent architectures are architectures that utilize multiple cooperative autonomous agents that collaborate on decision making and coordinating their actions to accomplish tasks beyond their individual capabilities [3], [4]Communication styles among these agents can be hierarchical, centralized, or distributed[5],[6]. Over the years, specialized languages have been developed for agent programming [7]. The research reported in this article does not utilize any of these languages.

Most new developments in agent architectures are driven by application needs. Application domains are varied including areas like traffic management[8], [9], cooperating robots[10], supply chain management [11], and smart electric grid management[12]. The research reported here follows this trend by customizing the agent architecture to the needs of the application domains. We elected to do our own development rather than rely on a general purpose architecture for a more efficient execution and a higher level of flexibility.

III. BASIC ARCHITECTURE

Our control architecture is divided into four basic modules with an additional weather data gathering module that we found to be useful in several of our developed applications. These modules are the User Input module, the Knowledge-based System, the information delivery module, and the Timer module. These modules are connected centrally to a database. The database we used is Microsoft Access and the system has also been tested with SQL Server thus making it more flexible. The use of an intelligent-agents approach has allowed the development of a user-friendly system that can be applied to many monitoring systems.

A. System Features

- Allows the users to enter their information for performing daily activities
- Stores the information in a database
- Agent parses the information and stores it
- Can connect to the web and collects the weather information
- Expert System integrates with the agents and accesses the user database to make intelligent decisions
- Agents collect the information from the Expert System
- Agents convert the information to appropriate forms as needed for user communication, such as Text or Wave for voice communication
- Telephony Application Programming Interfaces (APIs) can call the users with the data stored in the Agents

using standard telephony or any of an array of Voice Over Internet Protocol (VOIP) applications

- Users are contacted using their preferred communication method (voice, text, email) and within each method, they are given the capability of interacting with the system.
- The system is maintained by a timer, which runs every morning by default and checks the data for the users. Users can customize the timer schedule.

B. *User Input Module*

The user interface is a critical part of any solution and should be very user friendly. We developed a web-based user-input module. The User can enter their weekly information in the system. The system is smart and updates its information every time a user comes into the system. The user is allowed to make their personal profile, which is password protected. Options provided for the user are customized based on the type of application such as farming, or home automations as discussed in the next section. The system also collects the user's preferred contact method and their needed credentials so they can be contacted as needed using the information delivery module. The data stored in the database is used by the expert system module to compare the data and generate appropriate results. These web pages are running on an Internet Information Server and are connected to the database.

C. *Knowledge-Based System Module*

Knowledge-basedsystems (sometimes referred to as Expert Systems) are computer systems, which provide expert quality advice, such as diagnoses, and recommendations given real-world problems. They are intelligent systems, which have knowledge stored in them and can make decisions, which normally require human expertise. It receives as input a problem and through its knowledge base makes decisions to give a solution to the problem. Knowledge-based Systems have been used in different areas such as medicine, robotics, mathematics, and various other fields. We include a generic template for a knowledge-based system in our architecture. This template needs to be customized for each application as discussed in the next section.

The knowledge-basedsystem is designed to access the central database and check the requirements for every user that were entered through the user interface and based on the given rules, it makes its decisions using the information stored in the Data Base Management System(DBMS) agent.

The Knowledge-based systemis triggered based on the schedule stored in the timer module to avoid unnecessarily using the system resources and skips processing the users who are inactive in order to minimize the resources used by the agents, the CPU time, and the memory. The knowledge-based system invokes the information delivery agent discussed below to alert the user as needed.

D. *Information Delivery Module*

The information delivery module is another crucial part of the system. This module is responsible for delivering the results; the useful information generated from the expert system to the user and acquiring any feedback from the user. There are diverse ways of communication available today. Multiple agents are provided and can be activated according to the user's availability and wishes. Each agent is responsible for one communication method, an agent for agent-initiated phone communications, an agent for agent-initiated e-mail communications, an agent for user-initiated web-based communications, as well as an agent for VOIP communication that can be customized with any of several available VOIP applications (Skype, Messenger, WhatsApp for now but others can be added). This multi-modal communication provides efficient, dependable, and accessible interaction with the users regardless of their physical location.

This module manages the call processing. This is a multi-function module. It performs the function of opening the line, making a live connection, and then passing the data with a two-way interaction between the user and the automated program. This module goes through the list of users generated by the knowledge-based system and plays a file for each user.

This module also includes another set of agents known as sound agents. For every user, a sound agent is generated. These agents perform the function of converting any necessary information to be communicated to the user into wave files. We have used the Speech Application programming Interfaces to generate the wave files. These files are then played to the user who gets called by the call processing system.

E. *Timer Module*

This module controls the invocation of the knowledge-basedsystem module and if needed the Web data gathering, which in-turn triggers the information delivery module. We defined a default schedule that runs once a day This schedule can be customized to meet any specific user needs.

Figure 1 shows the overall diagram of the general control architecture with its components and shows their interactions.

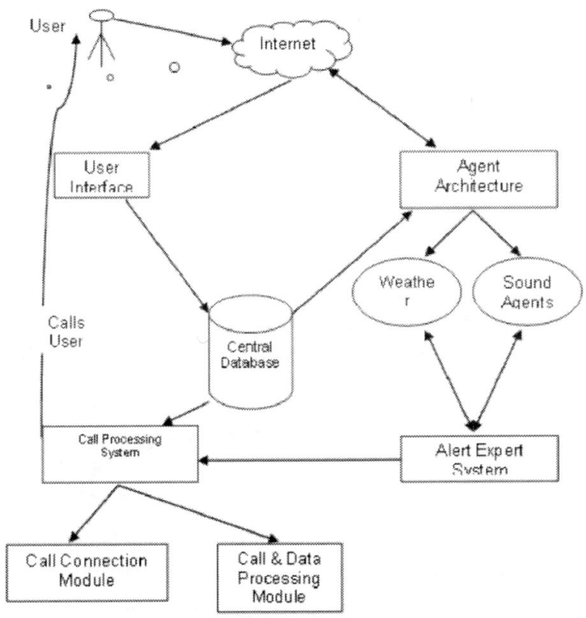

Figure 1. General Agent-Based Control Architecture

F. *Weather Data Gathering Module*

Since several of our applications rely on weather data. We designed a weather agent and included it with the basic architecture for use in any control situation that needs it.We included a collection of agents with one agent for each day of the week. While the choice of having an agent for each of the days of the week seems arbitrary, the choice was driven by our first application area in farming where we found that many of our famer collaborators are used to performing different tasks on different days of the week so having a different agent for each of the days of the week allows customization for each day in terms of the weather parameters needed. They use the web to collect information from weather web sites. They are also responsible for parsing the data and extracting the required data for their respective days. We developed these agents in Visual C++ and programmed them to use HTTP APIs to get the data. The Agent architecture looks for the web site URL, parses it and returns the type of service and its components. It then opens an HTTP connection and opens the source of the web page for data processing. The page contains the weather information for the given input parameters (location, time, needed weather data points).

There are seven weather agents, each holds a day's weather information and these intelligent agents in our system interact with the knowledge-based system. This interaction can occur in either direction. The knowledge-based system can trigger the weather agents if it needs weather information.The weather agents can also trigger the knowledge-based system if they detect a significant change in weather conditions.

G. *The Database*

There is another important agent, the DBMS Agent that retrieves the information from the database for the users. This agent gets updated during processing of different users. This agent works closely with the knowledge-based system and interacts with the above agents to facilitate decision-making. This agent carries the information for a specific user in a dedicated manner and holds that information until the decisions are created for that user.

IV. APPLICATIONS

We applied our control to several application domains. In this section, we present two of these applications; weather data monitoring for use in a farm control setting[13]and monitoring of incoming technical support phones for routing to appropriate technicians[14].

A. *Weather Monitoring*

Our weather monitoring system[14] is intended as a helper application to a farm management system we developed in the past to manage a wheat farm [1].

The agriculture community has always been dependent for their work on weather conditions, and it takes significant planning and money investment for them to perform their daily farming activities. If they are not well informed of the upcoming weather conditions, they are prone to revenue loss. Through this agent-based system, we provide this community an opportunity to prevent the waste of their resources and effectively utilize them by pre-informing them about valuable weather data based on their plans which we capture online in their personal accounts. There are seven weather agents, each holds a day's weather information and these intelligent agents in our system interact with the interactive decision criteria Alert Expert System, which activates these agents based on the management plans in the system. These plans include aspects such as irrigation and fertilization schedules which are typically extremely sensitive to changing weather conditions. Example conditions that the expert system module is trained to monitor include:

- Fertilization and Irrigation: Heavy Rains
- Spraying: Strong winds/Windy or rains
- Planting and Sowing: Rains

A top-level view of this system is shown in figure 2.

We tested this system with several collaborating farmers and all of them reported a high level of satisfaction with the alerts received from the system.

B. *Smart Call Routing*

In this application [2], we utilized our architecture to develop an agent system to route incoming technical support calls to appropriate technicians based on the needs of the users and the areas of expertise of the different technicians.

Traditionally, corporate computing systems consisted of hardware and software systems purchased from one or more vendors and maintained on site typically by local information technology staff. In recent years, a gradual shift occurred to a

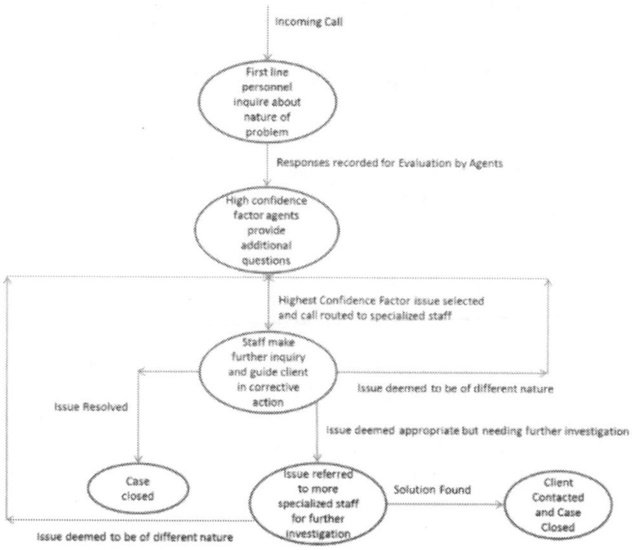

Figure 2. Top Level View of Weather Alert System

managed system model where corporations contract a vendor to install and support integrated IT systems. This shift was accompanied by a shift of the help desk support from the corporate IT department to the vendor's own staff. As a result, vendors set up large help desk installations where staff accept calls from personnel at a large number of corporate clients and attempt to troubleshoot a variety of issues.

The goal of this system is to assist the first line technicians in routing the calls to the appropriate service technicians. Figure 3 shows a top-level view of this system.

As reported in [2], this system resulted in the reduction of the average number rerouting incidents of incoming calls from 5.6 to 2.4 when used to replace an existing manual call routing system. This resulted in a higher level of satisfaction among surveyed callers.

V. Conclusions

In this paper, we presented a framework for communication agents embedded within an architecture for control based on a set of collaborating agents. The control architecture involves the users through communication between the users and the agent system. Multi agents are provided to enable intelligent decision making and interaction among users and their agents regardless of their physical location. We demonstrated the use of the developed architecture in two different control situations.The first application is for monitoring the web for the occurrence of an event such as a weather alert that would interact with predefined crop management plans. The other application is for routing incoming technical support calls to appropriate technicians based on their areas of expertise.

We are currently planning to apply this same architecture to other domain areas.

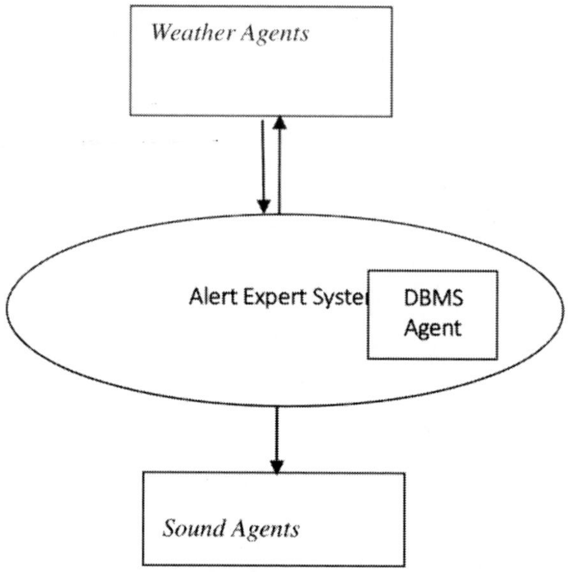

Figure 3: Top Level View of Call Routing System

References

[1] A. Kamel, "Agent-Based Design of Agricultural knowledge Based Systems," International Journal of Computers and Their Applications, pp. 228-232, 4 2005.

[2] A. Kamel, "Smart Call Routing Utilizing a Multi-Agent Architecture," in The Eighteenth International Multi-Conference on Computing in the Global Information Technology, Barcelona, Spain, pp. 1-4 2023.

[3] P. Stone, and M. Veloso, "Multiagent systems: A survey from a machine learning perspective," Journal of Artificial Intelligence Research, vol. 11, pp. 216-252, 2000.

[4] M. Tambe, P. S. Rosenbloom, "Towards intelligent agent architectures: A survey.," in Firts International Conference on Multiagent Systems, San Fransisco, CA, 1997.

[5] W. Van der Hoek, J. J. Meyer, C. Witteveen, "Agent architectures and their evaluation: Who is afraid of a benchmark?" Artificial Intelligence, vol. 131, no. 1, pp. 181-213, 2001.

[6] J. F. Hubner, J. S, Sichman, O. Boissier, "Developing multi-agent systems with a FIPA-compliant agent framework.," Software: Practice and Experience, vol. 34, no. 2, pp. 159-189, 2004.

[7] M. Wooldridge, N.R. Jennings, "Intelligent agents: Theory and practice.," in First International Workshop on Agent Theories, Architectures, and Languages (ATAL'94), The Netherlands, 1995.

[8] J. Ma, L. Chen, Y. liu, "Multi-agent systems for traffic management: A review.," IEEE Transactions on Intelligent Transportation Systems, vol. 17, no. 2, pp. 308-320, 2016.

[9] J. Ma, L. Chen, Y. liu, "Multi-agent systems for traffic management: A review.," IEEE Transactions on Intelligent Transportation Systems, vol. 17, no. 2, pp. 308-320, 2016.

[10] M. Smadi, A. Kamel "A Knowledge Based Traffic Signal Control Application," in Fifteenth International Conference on Computer Applications in Industry and Engineering, San Diego, CA, 2002.

[11] A. Agah, G. A. Bekey, "Multi-robot assembly system using evolutionary multi-objective optimization and self-adaptive multi-agent systems.," Robotics and Autonomous Systems, vol. 43, no. 3-4, pp. 171-186, 2003.

[12] X. Li, D. Li, C. Huang, "A multi-agent architecture for intelligent supply chain management.," Journal of Systems Science and Systems Engineering, vol. 22, no. 4, pp. 445-466, 2013.

[13] T. Pinto, H. Morais, Z. Vale, P. Faria "Multi-agent systems for integration of distributed energy resources in power systems: Models, applications, and future trends.," Renewable and Sustainable Energy Reviews, vol. 49, pp. 345-357, 2015.

[14] D. Seth and A. Kamel, "An Intelligent-Agent Based Automated Weather Alert System," in Third International Conference on Computer Science, Software Engineering, Information Technology, E-Business, and Applications, Cairo, Egypt, pp. 48-63, 2004.

ECG-based Seizure Prediction Utilizing Transfer Learning with CNN

Chia-Yen Yang and Pin-Chen Chen
Department of Biomedical Engineering
Ming-Chuan University
Taoyuan, Taiwan
e-mail: cyyang@mail.mcu.edu.tw

Abstract—**Clinically, electroencephalography (EEG) is the most common tool used to diagnose epilepsy. However, if considering practicality and convenience, electrocardiogram (ECG) is more suitable for use in non-medical institutions. Its problem that needs to be overcome is the improvement of accuracy. Therefore, this study attempted to apply transfer learning strategy to develop a seizure prediction system based on ECG for detecting interictal and preictal periods. We trained a nonpatient specific epilepsy prediction model based on Convolutional Neural Network (CNN), and then used transfer learning to fine-tune parameters with the goal of reducing the model development time and improving the performance for each specific patient. ECG data were obtained from two open-source datasets, the Siena Scalp EEG database and Zenodo, including 13 and 14 patients, respectively. The results show that the patient-specific model with six frozen layers achieved accuracy, sensitivity, and specificity of 100% for nine patients and required only 40 s of training time. By applying transfer learning, the model could directly use raw ECG signals, eliminating the time and manpower in extraction of features and greatly speeding up the training process. Furthermore, it achieved the purpose of personalized and accurate detection that could increase the practicality of seizure prediction in daily life.**

Keywords- electrocardiography (ECG); Convolutional Neural Network (CNN); seizure prediction; transfer learning.

I. INTRODUCTION

According to statistics report of the World Health Organization, epilepsy is one of the most common neurological diseases in the world, with about 50 million patients worldwide. It refers to the occasional, excessive, and disorderly discharge of brain neurons, resulting in limb movement disorders and perception, language, or other cognitive dysfunctions. Clinically, electroencephalography (EEG) is the most common tool used to diagnose epilepsy. However, its measurement environment is limited, and the operation requires the assistance of professionals. Besides, the interpretation of complex signals requires extensive work as well. Therefore, many researchers have used machine learning or deep learning technology to build an automatic epilepsy detection system (e.g., [7]). The recognition accuracies of those EEG models for epileptic seizures detection could reach more than 90%. However, if such signals were to be collected using a wearable device at home, various factors would have to be considered, including easy operation by a nonprofessional, and user comfort. Hence, some researchers have begun to investigate the potential of using other physiological signals, such as electrocardiogram (ECG), as an alternative (e.g., [6]). Because epileptic seizures often affect the autonomic nervous system, leading to effects on cardiovascular, respiratory, gastrointestinal, and urinary functions during or shortly after seizures, cardiovascular changes are gaining attention because of their ability to cause sudden unexpected death in epilepsy [8]. That means excessive neural activation associated with seizures affects central autonomic network function, regulates parasympathetic and sympathetic heart rhythm and contractility, and thereby reflects in heart rate and ECG waveforms [9][10]. Although they concluded that ECG is quite feasible in practice for at home monitoring, effectively improving the low accuracy of this method would be challenging. Therefore, this study attempted to apply transfer learning strategy to develop a seizure prediction system based on ECG for detecting interictal and preictal periods. We trained a nonpatient specific epilepsy prediction model based on Convolutional Neural Network (CNN), and then used transfer learning to fine tune parameters with the goal of reducing the model development time and improving the results for each specific patient.

The rest of this paper is organized as follows: Section 2 provides the classification method for CNN model. Section 3 describes the performance of the model and the comparison results of the different models. Section 4 includes conclusion and future.

II. MATERIALS AND METHODS

The followings describe the datasets, the analysis methodology and the evaluation metrics used in our study.

A. Datasets

ECG data were downloaded from two data sets: the Siena Scalp EEG database (including 13 patients; mean ± standard deviation age 42.6 ± 13.8 years) [3][5] and Zenodo (including 14 patients; mean ± standard deviation age 17.4 ± 9.6 years) [1]. For each patient, the diagnosis of epilepsy and classification were made by a doctor. All patients provided written informed consent approved by the Ethics Committee of the University of Siena.

B. Data Analysis

ECG signals were preprocessed using MATLAB in three steps: detrending, 80Hz lowpass filtering and 60Hz notch filtering. After preprocessing, the signals were truncated by using 10s overlapping windows with 8 s of overlap and divided into four epileptic states: seizure, preictal 20–10, preictal 30–20, and preictal 40–30. A total of 12,222 samples were obtained for each state (Figure 1).

C. *Classification and Performance Evaluation*

The CNN model was modified from the model of Wang et al. [7] and implemented using Python. It comprised four convolutional layers, five pooling layers, and three FC layers (Figure 2). Three approaches were used for training: recordwise (i.e., mixed datasets), subjectwise (i.e., cross dataset) and patient-specific (i.e., transfer learning). For all approaches, 10-fold cross-validation was used to evaluate the trained models. The optimized model was then validated on the testing dataset by calculating its accuracy, specificity, and sensitivity. These processes were performed five times.

III. RESULTS

Effectiveness of the three training approaches for establishing a CNN-based epilepsy prediction model was investigated. The results for recordwise training revealed that the performance for classifying interictal and three preictal states were all greater than 97%; the training times for all three models were approximately 2 h (Table I). The results for subjectwise training revealed that the performance for classifying interictal and three preictal states were greater than 78%; the training times were approximately 2 h. A comparison of the results for recordwise and subjectwise training revealed that if the novel subject data were not used for model training, the test accuracy, sensitivity, and specificity decreased but the training time remained constant. Finally, the results for patient-specific transfer learning differed from those for recordwise and subjectwise training (Table II). The models with 12 frozen layers and used to classify interictal and three preictal states achieved performance of greater than 94% with training times of approximately 1 min. Models with nine and six frozen layers classifying interictal and three preictal states achieved performance of 100% with training times of approximately 40 s and 45 s, respectively. Those with three frozen layers achieved performance of 97% with training times of approximately 50 s. In summary, freezing 9 layers led to the highest accuracy (i.e., 100%) and the shortest training time (~40 seconds), which further indicated that transfer learning was superior to recordwise or subjectwise learning.

We then compared the accuracy rates of our model with those of models reported by other studies on epileptic seizure prediction using ECG data (Table III). De Cooman et al. [11] proposed a support vector machine with transfer learning approach for seizure detection using single lead ECG data from 24 temporal lobe epilepsy patients. Their personalized approach resulted in an overall sensitivity of 71% with an average decrease in false detection rate of 37%. Baghersalimi et al. [12] designed a standard federated learning framework in the context of epileptic seizure detection using a deep learning-based approach, which operates across a cluster of machines. They evaluated the accuracy on the EPILEPSIAE database consisting of one-lead ECG from 29 patients. Their framework achieved a sensitivity of 81.25%, a specificity of 82.00%, and a geometric mean of 81.62%. The comparison result shows that ours had the best accuracy, specificity, and sensitivity.

IV. CONCLUSION AND FUTURE WORK

EEG is currently the main tool used to diagnose epileptic seizures. Many studies have utilized deep learning technology for prediction of epileptic seizures (e.g., [2]); however, if considering practicality and convenience, ECG is more suitable for use in nonmedical institutions, while the problem that needs to be overcome is the improvement of accuracy [4]. Therefore, this study used three different training methods to evaluate ECG-based classification models. Recordwise training was used to test the architecture of our model. The performance could reach more than 97%. Subjectwise training was used to simulate practical situations, i.e., the test data are independent and unrelated to the training data. The performance was over 78%. Due to the sharp drop in model performance, we applied transfer learning approach to develop a patient-specific model. The results show that the training effect of freezing 6 layers was the best: the accuracy, specificity, and sensitivity for 9 subjects all reached 100%, and the training time was less than 40 seconds. By applying transfer learning, the model could directly use raw ECG signals, eliminating the time and manpower in extraction of features and greatly speeding up the training process. Furthermore, it achieved the purpose of personalized and accurate detection that could increase the practicality of seizure prediction in daily life. For future practical applications, such as wearable devices employed for seizure prediction, studies on more or larger datasets should be conducted to validate the reliability of the model.

ACKNOWLEDGMENT

This study was supported in part by the National Science and Technology Council (MOST 111-2221-E-130-001-MY3), Taiwan.

REFERENCES

[1] L. Billeci, D. Marino, L. Insana, G. Vatti, and M. Varanini, "Patient-specific seizure prediction based on heart rate variability and recurrence quantification analysis," PLoS ONE, vol. 13, pp. e0204339, April 2018.

[2] H. Daoud and M. A. Bayoumi, "Efficient epileptic seizure prediction based on deep learning," IEEE Trans. Biomed. Circuits Syst., vol. 13, pp. 804–813, October 2019.

[3] P. Detti, G. Vatti, and M. D. L. Zabalo, "EEG synchronization analysis for seizure prediction: A study on data of noninvasive recordings," Processes, vol. 8, pp. 846, June 2020.

[4] K. Fujiwara et al., "Epileptic seizure prediction based on multivariate statistical process control of heart rate variability features," IEEE Trans. Biomed. Eng., vol. 63, pp. 1321–1332, June 2016.

[5] A. L. Goldberger et al., "PhysioBank, PhysioToolkit, and PhysioNet: components of a new research resource for complex physiologic signals," Circulation, vol. 101, pp. 215–220, June 2000.

[6] A. Jahanbekam et al., "Performance of ECG-based seizure detection algorithms strongly depends on training and test conditions," Epilepsia Open, vol. 6, pp. 597–606, July 2021.

[7] X. Wang et al., "One dimensional Convolutional Neural Networks for seizure onset detection using long-term scalp and intracranial EEG," Neurocomputing, vol. 459, pp. 212–222, October 2021.

[8] F. Leutmezer et al., "Electrocardiographic Changes at the Onset of Epileptic Seizures," Epilepsy, vol. 44, March 2003.

[9] M. Zijlmans, D. Flanagan, and J. Gotman, "Heart rate changes and ECG abnormalities during epileptic seizures: prevalence and definition of an objective clinical sign," Epilepsy, vol. 43, August 2002.

[10] T. Yamakawa et al., "Wearable epileptic seizure prediction system with machine-learning-based anomaly detection of heart rate variability," Sensors, vol. 20, no. 14, pp. 3987, May 2020.

[11] T. De Cooman et al., "Personalizing heart rate-based seizure detection using supervised SVM transfer learning," Front. Neurol., vol. 11, pp. 145, February 2020.

[12] S. Baghersalimi et al., "Personalized real-time federated learning for epileptic seizure detection," IEEE J. Biomed. Health Inform., vol. 26, no. 2, pp. 898-909, February 2022.

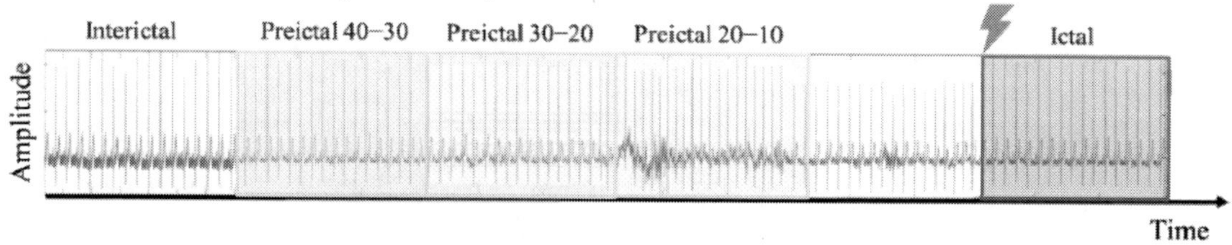

Figure 1. Illustration of four epileptic states in ECG signals.

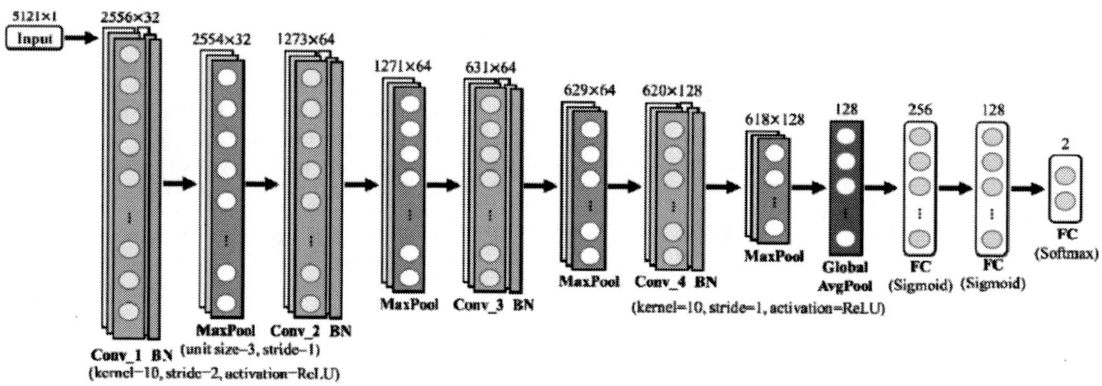

Hyperparameters: optimizer=Adam, batch size=128, learning rate=0.0002 (reduce_lr: min_lr=0.00001)

Figure 2. CNN architecture for classification of preictal and interictal periods.

TABLE I. PERFORMANCE OF THE RECORDWISE AND SUBJECTWISE TRAINING APPROACHES.

	Recordwise training			
	Accuracy (%)	Sensitivity (%)	Specificity (%)	Time
Preictal 10-20	98.96(± 0.05%)	99.09(±0.11%)	98.82(± 0.15%)	1hr48min40sec
Preictal 20-30	98.13(± 0.08%)	98.50(± 0.16%)	97.77(± 0.08%)	1hr54min39sec
Preictal 30-40	99.89(± 0.04%)	99.94(± 0.06%)	99.84(± 0.05%)	1hr44min26sec
	Subjectwise training			
	Accuracy (%)	Sensitivity (%)	Specificity (%)	Time
Preictal 10-20	85.88(± 0.68%)	83.24(± 0.32%)	88.52(± 1.57%)	1hr51min21sec
Preictal 20-30	84.90(± 0.87%)	82.66(± 1.18%)	87.13(± 0.89%)	1hr33min47sec
Preictal 30-40	83.33(± 1.54%)	78.51(± 3.39%)	88.15(± 1.24%)	1h37min58sec

TABLE II. CLASSIFICATION ACCURACY, SENSITIVITY, AND SPECIFICITY (MEAN VALUES) OF THE PATIENT-SPECIFIC INTERICTAL AND PREICTAL CLASSIFICATION TRANSFER LEARNING MODELS.

NO.	# of frozen layers	preictal 20-10				preictal 30-20				preictal 40-30			
		Acc (%)	Sen (%)	Spe (%)	Time (sec)	Acc (%)	Sen (%)	Spe (%)	Time (sec)	Acc (%)	Sen (%)	Spe (%)	Time (sec)
2	3	100	100	100	42	99.5	98.8	100	39	98.5	100	97	56
	6	100	100	100	40	100	100	100	37	100	100	100	45
	9	100	100	100	35	100	100	100	46	100	100	100	41
	12	100	100	100	104	97.5	94.4	100	112	100	100	100	102
4	3	100	100	100	46	100	100	100	46	100	100	100	39
	6	100	100	100	35	100	100	100	37	100	100	100	36
	9	100	100	100	38	100	100	100	32	100	100	100	34
	12	100	100	100	111	100	100	100	109	100	100	100	90
5	3	100	100	100	44	100	100	100	43	100	100	100	44
	6	100	100	100	43	100	100	100	36	100	100	100	35
	9	100	100	100	36	100	100	100	35	100	100	100	31
	12	100	100	100	58	100	100	100	81	100	100	100	76
7	3	100	100	100	50	100	100	100	51	100	100	100	40
	6	100	100	100	46	100	100	100	41	100	100	100	37
	9	100	100	100	34	100	100	100	39	100	100	100	32
	12	100	100	100	94	97.5	95.6	100	76	100	100	100	93
8	3	100	100	100	43	100	100	100	49	100	100	100	46
	6	100	100	100	38	100	100	100	45	100	100	100	36
	9	100	100	100	36	100	100	100	36	100	100	100	36
	12	100	100	100	109	94.9	94.1	95.6	112	100	100	100	107
9	3	100	100	100	38	100	100	100	49	100	100	100	42
	6	100	100	100	36	100	100	100	38	100	100	100	37
	9	100	100	100	37	100	100	100	31	100	100	100	30
	12	100	100	100	88	100	100	100	110	100	100	100	108
10	3	100	100	100	59	100	100	100	48	100	100	100	46
	6	100	100	100	45	100	100	100	38	100	100	100	36
	9	100	100	100	45	100	100	100	38	100	100	100	33
	12	100	100	100	73	100	100	100	78	100	100	100	59
11	3	100	100	100	42	100	100	100	45	100	100	100	41
	6	100	100	100	41	100	100	100	38	100	100	100	35
	9	100	100	100	40	100	100	100	33	100	100	100	35
	12	100	100	100	71	100	100	100	75	100	100	100	56
13	3	100	100	100	49	100	100	100	56	100	100	100	46

6	100	100	100	37	100	100	100	39	100	100	100	37
9	100	100	100	39	100	100	100	35	100	100	100	38
12	100	100	100	107	100	100	100	57	100	100	100	71

TABLE III. PERFORMANCE OF DIFFERENT SEIZURE PREDICTION SYSTEMS BASED ON CNNS WITH ECG SIGNALS.

Study	Dataset	Input	Model	Training Type	ACC(%)	SEN(%)	SPE(%)
De Cooman et al. [11]	Self-recorded	HRI and HR peaks	SVM+TL	P-spc	-	71%	-
Baghersalimi et al. [12]	EPILEPSIA	Raw data	Res1DCNN+FL	P-spc	81.62%	81.25%	82.00%
			1DCNN+FL		76%	69.25%	82%
			MLP+FL		74.00%	77%	71.50%
This study	Siena EEG+ Zenodo	Raw data	1D-CNN+TL	P-spc	99.94%	99.86%	100%

An Innovative Immersive Environment to Assess Non-Technical Skills: A Pilot Study

Dinet Jerome
2LPN, UR 7489
University of Lorraine
Nancy, France
jerome.dinet@univ-lorraine.fr

Pignault Anne
2LPN, UR 7489
University of Lorraine
Nancy, France
anne.pignault@univ-lorraine.fr

Linot Beatrice
SDIS 57 and 2LPN
SDIS and U. of Lorraine
Metz, France
beatrice.linot@sdis57.fr

Battarel Carole
Virtual Rangers Company
Virtual Rangers
Luxembourg, Luxembourg
info@virtual-rangers.com

Saint-Dizier De Almeida Valérie
2LPN, UR 7489
University of Lorraine
Nancy, France
valerie.saint-dizier@univ-lorraine.fr

Grayo Franck
Groupe EDF
Nuclear Power Plant of Cattenom
Cattenom, France
Franck.grayo@enedis.fr

Chevrier Pierre
ENIM
National School of Engineering
Metz, France
pierre.chevrier@univ-lorraine.fr

***Abstract*—Because non-technical skills are more and more important to improve safety in industry, this paper is aiming to present an innovative tool to assess these non-technical skills, by using an immersive environment. Even if all existing assessment methods (e.g., simulated clinical scenarios, objective structured clinical examinations, and questionnaires or written assessments) provide interesting data, they present several limitations (weakness of their theoretical background, only based on subjective and individual data). The main goal of this paper is to present an innovative tool to assess non-technical skills, by using an immersive environment, allowing collection of quantitative and objective data for several individuals engaged in a collaborative and a complex cooperative task. Performances of the team, performances, verbalisation and behaviors of each participant/player are automatically recorded by the immersive system and a debriefing session was realized with all participants/players at the end of each game. Our results obtained with 35 participants tend to confirm that technology such as an immersive environment created by Virtual Rangers can offer a new and positive model for assessing non-technical skills. Finally, advantages of this iterative and incremental human-centered design are discussed in the domain of the assessment of non-technical skills.**

***Index Terms*—virtual reality; human factors; behavioral science; human-computer interaction**

I. Introduction

Many 21st century operations are characterised by teams of workers dealing with significant risks and complex technology, in competitive, commercially-driven environments. Informed managers in such sectors have realised the necessity of understanding the human factors to their operations if they hope to improve production and safety performance. While organisational safety culture is a key determinant of workplace safety, it is also essential to focus on the non-technical skills of the system operators based at the 'sharp end' of the organisation [1].

In this context, a consortium has been created through an industrial chair. The "Behavior" chair held jointly by National Engineering School of Metz (ENIM) and the research unit 2LPN (Lorraine Laboratory of Psychology and Neuroscience of Behavioral Dynamics, UR7489) related to University of Lorraine (France). This Chair promotes collaboration between three main stakeholders: expert researchers in human factors, professionals in industrial field and experts in scripting and development of virtual environments. All of the stakeholders have opted for a training program enriched by an approach human-centered, i.e., centred to their behaviors and psychological factors underlined. The objective of the "Behavior" Chair is to develop innovative pedagogical innovations to train future engineers, professionals in industry, executives and managers in the industrial field or civil security in the behavioral approach to risk management in companies. More specifically, the challenge is to develop and validate tools (through virtual reality simulation) aimed at developing non-technical skills associated with collective tasks in an emergency or risk context. The tools developed by the "Behavior" Chair are used in training courses to assess the technical and non-technical skills mobilized in situation, and to engage the trainees in reflexive processes promoting the development of good practices and the associated skills.

This paper is aiming to present (i) one of the digital tools (i.e., an immersive environment) developed in this "Behavior" Chair oriented to the assessment of non-technical skills and (ii) the results issued from the first pre-validation testing of this digital tool conducted with 35 volunteers. In Section 1, the importance of non-technical skills in workplace safety and the different techniques used to assess them are presented; Section 2 is dedicated to the methodology used in our experiment by describing the characteristics of participants, the immersive environment specifically created, and the protocol and the procedure; In Section 3, the first results obtained in our pre-validation testing conducted with our 35 participants are described by distinguishing quantitative and qualitative data; Finally, in Section 4, perspectives and implications are discussed.

A. Non-Technical Skills to Improve Workplace Safety

From a historical point of view, non-technical skills emerged from research into aviation accidents which occurred in the late 1970s, such as the Tenerife airport disaster in 1977. As technology improved, the human contribution to accidents had become more apparent. Rather than there being any technical fault with the aircraft, it became clear from subsequent investigations that things, such as poor communication between pilots and air traffic control could be primarily responsible for these crashes. Since these disasters, a lot of other domains focused attention to non-technical skills, particularly in industry [17]. Because the modern complexities of healthcare delivery and rapid expansion of medical knowledge necessitate a high-functioning team approach, which requires human factors engineering and non-technical skills to operate effectively, multiple tools have been developed for the assessment of non-technical skills in healthcare [2] [7] [9]. Failure of non-technical skills has been linked to poor quality and safety of care [3]. For instance, a series of studies found a strong correlation between surgical team situational awareness and fewer technical errors [4] and a 3-year retrospective review of fatal medical accidents submitted to a third-party safety organisation found roughly half to be due to failures of non-technical skills, most often related to situational awareness, teamwork and decision-making [5].

While authors do not agree about the number of non-technical skills (e.g., from 11 for [1] to 22 for [12], a consensus exists about some crucial non-technical skills existing in all domains (Figure 1): time and stress management, situation awareness, communication, adaptability, creativity. In other words and in accordance with [14], we define non-technical skills as "intra- and inter-personal (socio-emotional) skills, essential for personal development, social participation and workplace success. They include skills, such as communication, ability to work on multidisciplinary teams, adaptability, etc.; these skills should be distinguished from technical, or "hard skills". We characterized them as "skills" in order to emphasize the fact that they can be learned/developed by suitable training efforts, and they can also be combined, towards the achievement of complex outcomes.

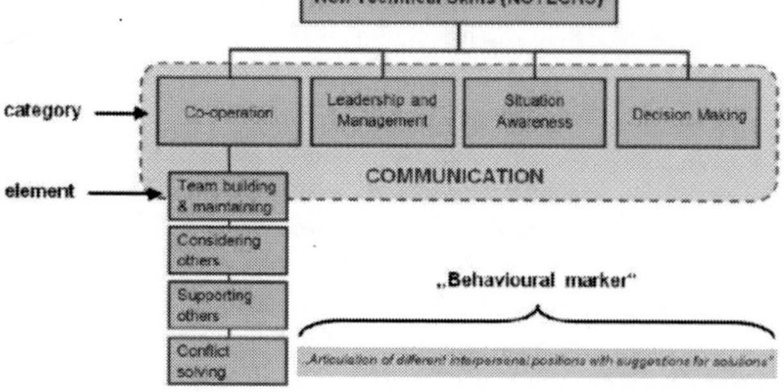

Fig. 1. Non-technical skills according to [5] and [6]

In other words, non-technical skills are defined as the social (teamwork, leadership, communication), cognitive (situation awareness, decision-making, cognitive readiness, task management) and personal management (stress and fatigue management) skills necessary for safe and effective performance. In other words, non-technical skills are the cognitive and social skills required for efficient and safe operations. In some domains such as civil aviation, nuclear power plant, high risk industry, it has long been appreciated that the majority of accidents could have been prevented if better non-technical skills had been demonstrated by personnel operating and maintaining the system. Whatever the domain (healthcare, industry, services, transportation, etc.) and whatever the activity (maintenance, problem solving, monitoring, etc.) when applied well, non-technical skills are invaluable in maintaining system safety and ensuring efficient and effective operations. For example, people often need to work in teams and communicate with one another to get a particular job done. Learned through training and practice, the best operators possess good non-technical skills which enables them to, for example, work well with others, work more safely, have a good "situation awareness" and communicate more effectively.

B. Assessment of Non-Technical Skills

Assessment methods related to non-technical skills fell into three categories [8]: simulated clinical scenarios, objective structured clinical examinations, and questionnaires or written assessments. Even if all these tools provide interesting data, they present the following limitations:

- Tools to assess non-technical skills were often developed locally, without reference to conceptual frameworks. Consequently, the tools were rarely validated, limiting dissemination and replication.
- Tools to assess non-technical skills are essentially based on qualitative and subjective data issued from verbalization or written data.
- Activity used to assess non-technical skills are often individual and "simple" activity (i.e., one people is asked to complete one specific task).
- The assessment of soft skill is therefore widely practised, but there is little in the way of research or evidence on how well this assessment is done.

. The main goal of this paper is to present an innovative tool to assess non-technical skills, by using an immersive environment, allowing collection of quantitative and objective data for several individuals engaged in a collaborative and a complex task.

The immersive environment created to assess non-technical skills has been elaborated by taking account of data issued from a large literature review suggesting that non-technical skills standards and assessments should [16]):

- Be aligned with the development of significant, soft skills goals.
- Incorporate adaptability and unpredictability.
- Be largely performance-based.

- Add value for teaching and learning.
- Make students' thinking visible.
- Valid for purpose.
- Generate information that can be acted upon and provides productive and usable feedback for all intended users.
- Provide productive and usable feedback for all intended users.
- Be part of a comprehensive and well-aligned system of assessments designed to support the improvement of learning at all levels of the educational hierarchy

.

II. METHOD

In this section, details are provided about the immersive environment created by Virtual Rangers to assess the non-technical skills, and about the design and procedure of the pilot study. This environment offers a role-playing simulation.

A. *The Immersive Environment*

The specific immersive environment created by Virtual Rangers to assess non-technical skills has been elaborated in accordance to Boud's ideas [15], having summarised a body of research on assessment, who listed desirable attributes of assessment as including:

- Assessment should be authentic (reliable).
- Assessment should be process rather than results oriented.
- the act of assessment signals the importance of what is being assessed, so assessment is a driver for learning; and assessment activities need to be seen by students as worthwhile and interesting activities.

. The use of immersive environment to assess non-technical skills is recent (e.g., [9] [18] [22]). Traditionally, immersive environments have been used in the development or the assessment of hard skills, particularly in technical areas such as health, engineering, defence or the environment [19] [21]. However, they can also be applied in the assessment and development of soft skills [20], which are increasingly key competencies for an individual in the twenty-first century [11] [12].

Fig. 2. Screenshot of the submarine viewed by each participant.

On the one hand, immersive environment headsets provide an immersion that focuses the user's attention on her/his actions in the virtual environment. On the other hand, the controllers/joysticks allow natural gestures to be reproduced to catch, use or throw objects. Tactile interactions are also simulated to reproduce screen interfaces.

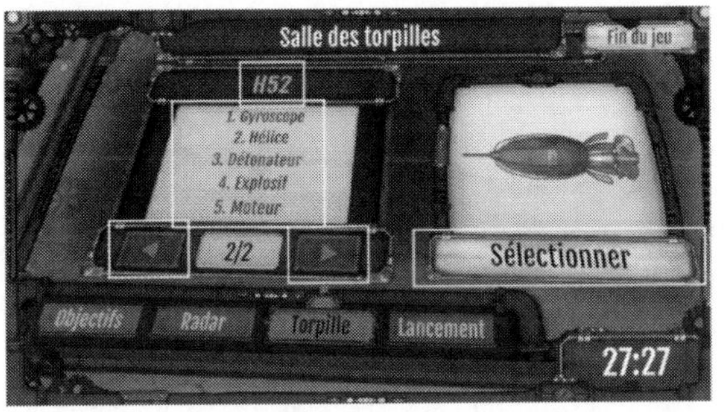

Fig. 3. Screenshot of the desk viewed by one of the players.

B. *Participants*

For this pre-validation testing session, thirty-five participants/players have been recruited to test the immersive environment specifically created. All are adults, volunteers, native French-speakers, and have no experience with immersive environment or have a very low level of experience with this kind of digital tool.

C. *Task and Procedure*

The assessment of the non-technical skills performed with our specific immersive environment has several successive steps:

- First, participants/players are asked to take a seat a the specific room to use the immersive environment (Figure 2). The situation/room can accommodate from 2 to 6 players.
- Then, each participant/player is equipped with a VR headset and is asked to take the two associated controllers/joysticks.
- After a training session, participants/players are informed that they will perform a collaborative task in a specific environment (i.e., a submarine; Figure 3). The topic (i.e., the submarine) has been chosen for the following reasons: a priori, no participant has experience in a submarine; to prevent falls, all tasks can be performed while the participant/player is seating down; and no specific technical skills are required to perform the different missions. Randomly, one of the participants/players is designated as a captain.
- To perform the collective task, each participant/player must realize specific tasks (Figure 4). They received instructions that they have to accomplish missions that will require precise synchronization and collaboration to achieve the objective of the module.. To do that, s/he is asked to listen and to understand to the instructions given by the captain, to use displayed information in front of

her/him, to use her/his hands to perform specific tasks and finally, to communicate with other participants/players.
- All interaction between participants/players are recorded to provide qualitative information about their behaviors, their verbalization and their attitudes.
- In parallel, all performances and all quantitative behaviors (e.g., time spent to perform the task, numbers and types of errors) are automatically recorded by the digital system.
- At the end of the game, a debriefing session is conducted with all participants/players. S/he is invited to comment freely their own behaviors, their difficulties, their limits or misunderstandings, etc. This debriefing session is supervised by an expert in ergonomics or work psychology.

Fig. 4. Example of a session performed in the Meta Behavior room by 6 participants.

III. Pre-Validation Testing: First results

The immersive environment several full iterations of software development, and after every iteration, the environment was tested in order to gain information about key elements: in particular, those elements that we believe can play the most prominent role in the efficacy, usability and acceptability of the immersive environment as a training and assessment tool. Iterations of development and testing are fundamental for assessing the development phase and make sure that the objectives are met to an acceptable extent. After the several iterations presented here, the immersive environment was released for an extensive validation phase

A. Quantitative Data

Performances of the team, performances, verbalisation and behaviors of each participant/player are automatically recorded by this system. By this way, it is easy to collect quantitative data such as the rate of success/failure, time spent to complete the tasks, the number and the type of each failure, etc. For instance:

- As Figure 5 shows, the more players there are, the greater the number of errors (Person's $r = .557$, $p=.0001$).
- As Figure 6 shows, the more players there are, the longer it takes to complete the mission Person's $r = .622$, $p=.0001$).
- But, finally, as Figure 7 shows, the number of errors has no significant impact on the success rate (Student't = .543, df=33, $p=.591$).
- And, in the same way, as Figure 8 shows, there is no significant relationship between the numbers of errors (x-axis) and time spent to complete the mission (Person's $r = .361$, $p=.033$).
- Some failures are particularly frequent. For instance, during the game, each participant/player was asked to take the good Personal Protective Equipment (PPE), i.e., a glove worn to minimize exposure to hazards that cause serious workplace injuries and illnesses. Each participant/player must choose the right gloves for the type of hazard (chemical, electrical, ...), this glove can be different among the player. Several participants/players did not choose the correct glove because they did not spend attention about the characteristics of the material.

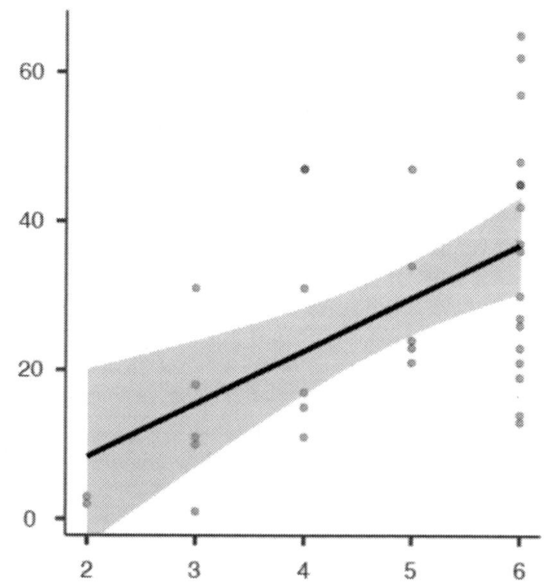

Fig. 5. Correlation between number of participants/players (x-axis, from 2 to 6) and number of errors (y-axis): Persaon's $r = .622$, $p=.001$

B. Qualitative Data

As explained in the Method part, a debriefing session was realized with all participants/players at the end of each game. Each participant/player was invited to comment freely their own behaviours, their difficulties, their limits or misunderstandings, etc. This debriefing session was always supervised by an expert in ergonomics or work psychology.

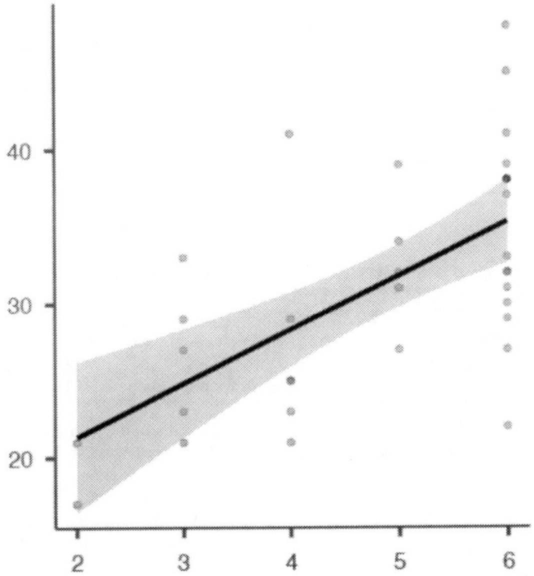

Fig. 6. Correlation between number of participants/players (x-axis, from 2 to 6) and time spent to complete the mission (y-axis, in minutes): Persaon's r = .557, p=.001

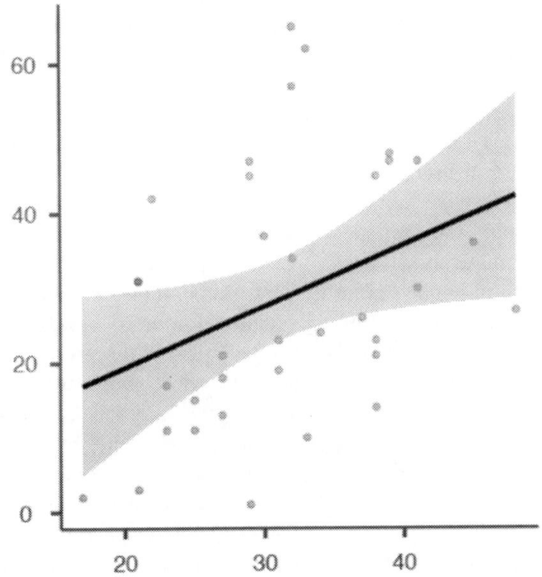

Fig. 8. Correlation between the numbers of errors (x-axis) and time spent to complete the mission (y-axis)

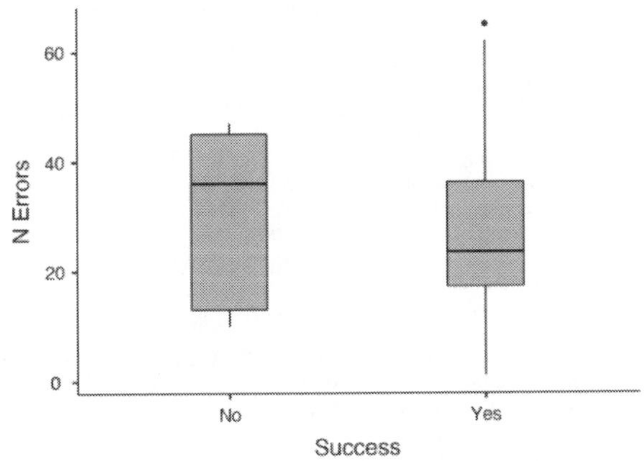

Fig. 7. Impact of the number of errors on success

A lot of interesting qualitative and complementary information has been obtained during this debriefing session. For instance, from a spontaneous manner, some participants/players evoked specific difficulties such as: "s/he didn't understand what s/he must to do, because s/he didn't listen me!" "S/he didn't respect the instructions given by the captain." "I was too stressed because the other individuals didn't' give feed backs about their own behaviours".

Moreover, some verbalisation allow to determine some problems or difficulties in the immersive environment or in the game design. For instance, some participants underlined the existence of irregularities in the synchronisation between the physical location of each other participants in the digital environment and their voices (e.g., "I saw him/her in front of me in the submarine but I heard her/his voice on the right side").

As we can see, debriefing provides information about the immersive environment itself (i.e., its usability, its acceptability, some technical problems) but debriefing is particularly crucial to allow participants/players to reflect on their experience, support each other, share perspectives, identify difficulties and finally, to develop understanding about some non-technical skills involved .

IV. Discussion

First, our results obtained with 35 participants tend to confirm that technology such as an immersive environment created by Virtual Rangers can offer a new and positive model for assessing non-technical skills. A crucial feature of non-technical skills is the fact that they can be developed through training, education and development programs and, besides the training, such non-technical skills can also be assessed using quantitative methodologies.

Second, we assume that the collaboration between scientists, industrial partners and designers is necessary to conceive a relevant assessment tool human-centred and oriented to non-technical skills.

Third, if the use of digital tool as immersive environment is relevant to assess non-technical skills, debriefing after the use is also important because it allows professional teams to reflect on their experience, support each other, share perspectives, identify learning opportunities and agree on improvement needs. In other words, we assume that an iterative and incremental human-centered design is a problem-solving technique that puts real people at the center of the development process, enabling us to create products and services such as immersive environments that resonate and are tailored to our audience's needs.

Our experiment has several limitations preventing generalization. For instance, several individual characteristics of each player/user (e.g., level of expertise, status in his/her company) were not assessed although we know that these individual characteristics can have an effect on participation or communication.

From an applied point of view, our immersive environment can be a complementary educational tool to assess and to teach non-technical skills. Non-technical skills are more and more important in industry for safety while some authors such as [23] discussed a mismatch between the goals of technical depth demanded by recruiters and line managers and the broader intellectual skills sought by corporate leadership. This can be described as the tension between needing graduates to be productive and to have safety behaviours today and the desire to harness and grow creative, innovative, and managerial talents. Non-technical Skills are more and more strategic to be successful in personal and professional life then are essential for a candidate when he tries to obtain any kind of job [24]. The quality of the industry, in terms of quality of the product, of the organization, of the services and of the workers' life and safety, strongly depends on the non-technical Skills possessed by personnel at any level. In other words, as an implication, universities and school of engineering need to equip students not just with intellectual and technical capabilities but also applied practical non-technical skills which make them more "work ready" to being focused in safety [25].

ACKNOWLEDGMENT

This research is supported by a grant issued from the industrial "Behavior" Chair ((https://chaire-behaviour.com/). We are very grateful to all the people who have participated in our experiment, and we want to thank all the partners related to the "Behaviour" Chair, this project being supported by a grant issued from Department de la Moselle (CD 57), the Center of Firefighting of Moselle (SDIS 57), Fondation ENIM, Fonds de dotation Mercy, EDF CNPE Cattenom, Virtual Rangers company, Demathieu Bard company, Eurometropole de Metz.

REFERENCES

[1] R. Flin, P. O Connor, and M. Crichton, "Safety at the Sharp End: A Guide to Non-technical Skills", 2013, pp. 1-317.

[2] H. Higham, et al., "Observer-based tools for non-technical skills assessment in simulated and real clinical environments in healthcare: a systematic review", BMJ Quality and Safety, vol. 28(8), pp. 672-686, 2019.

[3] R. Flin, G. Youngson, and S. Yule, "Enhancing surgical performance : a primer in non-technical skill", Boca Raton, FL: CRC Press, 2016.

[4] A. Mishra, K. Catchpole, T. Dale, and P. McCulloch, "The influence of non-technical performance on technical outcome in laparoscopic cholecystectomy", Surgical endoscopy, 22, pp. 68-73, 2008

[5] M. Uramatsu, et al., "Do failures in non-technical skills contribute to fatal medical accidents in Japan?" A review of the 2010–2013 national accident reports. BMJ open, vol. 7(2), e013678, 2017.

[6] P. Gontar, H. J. Hoermann, J. Deischl, and A. Haslbeck, "How Pilots Assess Their Non-Technical Performance–A Flight Simulator Study", Advances in human aspects of transportation. part i, pp. 119-128, 2014.

[7] A. L. Hamilton, J. Kerins, M. A., MacCrossan, and V. R. Tallentire, "Medical Students' Non-Technical Skills (Medi-StuNTS): preliminary work developing a behavioural marker system for the non-technical skills of medical students in acute care. BMJ Simulation and Technology Enhanced Learning", vol. 5(3), pp. 130, 2019.

[8] M. Gordon, et al., "Non-technical skills assessments in undergraduate medical education: a focused BEME systematic review", BEME Guide No. 54. Medical teacher, vol. 41(7), pp. 732-745, 2019.

[9] R. Flin, and N. Maran, "Identifying and training non-technical skills for teams in acute medicine", BMJ Quality and Safety, vol. 13(suppl 1), pp. i80-i84, 2004.

[10] F. Almeida, and Z. Buzady, "Development of soft skills competencies through the use of FLIGBY", Technology, Pedagogy and Education, vol. 31(4), pp. 417-430, 2022.

[11] H. Tadjer, Y. Lafifi, H. Seridi-Bouchelaghem, and S. Gülseçen, "Improving soft skills based on students' traces in problem-based learning environments, Interactive Learning Environments", vol. 30:10, pp. 1879-1896, 2022.

[12] V. Dolce, F. Emanuel, M. Cisi, and C. Ghislieri, "The soft skills of accounting graduates: perceptions versus expectations", Accounting Education, vol. 29:1, pp. 57-76, 2020.

[13] C. Succi, "Are you ready to find a job? Ranking of a list of soft skills to enhance graduates' employability", International Journal of Human Resources Development and Management, vol. 19(3), pp. 281-297, 2019.

[14] K. Kechagias, "Teaching and assessing soft skills", 2011, European Union. Retrieved online: http://hdl.voced.edu.au/10707/363495.

[15] D. Boud, "Enhancing learning through self assessment", Routledge, 1995.

[16] M. Binkley, et al., "Defining 21st Century Skills. Draft White Papers. Melbourne: Assessment and Teaching of 21st Century Skills (ATCS21), 2010.

[17] S. Prihatiningsih, "A Review of Soft-skill Needs in in Terms of Industry", In IOP Conference Series: Materials Science and Engineering, vol. 306, No. 1, pp. 012117, IOP Publishing, 2018.

[18] L. Hickman, and M. Akdere, "Exploring Virtual Reality for Developing Soft-Skills in STEM Education," 2017 7th World Engineering Education Forum (WEEF), Kuala Lumpur, Malaysia, 2017, pp. 461-465, doi: 10.1109/WEEF.2017.8467037.

[19] B, Eberhard, and T. Haase, "Virtual reality platforms for education and training in industry", Advances in Databases and Information Systems: Associated Workshops and Doctoral Consortium of the 13th East European Conference, ADBIS 2009, Riga, Latvia, September 7-10, 2009. Revised Selected Papers 13. Springer Berlin Heidelberg, 2010.

[20] F. Górski, "Building virtual reality applications for engineering with knowledge-based approach", Management and Production Engineering Review, vol. 8.4, pp. 64-73, 2017.

[21] D. Gorecky, M. Khamis, and K. Mura, "Introduction and establishment of virtual training in the factory of the future", International Journal of Computer Integrated Manufacturing, vol. 30(1), pp. 182-190, 2017.

[22] D. Eckert, and A. Mower, "The effectiveness of virtual reality soft skills training in the enterprise: a study", Price Waterhouse Coopers, 2020.

[23] J. J. Duderstadt, "Engineering for a changing road, a roadmap to the future of engineering practice, research, and education", Millennium Project, 2007.

[24] B. Cimatti, "Definition, development, assessment of soft skills and their role for the quality of organizations and enterprises", International Journal for quality research, vol.10(1), pp. 97, 2016.

[25] N. Khalid, et al., "Importance of soft skills for industrial training program: employers' perspective", Asian Journal of Social Sciences and Humanities, vol. 3(4), pp. 10-18, 2014.

Evaluation of Different Types of Stimuli in a ERP-Based Brain-Computer Interface Speller under RSVP

Ricardo Ron-Angevin and Álvaro Fernández-Rodríguez
Departamento de Tecnología Electrónica, Universidad de Málaga
Malaga, Spain
email: rron@uma.es, afernandezrguez@uma.es

Véronique Lespinet-Najib, Charlotte Chamard, Maëva Fortune, Antoine Hardouin, Inès Lefevre, Diane Vacherie and Jean-Marc André
Laboratoire IMS,
CNRS UMR5218, Cognitique Team, Bordeaux INP-ENSC
Talence, France
email: veronique.lespinet@ensc.fr, chchamard@ensc.fr, maefortune@ensc.fr, ahardouin001@ensc.fr, ines.lefevre@ensc.fr, dvacherie@ensc.fr, jean-marc.andre@ensc.fr

Abstract— **Rapid Serial Visual Presentation (RSVP) is currently one of the most suitable gaze-independent paradigms to control a visual brain-computer interface based on event related potentials (ERP-BCI) by patients with a lack of ocular motility. However, gaze-independent paradigms have not been studied as closely as gaze-dependent ones in reference to the type of stimuli presented. Under gaze-dependent paradigms, faces have been shown to be the most appropriate stimuli, especially when they are red. Therefore, the aim of the present work is to evaluate whether these results of the color of faces as visual stimuli also has an impact on ERP-BCI performance under the RSVP paradigm. In this preliminary study, six participants tested the ERP-BCI under RSVP using four different conditions for a speller application: letters, blue faces, red faces, and green faces. These preliminary results showed non-significant differences in accuracy or information transfer rate. The present work therefore shows that, unlike under gaze-dependent paradigms, the stimulus type has no impact on the performance of an ERP-BCI under RSVP. This finding should be considered in future ERP-BCI proposals aimed at users who need gaze-independent systems.**

Keywords – Brain-Computer Interface (BCI); Event-Related Potential (ERP); Rapid Serial Visual Presentation (RSVP); stimulus; speller

I. INTRODUCTION

An Event Related Potential (ERP)-based Brain-Computer Interface (BCI) is a type of Assistive Technology (AT) that allows a user to communicate with his/her environment using only brain signals [1]. In addition to ERP-BCIs, there are several types of ATs, such as eye-trackers, head-pointing devices, or low-pressure sensors. However, some injuries or diseases, such as Amyotrophic Lateral Sclerosis (ALS), can lead to situations in which the muscular channel and even eye movements can be affected [2]. Therefore, in severe motor limitations, most of these examples of AT may no longer be useful because they depend on some type of muscular channel that may be affected in the patient. This makes ERP-BCIs a promising option in severe cases of lack of muscular control.

ERPs are changes in the voltage of the electrical activity of the brain caused by the presentation of a specific event. These events can be external stimuli presented in various forms, like visual, auditory or tactile events [3]. The form used in the present work is the visual one. Based on the review presented in [3], this form generally provides the best results for the control of an ERP-BCI. Furthermore, under certain presentation paradigms, the visual modality can be used even if the user has no ocular control. A paradigm that does not require eye movement is Rapid Serial Visual Presentation (RSVP) [4]. In the following, we explain how RSVP is used for control of a visual ERP-BCI.

The main feature of RSVP is that the visual stimuli are presented serially—one after the other—in the same spatial location. For the control of a visual ERP-BCI, different visual stimuli are presented to the user, who must attend to one of them. Paying attention to the desired stimulus (for example, a letter in the case of a speller) should elicit a different electrical signal in the brain than the signal associated with undesired stimuli. Hence, the objective of an ERP-BCI is to discriminate between the desired or attended stimulus (target) and undesired or non-attended stimuli (non-target) based on the user's brain signals. The main component used by these systems is the P3 signal (also called P300). This P300 corresponds to a positive deflection in the amplitude of the brain's electrical signal that begins approximately 300–600 ms after the presentation of a stimulus that the user is expecting. However, an ERP-BCI generally uses all possible ERPs involved in the observed time interval (e.g., P2, N2, or a late positive potential). That is, any signal that helps to discriminate the attended stimulus (target) from unattended ones (non-target) will be used in the selected interval time (e.g., 0–800 ms after stimulus onset).

As mentioned above, the target population for a visual ERP-BCI may be patients who have lost even the ability to control their eyes. It is therefore important that the interfaces offered to this type of user are adapted to their abilities. For example, performance worsens considerably if the user cannot directly attend to stimuli with the gaze [5] [6]. This makes it convenient to employ paradigms that do not require eye control to yield adequate performance, such as RSVP. Other works have shown that parameters, such as (i) the spatial distribution of the stimuli [7], (ii) the stimulus duration [8] and (iii) the type of stimulus employed [9] have an impact on performance.

The type of stimulus used in an ERP-BCI has been a widely studied factor in gaze-dependent paradigms, such as matrix-based ones, in which stimuli are presented in subsets on a matrix of letters and the subject can gaze at any symbol. For example, the most used matrix-based paradigm is the Row-Column Paradigm (RCP). In this paradigm, rows and columns are flashed (i.e., highlighted from grey to white) one by one. To select a character, the user pays attention to the flashing of a specific target character, as this acts as the task-relevant stimulus that elicits the ERP component (e.g., the P300 potential). Once the ERP has been linked to a specific row and column, the BCI is able to determine the user's target character. In these matrix-based paradigms, faces have been one of the best performing stimuli [10], and continuing this trend, further work has shown how even the color of the face can influence performance. Specifically, in [11], it was shown that semitransparent green faces performed better than normal color semitransparent faces. Afterwards, in [12] the effect of using semitransparent faces of different colors—blue, green and red—superimposed on the letters was studied (Figure 1). In that study, it was shown that red faces performed better than green and blue faces. However, it should be considered that what was obtained, in terms of performance and the type of stimulus used, under paradigms other than RSVP need not be similar to what was obtained under RSVP [13]. It may be interesting to ask whether this effect on face color performance could also be obtained under RSVP. Therefore, the aim of this study is to replicate the experiment proposed in [12] but under the RSVP modality.

In summary, RSVP is a suitable gaze-independent control paradigm used in the field of BCIs in case users do not have oculomotor control. However, the effect previously found under gaze-dependent paradigms on the color of faces used as visual stimuli has not been studied under RSVP. Therefore, to study the effect of stimulus type on performance in an ERP-BCI under RSVP could be a significant contribution.

This paper is organized as follows: Section 2 describes the experimental setup, and presents details about the spelling paradigms. The results and discussion are presented in Section 3, followed by the conclusion and future works in Section 4.

II. Material and Methods

A. *Participants*

Six healthy French university students participated in this study. None of them had previous experience using a BCI system. The study was approved by the Ethics Committee of the University of Malaga and met the ethical standards of the Helsinki Declaration. According to self-reports, all participants had no history of neurological or psychiatric illness, had normal or corrected-to-normal vision, and gave informed consent trough a protocol reviewed by the ENSC-

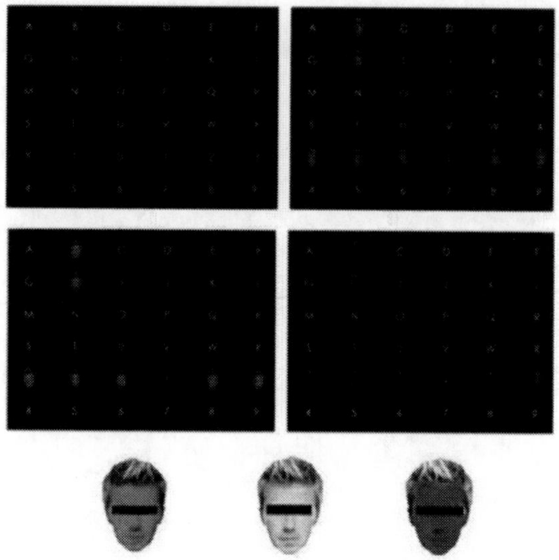

Figure 1. Stimulation pattern used in the study conducted by S. Li et al. [12] in which red, green and blue semitransparent faces were used as stimulation.

IMS (École Nationale Supérieur de Cognitique – Intégration du Matériau su Système) Cognitive and the UMA-BCI teams from the University of Malaga.

B. *Data acquisition and Signal Processing*

The EEG was recorded using the electrode positions: Fz, Cz, Pz, Oz, P3, P4, PO7 and PO8, according to the 10/10 international system. All channels were referenced to the right earlobe, using FPz as ground. Signals were amplified by a 16 channel gUSBamp amplifier (Guger Technologies). The amplifier settings were from 0.5 Hz to 100 Hz for the band pass filter, the notch (50 Hz) was on, and the sensitivity was 500 μV. The EEG was then digitized at a rate of 256 Hz. EEG data collection and processing were controlled by the UMA BCI Speller software [14], a BCI speller application developed by the UMA-BCI group which provides end users with an easy to use open-source BCI speller. This software is based on the widely used platform BCI2000 [15] so, it takes advantage of the reliability that such a platform offers. The UMA-BCI Speller wraps BCI2000 in such a way that its configuration and use are much more visual and, therefore, easier. As with any BCI speller developed with BCI2000, a Stepwise Linear Discriminant Analysis (SWLDA) of the data was performed to obtain the weights for the P300 classifier and to calculate the accuracy (using the BCI2000 tool called *P300classifier*). A detailed explanation of the SWLDA algorithm can be found in the P300Classifier user reference [16].

C. *The spelling paradigms*

Four different RSVP paradigms were evaluated in the present work. The only difference between paradigms was the type of stimulus used: (i) Gray Letters (GL), (ii) semitransparent gray letters with a Blue Famous Face (BFF), (iii) semitransparent gray letters with Green Famous Face

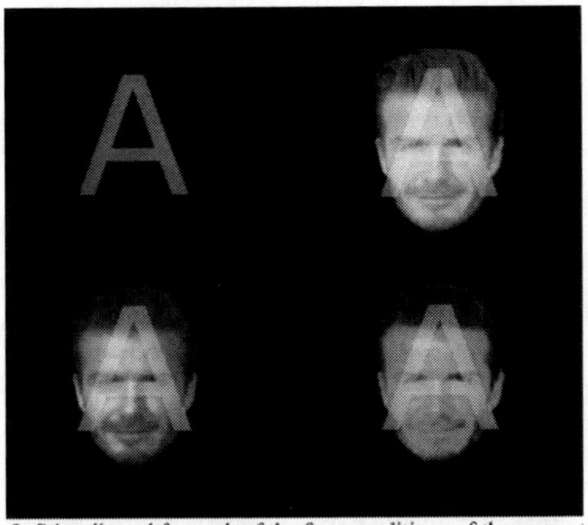

Figure 2. Stimuli used for each of the four conditions of the present study.

(GFF), and (iv) semitransparent gray letters with Red Famous Face (RFF) (Figure 2). Each paradigm presented six different letters that would be used during the experiment for writing words (A, E, I, N, R, and S, arial font). The number of letters was selected to avoid a target selection time that was too long, as the aim of this study was to validate the different sets of stimuli under RSVP for communication purposes. In previous studies with this kind of paradigm, the same number of elements has been used to validate hypotheses [9] [17]. The famous face of David Beckham was used as stimulus, as other authors did on [11]. The dimensions regarding the type of stimuli were as follows: letters, around 6 × 6 cm (the letter N was used as a reference); and faces, around 6 × 8 cm. The background used for the interface was black, and the stimuli were presented in the center of the screen. Also, at the top of the screen, both the letters to be selected and those previously selected were indicated.

The duration of each stimulus presentation was equal to 187.5ms and the Inter Stimuli Interval (ISI) was equal to 93.75ms. Therefore, the Stimulus Onset Asynchrony (SOA) had a duration equal to 281.25ms. The time for completing a sequence (i.e., single presentation or flashing of every stimulus) was 1687.5 ms. The pause time between one selection and the start of the next (i.e., between completed sets of sequences) was equal to 5 s. The flashing stimuli were presented in the center of the screen.

D. *Procedure*

A within-subject design was used, so that all users went through all experimental conditions. The experiment was carried out in one session. The order of the paradigms was counterbalanced across participants to prevent any undesired effects, such as learning or fatigue. Each condition consisted of two parts: (i) an initial calibration phase to obtain the specific signal patterns associated with each user and (ii) an online phase in which the user actually controlled the interface. Therefore, the main difference between both phases was that in the first phase the user did not receive any feedback.

For both phases, the task was to write different French four-letter words. In the case of the calibration phase, the participant had to write four words ("ASIE", "REIN", "NIER", and "SAIN"), so the total number of selections for this task was 16 letters. On the other hand, for the online phase, the user had to write three words ("ANIS", "REIN" and "SERA"), so the number of selections would be 12 letters. In case the user made a mistake when selecting a letter in the online phase, he/she had to continue with the next letter. For both phases, a short break between words (variable at the request of the user) was employed. The number of sequences (i.e., the number of times that each stimulus—target and non-target—was presented) was fixed to 10 in the calibration phase. Otherwise, for the online phase, the number of sequences selected was two more sequences than the minimum number of sequences required to obtain 100% accuracy in the calibration phase.

E. *Evaluation*

Two parameters were used to evaluate the effect of the RSVP paradigm and stimulus type on performance: i) the accuracy in the calibration and online phases, and ii) the Information Transfer Rate (ITR) in the online phase. The accuracy (%) was defined as the percentage of correctly predicted selections. While for the online task this last definition was applied, for the calibration phase, the accuracy was computed by the signal classifier after the classification of the word using the data from each sequence. The ITR (bit/min) is an objective measure to determine the communication speed of the system [18]. This parameter considers accuracy, the number of elements available in the interface and time to select one element:

$$\mathrm{ITR} = \frac{\log_2 N + P\log_2 P + (1-P)\log_2 \frac{1-P}{N-1}}{T}$$

where P is the accuracy of the system, N is the number of elements available at the interface and T is the time needed to complete a trial (i.e., select an element). It should be noted that the pause between selections was not considered when calculating the ITR.

III. Results and Discussion

A. *Calibration phase*

The *P300classifier* tool provides the performance obtained in the calibration phase according to the number sequences (Figure 3). In reference to accuracy in the calibration phase, the performance shown has been satisfactory, exceeding 90% average accuracy for all conditions from the third sequence. A three-way repeated measures ANOVA (4 × 10) including the conditions (GL, BFF, GFF and RFF), and sequence (from sequence 1 to 10) factors was carried out. The analysis only showed significant differences for the sequence factor (F (9, 45) = 37.322; $p < 0.001$), but not for the condition factor (F (3, 15) = 1.427; p = 0.274) or the interaction between them (F (27, 135) = 0.999; p = 0.475). Therefore, as can be observed in Figure 3, it seems that the accuracy obtained depends on the number of sequences carried out, but not on the type of stimulus used.

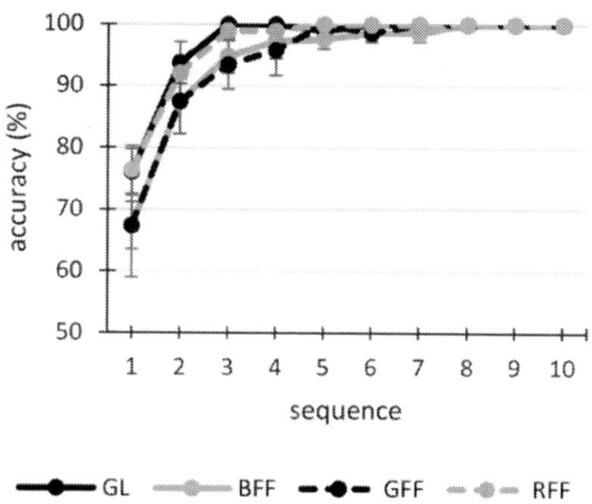

Figure 3. Accuracy (mean ± standard error) of the different conditions—gray letters (GF), semitransparent blue famous face (BFF), semitransparent green famous face (GFF), and semitransparent red famous face (RFF)—as a function of the number of sequences.

B. Online phase

In reference to the online phase, it can also be affirmed that the results obtained were adequate, with an accuracy and ITR higher than 85% and 15 bits/min for all conditions (table 1). Two three-way repeated measures ANOVA (4) including the condition factor (GL, BFF, GFF and RFF) were performed using each one accuracy and ITR as dependent variable. These analyses showed no significant results for either the accuracy (F (3, 15) = 0.718; p = 0.557) or the ITR (F (3, 15) = 0.459; p = 0.715). Therefore, these results show that stimulus type has no significant effect on ERP-BCI performance under RSVP.

C. Related literature

The results obtained in the present work differs with those previously obtained by other proposals under gaze-dependent paradigms. In those proposals, it was shown that the use of faces as stimuli produced an improvement in performance compared to letters [10], and even differences depending on the color of the face [11], [12]. In the present work, under RSVP, no significant differences were even obtained between letters and red faces, which were supposed to be the best stimuli under a matrix-based paradigm. However, these results are in line with those obtained in previous works that showed that the enhancements produced by the type of stimulus depend on the presentation paradigm used. Specifically, other studies under RSVP have demonstrated that the type of stimulus used does not produce an improvement in performance compared to those obtained under other matrix-based paradigms [13], [20]. Therefore, it is necessary to consider the peculiarities of each paradigm to find out which variables are the ones that can allow an improvement in performance. Based on the results obtained in the present study, in the design of a RSVP-based speller, since no significant differences were found, the option of stimulating only with letters should be considered, that is, without adding other elements (e.g., images superimposed on the letters) that could even make it more difficult to detect the desired stimulus.

IV. CONCLUSIONS AND FUTURE WORK

The present preliminary study has shown that the color of the faces used as visual stimuli does not seem to affect ERP-BCI performance under RSVP. Therefore, it is possible that, at least to improve performance, the use of faces or colored faces is not necessary. In this line, in order to choose the type of stimuli used, it could be more convenient to be guided by other variables, such as the user's preferences or the type of application to be controlled. However, it is admitted that the present work shows its limitations since the sample size employed has been small and more metrics could have been added, such as an analysis of the ERP signal or questionnaires focused on evaluating the user experience. Thus, future work could go deeper into this type of assessment more extensively. It would also be interesting if further work aims to explain which variables affect the user experience using an ERP-BCI under RSVP and how they can be manipulated to improve performance.

ACKNOWLEDGMENT

This research is part of the SICODIS project (PID2021-127261OB-I00), which has been jointly funded by the Spanish Ministry of Science, Innovation, and Universities (MCIU); the Spanish State Investigation Agency (AEI); the European Regional Development Fund (ERDF); and the University of Malaga. This work has been carried out in a framework agreement between the University of Málaga and the University of Bordeaux (Bordeaux INP). Moreover, the authors would like to thank all participants for their cooperation.

TABLE I. MEAN ± STANDARD DEVIATION (SD) OF NUMBER OF SEQUENCES USED, ACCURACY AND INFORMATION TRANSFER RATE (ITR) FOR THE DIFFERENT CONDITIONS IN THE ONLINE TASK: WL, BFF, GFF, RFF.

Participant	Number of sequences				Accuracy (%)				ITR (bit/min)			
	GL	BFF	GFF	RFF	GL	BFF	GFF	RFF	GL	BFF	GFF	RFF
P01	3	3	3	6	91.67	100	100	100	23.44	30.63	30.63	15.32
P02	4	5	4	4	50	91.67	83.33	75	3.77	14.06	13.76	10.61
P03	4	3	5	4	83.33	83.33	100	100	13.76	18.35	18.38	22.98
P04	3	5	5	4	100	100	100	83.33	30.63	18.38	18.38	13.76
P05	4	4	3	4	100	100	100	100	22.98	22.98	30.63	22.98
P06	5	9	8	4	100	58.33	100	83.33	18.38	2.52	11.49	13.76
Mean	3.83	4.83	4.67	4.33	87.50	88.89	97.22	90.28	18.83	17.82	20.55	16.57
SD	0.75	2.23	1.86	0.82	19.54	16.39	6.8	11.08	9.28	9.38	8.26	5.2

REFERENCES

[1] J. R. Wolpaw, N. Birbaumer, D. J. McFarland, G. Pfurtscheller, and T. M. Vaughan, "Brain-computer interfaces for communication and control," Clin. Neurophysiol., vol. 113, no. 6, pp. 767–791, 2002, doi: 10.1016/S1388-2457(02)00057-3.

[2] G. Bauer, F. Gerstenbrand, and E. Rumpl, "Varieties of the locked-in syndrome," J. Neurol., vol. 221, no. 2, pp. 77–91, 1979, doi: 10.1007/BF00313105.

[3] B. Z. Allison, A. Kübler, and J. Jin, "30+ years of P300 brain–computer interfaces," Psychophysiology, vol. 57, no. 7, pp. 1–18, 2020, doi: 10.1111/psyp.13569.

[4] L. Acqualagna and B. Blankertz, "Gaze-independent BCI-spelling using rapid serial visual presentation (RSVP)," Clin. Neurophysiol., vol. 124, no. 5, pp. 901–908, 2013, doi: 10.1016/j.clinph.2012.12.050.

[5] P. Brunner et al., "Does the 'P300' speller depend on eye gaze?," J. Neural Eng., vol. 7, no. 5, p. 56013, 2010, doi: 10.1088/1741-2560/7/5/056013.

[6] S. Chennu, A. Alsufyani, M. Filetti, A. M. Owen, and H. Bowman, "The cost of space independence in P300-BCI spellers," J. Neuroeng. Rehabil., vol. 10, no. 1, pp. 1–13, 2013, doi: 10.1186/1743-0003-10-82.

[7] D. O. Won, H. J. Hwang, D. M. Kim, K. R. Müller, and S. W. Lee, "Motion-Based Rapid Serial Visual Presentation for Gaze-Independent Brain-Computer Interfaces," IEEE Trans. Neural Syst. Rehabil. Eng., vol. 26, no. 2, pp. 334–343, 2018, doi: 10.1109/TNSRE.2017.2736600.

[8] S. Lees, P. Mccullagh, L. Maguire, F. Lotte, and D. Coyle, "Speed of rapid serial visual presentation of pictures , numbers and words affects event-related potential-based detection accuracy," IEEE Trans. Neural Syst. Rehabil. Eng., vol. 28, no. 1, pp. 113–122, 2020, doi: 10.1109/TNSRE.2019.2953975.

[9] L. Chen et al., "Exploring Combinations of Different Color and Facial Expression Stimuli for Gaze-Independent BCIs," Front. Comput. Neurosci., vol. 10, no. January, p. 5, 2016, doi: 10.3389/fncom.2016.00005.

[10] T. Kaufmann, S. M. Schulz, C. Grünzinger, and A. Kübler, "Flashing characters with famous faces improves ERP-based brain-computer interface performance," J. Neural Eng., vol. 8, no. 5, p. 056016, 2011, doi: 10.1088/1741-2560/8/5/056016.

[11] Q. Li, S. Liu, J. Li, and O. Bai, "Use of a green familiar faces paradigm improves P300-speller brain-computer interface performance," *PLoS One*, vol. 10, no. 6, pp. 1–15, 2015, doi: 10.1371/journal.pone.0130325.

[12] S. Li et al., "Comparison of the ERP-Based BCI Performance Among Chromatic (RGB) Semitransparent Face Patterns," Front. Neurosci., vol. 14, no. January, pp. 1–12, 2020, doi: 10.3389/fnins.2020.00054.

[13] Á. Fernández-Rodríguez, M. T. Medina-Juliá, F. Velasco-Álvarez, and R. Ron-Angevin, "Different effects of using pictures as stimuli in a P300 brain-computer interface under rapid serial visual presentation or row-column paradigm," Med. Biol. Eng. Comput., vol. 59, no. 4, pp. 869–881, 2021, doi: 10.1007/s11517-021-02340-y.

[14] F. Velasco-Álvarez et al., "UMA-BCI Speller: an Easily Configurable P300 Speller Tool for End Users," *Comput.* Methods Programs Biomed., vol. 172, pp. 127–138, 2019, doi: 10.1016/J.CMPB.2019.02.015.

[15] G. Schalk, D. J. McFarland, T. Hinterberger, N. Birbaumer, and J. R. Wolpaw, "BCI2000: A general-purpose brain-computer interface (BCI) system," IEEE Transactions on Biomedical Engineering, vol. 51, no. 6, pp. 1034–1043, 2004, doi: 10.1109/TBME.2004.827072.

[16] "User Reference: P300Classifier," 2011. https://www.bci2000.org/mediawiki/index.php/User_Reference:P300Classifier. 2023/05/25.

[17] Á. Fernández-Rodríguez, M. T. Medina-Juliá, F. Velasco-Álvarez, and R. Ron-Angevin, "Preliminary Results Using a P300 Brain-Computer Interface Speller: A Possible Interaction Effect Between Presentation Paradigm and Set of Stimuli," in Lecture Notes in Computer Science (including subseries Lecture Notes in Artificial Intelligence and Lecture Notes in Bioinformatics), vol. 11506 LNCS, I. Rojas, G. Joya, and A. Catala, Eds. Springer International Publishing, 2019, pp. 371–381.

[18] J. R. Wolpaw, H. Ramoser, D. J. McFarland, and G. Pfurtscheller, "EEG-based communication: Improved accuracy by response verification," IEEE Trans. Rehabil. Eng., vol. 6, no. 3, pp. 326–333, 1998, doi: 10.1109/86.712231.

[19] T. Kaufmann and A. Kübler, "Beyond maximum speed - A novel two-stimulus paradigm for brain-computer interfaces based on event-related potentials (P300-BCI)," J. Neural Eng., vol. 11, no. 5, 2014, doi: 10.1088/1741-2560/11/5/056004.

[20] R. Ron-Angevin et al., "Performance Analysis With Different Types of Visual Stimuli in a BCI-Based Speller Under an RSVP Paradigm," Front. Comput. Neurosci., vol. 14, 2021, doi: 10.3389/fncom.2020.587702.

Cognitive Chrono-Ethnography (CCE) to Reveal Personal Walking Motivations and Nudging Habit Formation in Reaction

Max Hanssen
University of Tsukuba
Tsukuba, Ibaraki, Japan
Email: maxhanssen98@outlook.com

Muneo Kitajima
Nagaoka University of Technology
Nagaoka, Niigata, Japan
Email: mkitajima@kjs.nagaokaut.ac.jp

SeungHee Lee
University of Tsukuba
Tsukuba, Ibaraki, Japan
Email: lee.seunghee.gn@u.tsukuba.ac.jp

Abstract—**Cognitive Chrono-Ethnography (CCE) explores the qualitative nature of people's decision-making process through ethnographical field observation to identify human behaviors related to a daily activity. This paper shows how the results of previous CCE studies on habitual walking behavior possibly nudged people along the stages of the transtheoretical model. The interview results of 29 participants from past CCE studies showed that participants became more consciously aware of their appreciation for certain walking elements through either the one-on-one interview or the experience on an unfamiliar route. Moreover, the revealed walking motivations were matched to the six different stages of the transtheoretical model, assuming that people in the precontemplation and contemplation stages are motivated by exploration and a route plan, people in the preparation and action stages are motivated by the surrounding and social aspects, and people in the maintenance and termination stages are motivated by mental thinking, physical exercise, and a route plan.**

Keywords—Cognitive Chrono-Ethnography; Habit Formation; Walking Preferences; Nudges.

I. Introduction

Making a permanent change in behavior is rarely a simple process. It often involves a considerable commitment of effort, time, and emotion. In this regard, many researchers have studied the process of behavior change. Prochaska introduced the transtheoretical model of behavior change, which assess an individual's readiness to act on a new healthier behavior, and provides strategies, or processes of change to guide the individual [1]. In the transtheoretical model, change involves progress through the following six stages [1][2]:

1) Precontemplation: People have no intention to take action in the foreseeable future and are unaware of their behaviour.
2) Contemplation: People are aware of their behaviour, and intend to take action in the foreseeable future.
3) Preparation: People are intending to take action in the immediate future, and may begin taking small steps of behaviour change.
4) Action: People have made overt modifications in their behaviour or in acquiring new healthy behaviours.
5) Maintenance: People have been able to sustain their change for at least six months and are working to prevent relapse.
6) Termination: People have zero temptation and they are sure they will not return to their old behavior.

Past research mentioned various motivating factors for progression along the transtheoretical model stages. Accordingly, it is recognized that people at different stages are motivated by different messages. A smoker in precontemplation likely needs different information to move to contemplation than a smoker in the action stage who needs to move to the maintenance stage. Hence, it is important to develop persuasive interventions that match an individual's stage. Hereof, O'Keefe [3] noted that decisional balance and self-efficacy are important to create stage-matched persuasive messages.

This research considers the capability of the nudge theory to push people along the different stages of the transtheoretical model. Nudge theory is based on the concept that by shaping the environment, one can influence the likelihood that one option is chosen over another by individuals [4]. In other words, nudge theory proposes adaptive designs of the decision environment as ways to influence the behavior and decision-making of groups or individuals [4]. Therefore, a nudge makes it more likely for a person to make a particular choice, by altering the environment so that automatic cognitive processes are triggered to favour the desired outcome.

On this matter, Cognitive Chrono-Ethnography (CCE) as defined by Kitajima [5][6] could possibly be a nudge to promote habit formation in participants. CCE explores the qualitative nature of people's decision-making process through ethnographical field observation to identify human behaviors related to a daily activity. Afterwards, study parameters are identified through model-based simulation, which are used to find participants who suit the criteria. Consequently, a CCE study is conducted where participant's activity is recorded without interfering their usual behavior. For example, Kitajima, Nakajima, and Toyota [7] clarified visiting behaviors of 9 loyal baseball fans via CCE. They selected loyal fans based on web questionnaires and interviews, and asked them to watch three baseball games while their view, heart rate, and utterances were recorded. One week after each game, interviews were conducted. Each participant did 4 interviews, which created a fan history from 5 years ago until the present, showing what triggered them to stage-up and become a loyal fan. Among the participants, there was one fan who mentioned that looking back on his past made him a stronger fan [8]. Therefore, reflecting on one's own experience via CCE unconsciously nudged them on the transtheoretical model.

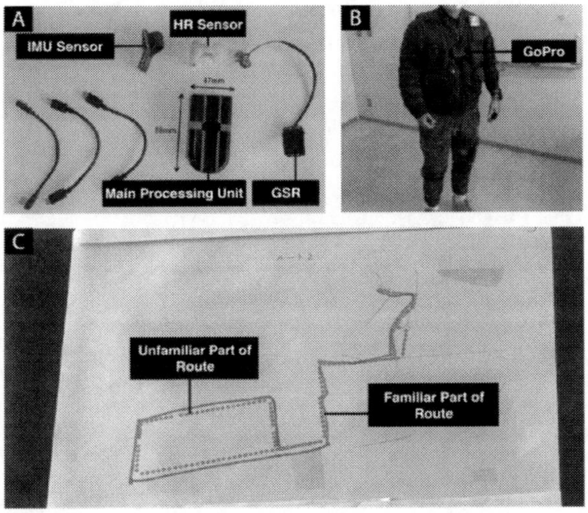

Figure 1. Walking experiences were recorded via (A) biometric data captured with a wearable device, (B) video footage captured with a GoPro camera, and (C) a map showing the familiar and unfamiliar parts of the route.

Similarly, past studies have used CCE to study individual walking experiences and identify individuals' walking motivations to promote healthy habitual behaviors [9][10][11]. During the studies, participants became aware of their appreciation for certain elements of a walk because of the experimental setting of CCE. Therefore, we hypothesized that participants of this study also unconsciously progressed on the transtheoretical model, because the personal walking motivations became apparent through the CCE study. However, research has not yet confirmed whether the past CCE studies also nudged participants to forming a walking habit. Therefore, the purpose of this study is to clarify how CCE revealed individuals' walking motivations, and consider how participation to the CCE study could nudge participants to make a permanent change in behavior.

This paper is organized as follows. In Section II, the methodology of this study is described. In Section III, the results of the 29 participants are shown regarding personal walking motivations. In Section IV, the relation between CCE, walking motivations, and nudge theory are discussed. Finally, Section V concludes the paper and shows how future works concerns CCE to promote healthy habit formation.

II. Methodology

In order to understand how CCE helps participants becoming aware of the walking elements that personally motivate them to take a walk, this study examined the experience of 29 participants from past CCE studies [9][10][11]. All participants walked two routes: firstly, a familiar route (A), and afterward, an unfamiliar route (B). Routes were discussed and decided together with participants beforehand to confirm participants' familiarity with the routes. As shown by Degen and Rose [12], taking repetitive walking routes makes people less sensitive to their surroundings. As a consequence, individuals, who enjoy the benefits of walking, might not be aware of all the elements that contribute to their good walk. This is further supported by the fact that walking is an automatic process performed unconsciously [13]. Hence, walking an unfamiliar route after a familiar route possibly helped to reveal underlying personal factors that are unconsciously valued by participants. Moreover, their activity was recorded via a wearable device to capture biometric data (Figure 1 (A)), an attachable GoPro camera to capture video footage (Figure 1 (B)), and a map where participants filled in their familiar and unfamiliar parts of the route (Figure 1 (C)).

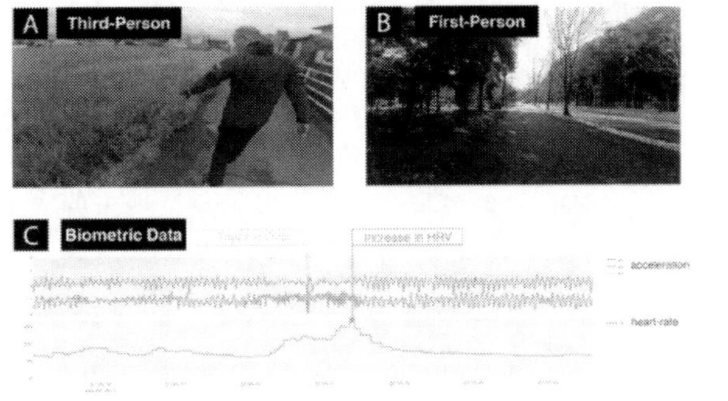

Figure 2. Activities of participants 1 to 5 were recorded via (A) third-person view, while participants 6 to 29's (B) first-person view was recorded, and (C) biometric data of all participant was visualized.

Consequently, after route A and after route B, 10-minute one-on-one interviews were conducted. Following the CCE approach, participants' walking experience was reproduced in chronological order by showcasing the captured video footage, biometric data, and route to make participants remember their experience to the best extent possible. During the interview, participants were asked about their activity by focusing on the decision-making process and satisfaction of their walks. Additional questions were asked about the walk's interesting moments, participants' walking preferences, and the good and bad parts of the walk.

Past research [9][11] transcribed and analyzed the interview answers using Thematic Analysis (TA) to relate participants' walking habit with the walking elements that they valued, and to clarify the events that triggered the feeling of value or satisfaction. TA is a method for identifying, and analyzing patterns of a dataset [14]. Hanssen et al. [9][11] first familiarized themselves with the interview answers, and marked interesting answers. Then, similar interesting answers were grouped into themes and further reviewed. Finally, each theme was named, and results were summarized.

III. Results

A. Activity Recording

As a result of the wearable device (Figure 1(A)) and the attached GoPro video camera (Figure 1(B)), camera footage and biometric data were recorded for all participants. Participants 1 to 5 participated in a separate CCE study [9] from participants 6 to 29 [11]. The video footage was recorded from

TABLE I. THE VALUES MENTIONED BY EACH PARTICIPANT DURING THE ONE-ON-ONE INTERVIEWS AFTER EACH WALK

Participant	Value 1	Value 2	Value 3	Value 4	Value 5	Value 6	Value 7
1	Safety	Unknown Scenery	Rhythm				
2	Safety	Daylight					
3	Conversation	Flora	Company	Surrounding	Nature		
4	Flora	Insects	Talking	Scenery	Nostalgic	Benefits	
5	Seeing Firework	Night	Nostalgic	Conversation	Relax	Scenery	
6	Sunny	Seeing pigeon	Seeing statue	Seeing playground	Seeing School	Seeing lake	Seeing trees
7	New Things						
8	New Things	Weather	Feelin Environment				
9	Safety	Air Quality	Scent	Weather			
10	Peaceful Atmosphere	Safety					
11	Less People	Scenery	Tempo and Music	Adventure			
12	Mental Thinking	Scenery					
13	Scenery	Sunny	Time	Less People			
14	Natural View	New Shops	Less People	Explore	Season	Flowers	
15	Physical	Oxygen	Thinking while Exercising	Road Condition			
16	Landmarks	Familiarity	Purpose	Fun Shops			
17	Sunny	Greenery	Peceful and Silent				
18	Safety	Scenery	No Cars				
19	Mentality	Weather					
20	Pedestrian Road	Plants	Season				
21	Relaxing						
22	Others	Nature	Scenery	No Noise	Explore		
23	Purpose	Solitude	Nature	Silence	See Others	Continuity	
24	Time	Freedom	With Someone	Purpose	Plan		
25	With Someone	Walkability	Scenery				
26	Scenery Changes	Newness	Nature	Walkability			
27	Physical Benefits	Purpose					
28	Familiarty	Adventure	Time				
29	Weather	New Things					

different perspectives for the two CCE studies. Therefore, the captured video footage was recorded from a third-person view for participants 1 to 5 (Figure 2(A)), and a first-person view for participants 6 to 29 (Figure 2(B)). Moreover, Figure 2(C) shows an example of the biometric data that was recorded with the wearable device shown in Figure 1(B). As part of a CCE study, these recordings were shown to participants during the one-on-one interviews to improve the memory of participants related to their experience.

B. One-on-one Interviews

During the interview participants discussed parts of the walk that impacted them and identified enjoyable walking elements that potentially motivated them to walk again. Table I summarizes all values that were mentioned by the 29 participants in the past research [9][11].

Many participants became aware of their appreciation for certain values through the interview itself. The review of the captured video footage, biometric data, and map of the route made participants remember their walking experience, enabling them to answer the questions asked by the researcher. Hereof, participants mentioned directly that they were unaware of their appreciation for certain elements that walking has to offer, but the experiment made them realize their appreciation for these walking elements. For example, participant 4 mentioned the values "Nostalgic" and "Benefits" during the interview. In this regard, he mentioned:

> *I felt nostalgic while walking because I used to take recreational walks in the past but not any more. My father used to walk with me everyday because I had many personal troubles after we moved to a different house. Now I realize that walking everyday gave me many benefits that helped me to overcome that situation.*

Other participants realized their appreciation for certain walking elements after they were introduced to an unfamiliar route after the usual familiar walk that they took. In this regard, participants 1 and 2 realized their appreciation for "Safety" after the unfamiliar route. For example, after walking a route with a narrower pedestrian road than usual, participant 1 told the interviewer:

> *The narrow pedestrian road was too close to the cars passing-by and made the route not enjoyable. Therefore, I think safety is the most important factor for a good walk.*

Similarly, participant 15 mentioned her appreciation for certain specific walking elements related to safety, such as "Road Condition" and "Thinking while Exercising." These became apparent to her after walking an unfamiliar route, which had a poorer road condition than she was used to with her familiar walks. She mentioned:

> *The poor condition of the pedestrian road made me focus on where I put my feet while walking. Because of this, I could not think about the things I want to think about while walking.*

However, many participants' experience were also positively influenced by the unfamiliarity of the second route, making their appreciation for "Newness" and "Exploration" apparent. For example, participant 26 mentioned the importance of

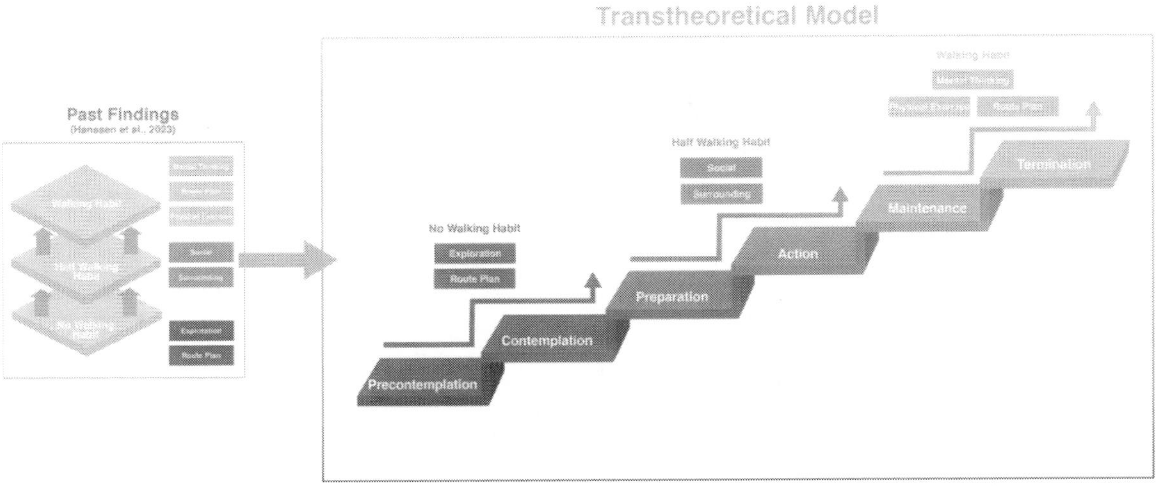

Figure 3. Walking motivations related to different stages of the Transtheoretical Model were found based on previous findings [9].

"Scenery Changes" and "Newness" after walking an unfamiliar route. Also, participants 7 and 8 mentioned "New Things" as important motivations for them to take a walk. Similarly, participant 14 mentioned the importance to explore during a walk. After having walked her unfamiliar route, she mentioned during the interview:

> *I like to explore during a walk. I saw new shops that looked interesting. It is nice to find new shops that I can maybe visit later in the future.*

The familiarity of the experience was not only determined by the route that participants walked, but also by the time of the day. Participant 2 usually takes a walk in the daylight. However, he walked the second unfamiliar route during the night. As a result, the familiarity of the overall walking experience further decreased. Moreover, participant 2 noticed the importance of daylight in order to have a satisfying walk. In this regard, he mentioned:

> *I needed to watch out where I walked because of the lack of light. Therefore, the walking experience felt less safe.*

C. Emerged Themes for Walking Motivations

The Thematic Analysis of the previous CCE studies showed that people with different walking habits valued different walking elements. As a result, Hanssen et al. [11] classified the values into the following six emerging themes to relate the values to walking habit stages:

- **Surrounding:** Elements related to natural features of our surroundings, considered in terms of their appearance, smell, and sound.
- **Social:** People's need for interactions with other people or need for solitude during the walk.
- **Exploration:** Wanting to explore "newness" during a walk by encountering unfamiliar events or objects.
- **Route Plan:** People with a walking habit benefited from the "safety" and "road condition" of the Route Plan, while people with no habit valued the "purpose" or "destination" of the Route Plan.
- **Physical Exercise:** Walking motivations that stem from wanting to move the body for healthy exercise.
- **Mental Thinking:** Walking helped to stimulate the people to think about desired things in their mind.

IV. Discussion

A. CCE to Identify Walking Motivations

Past studies took various approaches to study habit formation that improve physical health [15][16]. Lally et al. [15] documented experiences of habit development in participants who enrolled on a weight loss intervention. Tobias [16] developed a social psychological model of habit development by studying the effect of memory aid in habit development and analyzing time-series data from a behavior-change campaigns. Both studies found insights regarding behavior change. Lally et al. [15] revealed that behavior change is initially experienced as effortful but automaticity increased, as the performance becomes easier. Moreover, Tobias [16] provided a new understanding on the role of memory to support the performance of repeated behaviors. However, related works have not yet shown methods to reveal the valued walking elements of people that have different walking habits [1][2].

Nevertheless, the past CCE studies' results on people's walking experience raised awareness on personally valued walking elements [9][11]. In particular, some participants' one-on-one interview responses revealed that they were unaware of personal walking motivations beforehand, but the walks during the experiment and review of the captured activity recordings raised their awareness on the elements that motivated or satisfied them. These were summarized in Table I, and it could be argued that these stimulated them to walk regularly. In this manner, CCE contributed to healthy behavior change as it was able to identify the walking elements that motivate people to walk again.

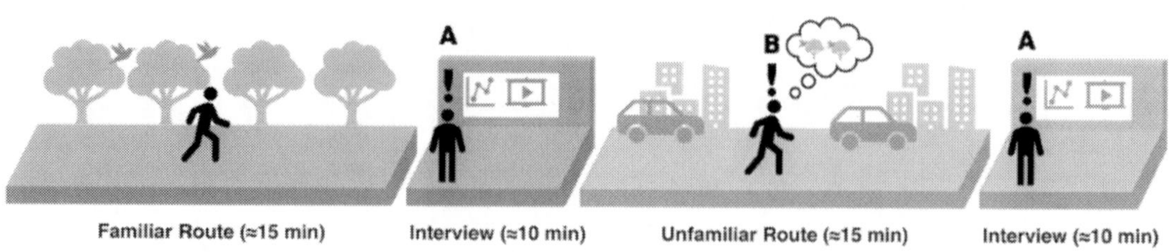

Figure 4. Personal walking motivations of participants were found during the CCE study by either (A) the review of the captured data during the interview or (B) the presence or lack of certain walking elements during the unfamiliar route.

Moreover, Hanssen et al. [11] further classified the valued walking elements into themes via Thematic Analysis. Six themes emerged, which were further related to people of different walking habit stages, identifying how people with a walking habit value different elements than people without a walking habit. This study built upon the previous findings by examining how the themes possibly relate to the different stages of the transtheoretical model, as shown in Figure 3.

In past research, three different walking habit stages were identified based on how often participants mentioned that they walked in their daily life. The three stages were the "No Walking Habit", "Half Walking Habit", and "Walking Habit" stages. Since previous research identified three habit stages and there are six stages in the transtheoretical model, this research matched the "No Walking Habit" stage to the "Precontemplation" and "Contemplation" stages, the "Half Walking Habit" stage to the "Preparation" and "Action" stages, and the "Walking Habit" stage to the "Maintenance" and "Termination" stages of the transtheoretical model. Therefore, this study assumes that people in each stage are motivated by the following values, as shown in Figure 3:

- **Precontemplation – Contemplation:** People at this stage are motivated to stage-up by values related to "Exploration" and "Route Plan" of walking. Specifically, the "Route Plan" needs a purpose and destination.
- **Preparation – Action:** People at this stage are motivated to stage-up by values related to "Social" and the "Surrounding" of walking.
- **Maintenance – Termination:** People at this stage are motivated to stage-up by values related to "Mental Thinking", "Physical Exercise" and "Route Plan" of walking. Specifically, the "Route Plan" needs to be have good road conditions and safety.

However, future works should concern how participants can be categorized to one of the six stages of the transtheoretical model. Currently, this research assumed relations between the three walking habit stages and the transtheoretical model, but these are only based upon the frequency that participants mentioned to walk in their daily life. Hence, more in-depth questions should be asked in future works to confirm the stage of the participant, and to reveal what walking elements motivated people in each of the six stages.

B. CCE as a Nudge for Walking Habit Formation

Not only researchers, but also the participants themselves became aware of the elements that motivated them. Therefore, participation to the CCE study enabled the participants to better understand their reasons and benefits for walking. It can be argued that better understanding the reasons and benefits of healthy activities motivates people to perform this activity regularly [17] . Therefore, past CCE studies were not only able to identify walking motivations, but also nudged participants to form a walking habit by letting them understand their personal walking motivations.

Hereof, CCE nudged people in two different manners. First, with the review of the video footage, map, and biometric data, as it helped participants to remember and understand their own experience better. Accordingly, when they were questioned about their walking motivations, they discovered that they had an appreciation for certain walking elements that they previously did not know (Figure 4(A)). An example can be seen in the response of participant 4. The interview and review of the captured data together with a researcher forced participant 4 to reflect on walking in general. Because of this, the participant realized the importance and benefits that he got from past walking experiences. In other words, it can be argued that the participant became more aware of the effect of daily walking, which possibly motivated him to walk more frequently.

Second, participants discovered their appreciation for walking elements during the unfamiliar route (Figure 4(B)). In this regard, participants either realized their personal walking motivations because the usual elements that they encounter in their familiar walk were not present during the unfamiliar walk, or because the unfamiliar walk introduced them to new elements that they immediately appreciated. For example, participants 1 and 15 noticed the lack of safety while walking the unfamiliar route compared to their familiar walking route. Participant 1 mentioned the pedestrian road being narrower than usual, and participant 15 mentioned the bad influence of the poor road condition on her experience. Therefore, they became more aware of the importance of safety to have their good walk. On the other hand, participant 14 noticed many new shops during the unfamiliar route that she had not seen before. Because of this, she became aware of her appreciation to explore and find new things during a walk.

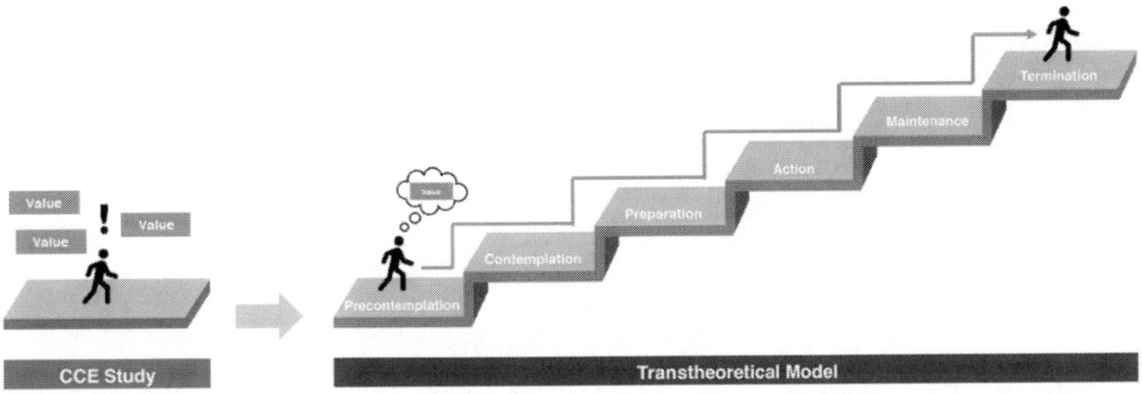

Figure 5. The influence of CCE to push people along the six stages of the transtheoretical model via the increased awareness on personal values was found

C. The Effect of CCE on the Transtheoretical Model

CCE's contribution to the transtheoretical model is shown in Figure 5. Participants become aware of an activity's benefits through CCE, which can motivate them to develop a habit. In this regard, it is assumed that participants in the precontemplation and contemplation stages are impacted to the greatest extent, as the results showed that participants in the higher stages were already more aware of their walking motivations.

V. CONCLUSIONS

This paper presents a new approach to understanding the personal motivations that people have to walk. The interview results from past CCE studies showed that participants became more aware of their appreciation for walking elements, possibly nudging them towards the next stage in the transtheoretical model. In this regard, CCE mainly identified motivations for habitual walking experiences in two different manners. First, the interviews helped participants to reflect on their experience. Second, participants realized what important walking elements were missing in the unfamiliar route.

Even though this paper explains CCE's ability to identify motivations for walking, it can be applied to any activity that requires progression through the transtheoretical model, such as psychological rehabilitation. By uncovering personal motivations and facilitating progression through the transtheoretical model, CCE can help individuals in psychological rehabilitation become more aware of the elements that contribute to their well-being and address any missing components in their therapeutic journey. CCE's ability to identify motivations extends its potential beyond walking, making it a valuable tool for promoting positive change and psychological recovery.

In conclusion, CCE can reveal what factors push people to advance to the following transtheoretical model stage. The revealed factors can be introduced to other people who are in the precontemplation or contemplation stage, but have the potential to fully develop a habit, so that they are successfully guided through the transtheoretical model stages. By participating in a CCE experiment about a healthy activity, participants can become aware of the activity's benefits, which potentially nudges them to the next stage in the transtheoretical model.

ACKNOWLEDGEMENT

Supported by JSPS KAKENHI Grant Number 20H04290.

REFERENCES

[1] J. O. Prochaska and W. F. Velicer, "The transtheoretical model of health behavior change," *American Journal of Health Promotion*, vol. 12, no. 1, pp. 38–48, 1997.

[2] J. O. Prochaska, "Transtheoretical model of behavior change," *Encyclopedia of Behavioral Medicine*, pp. 2266–2270, 2020.

[3] D. J. O'Keefe, *Persuasion: Theory and research*. SAGE, 2016.

[4] R. H. Thaler and C. R. Sunstein, *Nudge: Improving decisions about health, wealth, and happiness*. Penguin Books, 2009.

[5] M. Kitajima, H. Tahira, S. Takahashi, and T. Midorikawa, "Understanding tourists'in situbehavior: A cognitive chrono-ethnography study of visitors to a hot spring resort," *Journal of Quality Assurance in Hospitality & Tourism*, vol. 13, no. 4, pp. 247–270, 2012.

[6] M. Kitajima, "Cognitive Chrono-Ethnography (CCE): A Behavioral Study Methodology Underpinned by the Cognitive Architecture, MHP/RT," in *Proceedings of the 41st Annual Conference of the Cognitive Science Society*. Cognitive Science Society, 2019, pp. 55–56.

[7] M. Kitajima, M. Nakajima, and M. Toyota, "Cognitive chrono-ethnography: A method for studying behavioral selections in daily activities," *Proceedings of the Human Factors and Ergonomics Society Annual Meeting*, vol. 54, no. 19, pp. 1732–1736, 2010.

[8] M. Kitajima, "Cognitive Chrono-Ethnography (CCE): a methodology for anticipating future user needs," in *Work: A Journal of Prevention, Assessment and Rehabilitation (IEA 2012: 18th World congress on Ergonomics - Designing a sustainable future)*, vol. 41. Amsterdam, The Netherlands: IOS Press, 2012, pp. 5251–5258.

[9] M. Hanssen, E. Onchi, M. Kitajima, and S. Lee, "Subjective differences of walking behaviors between familiar and unfamiliar routes," *4th International Conference of the Korean Society on Emotion and Sensibility*, pp. 91–99, 2021.

[10] M. Hanssen, E. Onchi, L. Zhi, M. Kitajima, and S. Lee, "A cognitive chrono-ethnography approach for classifying walking motivations to understand the development of walking habits." *Spring Meeting of the Korean Society of Emotion and Sensibility*, pp. 53–56, 2022.

[11] M. Hanssen, M. Kitajima, and S. Lee, "The evaluation of beneficial walking elements to identify motivations for walking habit formation," *Emotion and Sensibility 27 [under review]*, 2023.

[12] M. M. Degen and G. Rose, "The sensory experiencing of urban design: The role of walking and perceptual memory," *Urban Studies*, vol. 49, no. 15, pp. 3271–3287, 2012.

[13] L. A. Malone and A. J. Bastian, "Thinking about walking: Effects of conscious correction versus distraction on locomotor adaptation," *Journal of Neurophysiology*, vol. 103, no. 4, pp. 1954–1962, 2010.

[14] V. Braun and V. Clarke, "Thematic analysis." *APA handbook of research methods in psychology, Vol 2: Research designs: Quantitative, qualitative, neuropsychological, and biological.*, pp. 57–71, 2012.
[15] P. Lally, J. Wardle, and B. Gardner, "Experiences of habit formation: A qualitative study," *Psychology, Health & Medicine*, vol. 16, no. 4, pp. 484–489, 2011.
[16] R. Tobias, "Changing behavior by memory aids: A social psychological model of prospective memory and habit development tested with dynamic field data." *Psychological Review*, vol. 116, no. 2, pp. 408–438, 2009.
[17] S. Mandic, H. Wilson, M. Clark-Grill, and D. O ' Neill, "Medical students ' awareness of the links between physical activity and health." *Montenegrin Journal of Sports Science and Medicine*, vol. 6, no. 2, pp. 5–12, 2017.

The Basis of Thinking from Behavior Elements

Peter Pfeifer
Sense Machine Project
Berlin, Germany
Email:
peter.pfeifer@sense-machine.com

Julian Pfeifer
Sense Machine Project
Berlin, Germany
Email:
julian.pfeifer@sense-machine.com

Niko Pfeifer
Sense Machine Project
Berlin, Germany
Email:
pfeifer.niko@gmail.com

Abstract—**In brain decoding research, one thing in particular is neglected: basic drives and their relationship to behavior. Basic drives 'drive' to fulfill basic needs that are important for survival, the situation of life, reproduction, and good social relationships. The brain controls the behavior needed to attain these goals. This work shows that behavior is based on thousands of combinations of only 5 drive-related basic behavior elements. Since these behaviors vary in more than 100 different areas of life, they add up to a large number of human behaviors. These 5 drive-related basic behavior elements are the components for thousands of behaviors and terms that describe behavior. They have representations in the brain that give thinking its basis. These elements are the basic building blocks for both behavior and thinking about that behavior. It is an approach to reduce the thinking processes in the brain from very many different to very few building blocks. It can be an approach that helps brain research to get closer to understanding thinking through this reduction of elements in the direction of think modules.**

Keywords-cognitive modeling; psycholinguistics; psychology; psychophysiology of cognition.

I. INTRODUCTION

In the science of the brain, considerations start with information processing and end with information processing. Psychophysiology of cognition examines the functionality of the brain in relation to sensory stimuli and thinking [1]. In contrast to this research, we do not start from single, stand-alone drives but from combinations of drives. With the combinations, it is possible to understand wide areas of human behavior.

This work offers a model of thinking that divides behavior and thinking into elements. Behavior and thinking elements, all of which are drive-related. Drive goals *and* the methods used to achieve them are related to basic drives. Drive goals and methods are combined. These elements exist in a scenario of memories, and the memories are connected to these drives.

One example is the feeling of hunger. When one sees delicious food, one feels the urge to eat it. The moment one sees it, memories of that food and how one ate it come to mind. But when there is no food available, one feels bad. However, if one has just eaten a good meal and filled one's stomach, the urge to eat will be less, and one will not feel bad.

When a drive is addressed, a feeling of attraction to a specific object arises. This feeling is supplemented by another one that indicates the degree of drive satisfaction in relation to this drive. If a drive is not satisfied for a long time, one feels bad.

A drive 'drives' in order to do something that leads to the achievement of the drive's goal. The associated feeling of the state of drive fulfillment has the task of accelerating the execution of the drive process if necessary.

Another example is the sexual attraction that arises between a man and a woman. When two good friends (males) are talking to each other and one of them says:

"Yesterday, I saw a very attractive woman!"

The listener immediately has a picture in his head. He has 'drive-related memories' of related situations. He remembers a moment when he has seen an attractive woman, and he remembers the feelings he has had. These feelings relate to basic drives that are important to the survival of animals and humans.

The basic genital drive attracts a man to get closer to an attractive woman. There are other basic drives that oppose it. For example, if someone is married, he must not get too close to other women. It is also a basic drive to hold on to his partnership, and a conflict within one person between his drives is possible.

In neurolinguistics, it has been shown that a speaker and a listener synchronize their brains in a conversation [2]. This is so easy because they have the same basic drives. Keywords addresses the same basic drive of the listener as of the speaker. Only scientific topics that are far from basic drives require more effort to be synchronized.

The drives, more precisely the driving moments experienced, are the keywords for our memories and the basic building blocks for our behaviors and our language, which describe our behaviors. Linguists call it background knowledge. It is necessary to know many things about corresponding human behavior, so that it does not need more than a short sentence to create a whole scenario of circumstances in the listener's head.

It was postulated that it is essential to have background knowledge in order to be able to understand statements correctly. In semantic frame theory [3], it is said that one can understand a word only if one knows all aspects of the situations related to that word. To define background knowledge, many texts are required for each scenario.

In many researches, the importance of the objects for the drives is neglected. For example, in Semantic Components [4], there was an endeavor to classify objects. For example, woman = human + female. However, the drive importance of a woman for a man (and vice versa) is not specified.

The following shows a way that does not require a lot of text but takes into account the importance of drives. Section II explains the fundamentals of the basic drives. Section III shows the components of behavior (behavior described by predicates). Section IV shows the diversity of basic drives in different areas of life. Section V presents the role of objects in achieving drive goals through coding. Section VI shows the complex construction of objects by concatenating basic drives. Section VII. explains methods of this work. Section VIII contains the conclusions.

II. Drive Basis

Today, the science of thinking deals with information, information processing, and language. Behaviors are neglected.

In the human past, there was a struggle for survival. Today people in Western society no longer have to fight wild animals and do not have to work the field by hand to laboriously get a daily meal. So, one is usually not aware that fundamental drives determine our lives.

Nevertheless, basic drives remain in our striving and behavior until today. Before language, only behavior was the point that made the difference between life and death. Drives have the task of ensuring the survival of the individual and - in the case of social beings - also of society. Without this function, humans would have died out millions of years ago.

For social beings like humans, two things are extremely important: giving and getting.

- When one gets nothing (for drive 1), no food, no money; one will die.
- When one has no home, no safe place to sleep, nothing that belongs to one, nothing that is available (drive 2). In winter, one would die very soon
- When someone not being able to achieve goals or move to destinations (drive 3). This person would only survive with help.
- Giving (more generally, helping others with their drives, including teaching (drive 4) is very important for the society.
- When one would be blind and deaf. One would not be able to get vital information (drive 5).

Behaviors have the task of fulfilling drives. The behaviors and their associated drive goals are organized in a special combination system. This work shows it by coding with numbers.

Each number represents a basic drive that relates to the entire drive scenario and the associated *drive-related memories*. With this system, it is possible to understand the logical connections between activities and objects. Identifying the drives within human behavior means understanding the behavior and the texts that describe the behavior.

These basics can be found in different quantities and sequences as building blocks for thousands of behaviors and at least several thousand objects. The basic drives run through all areas of human life and dominate human thinking.

In the following, the connections are to be grasped logically and to be understood logically. All rules and relations of the following were recognized and not created.

III. The Coding of Behaviors/Predicates

Predicates are mainly used to describe behaviors. There are numerous predicates that contain two or more basic drives in combination. One single predicate contains one activity (of a human) that consists of two or more basic drives, which are executed simultaneously.

A linguistic paper [5] uses the above 5 basic drives and shows that the most important predicates and objects are combinations of these 5 basic drives. Each drive is subject to variations depending on the current area of life, but they are always derived from the same drive root. (Areas of life are similar to domains.)

In the physical area of life (one of around 100 known areas), these are:

Drive 1. drinking, eating.
Drive 2. holding back.
Drive 3. moving.
Drive 4. letting go.
Drive 5. seeing, hearing, feeling - (perception).

For example, in the material area of life, the predicates/ behaviors play the basic role:

Drive 1. getting.
Drive 2. determining*/controlling (exercise of power).
Drive 3. striving/moving (for reaching goals).
Drive 4. good performing with work for others (to get money).
Drive 5. informing oneself (also curiosity).

(*Always determining in the sense of deciding.*)

These predicates are '*Basic Behavior Elements*' since they are elements of combinations, *the building blocks, and key elements of the material area.*

One can get objects like:

1. Food, meals (objects for drive 1).
2. Owned objects such as a house or apartment, furniture etc. (objects for drive 2).
3. Mobility aids such as a car (objects for drive 3).
4. Work equipment such as machines or hand tools (Objects for drive 4).
5. Information devices such as computers or TVs (Objects for drive 5).

- The food corresponds to basic drive number 1.
- House or apartment belongs to basic drive number 2 because this is where the owner has the most determination/control.
- A car belongs to basic drive number 3 because it can be used to reach destinations with it.
- The work equipment belongs to basic drive number 4, because it can be used to perform work particularly well and earn money.

- A computer connected to the internet belongs to basic drive number 5, because it can be used to obtain information.

Any of these five objects can be reused with the five base drives. Each of them can be:

1. got,
2. determined/controlled,
3. strived/moved for this as a goal,
4. good performed (and earned money) with it,
5. or obtained information about it.

Each drive object can be combined with each drive activity (5×5).

An activity is a behavior that consists of a combination of Basic Behavior Elements. Activities are described by predicates. To understand the combinations *within* an activity, two more concepts are required: Goal and assistance. Each of the Basic Behavior Elements can be used as a goal or/and assistance. The following are some examples of activities with their basic behavior elements.

The predicate -fetch- consists of two Basic Behavior Elements: The drive *striving/moving* (drive 3) and the drive *getting* (drive 1). It would be possible to explain: 'I want to get something, and it is not close, so I have to move to the position where it is. When I reach the position, I take it (again moving).'

This activity, reduced to its essentials, consists of moving and getting. The combination is drive 3 with goal 1. Both drives are combined with another.

Because drive 1 is the objective, it is marked as *goal*. The other drive is the *assistance* to reach the goal. There are many things that can be strived for or moved for, but the goal selects and constricts the type of moving to a specific direction, in this case to *get* something.

The predicate -bring about- consists of the drive *striving/moving* (drive 3) and the drive *determining/ controlling* a desired state (drive 2). It is related to striving. The goal is a thing, device or arrangement that functions as desired. (Example: Repair a device, build a device.) It is necessary to move and handle something so that the result reaches a desired state. The combination is drive 3 + goal 2.

The predicate -go- consists of the drive *striving/moving* (drive 3) and reaching a destination (goal drive 3). The combination is drive 3 + goal 3.

The predicate -manufacture- consists of the drive *striving/moving* (drive 3) and the drive (work) *performing* (drive 4). One has to make *striving/moving* to *perform* well (drive 3 + goal 4).

The predicate -look something up- consists of the drive *striving/moving* (drive 3) and the drive *informing* (drive 5). It comprises to *strive* to a position or to *move* something to a position, from which it is possible to see something that leads to *informing* (drive 3 + goal 5).

All examples above use the assistance drive 3 (*striving/moving*) and the second are the goals: The goal adjusts the assistance (which contains many possibilities) *to one activity*. The principle is: A special assistance is used to reach a special goal. The term special means: One of the 5 Basic Behavior Elements with their numbering 1 to 5.

Each drive can be used as *assistance and* the second complement (again each drive) is the *goal*. The goal selects the type of assistance activity. The meaning of a predicate can be indicated by 2 (or more) code numbers.

In the same way, one can use any of the 5 elements as assistance:

- The drive 3 striving/moving assists the other drives in Table I.
- The drive 5 informing assists the other drives in Table II.
- The drive 1 getting can also be assistance for the other drives in Table III.
- The helping drive 4 assists drives of the other people in Table IV.
- The drive 2 determining/controlling assists the other drives in Table V.

TABLE I. EXAMPLES USING THE ASSISTANCE DRIVE 3 (*STRIVING/MOVING*) AND DIFFERENT GOALS

Activity	Goal
Fetch	is for 1 *getting* =3//Goal 1
Bring about	is for 2 *determining/controlling* desired state=3//Goal 2
Go	is for 3 *striving / moving* (to a destination) = 3//Goal 3
Manufacture	is for 4 (work) *performing* =3//Goal 4
Look something up	is for 5 *informing (*oneself) = 3//Goal 5

TABLE II. EXAMPLES USING THE ASSISTANCE DRIVE 5 *(INFORMING)* AND DIFFERENT GOALS

Activity	Goal
Inquire supply	is for 1 *getting* =5//Goal 1
Weigh possibilities	is for 2 *determining/controlling* desired state=5//Goal 2
Search connection	is for 3 *striving / moving* (to a destination) = 5//Goal 3
Search customer	is for 4 (work) *performing* =5//Goal 4
Read, watch, listen	is for 5 *informing (*oneself) = 5//Goal 5

TABLE III. EXAMPLES USING THE ASSISTANCE DRIVE 1 (*GETTING*) AND DIFFERENT GOALS

Activity	Goal
Get	is for 1 have got = 1//Goal 1
Acquire	is for 2 *determining/controlling* (having) sth = 1/Goal 2
Buy a ticket	is for 3 *striving / moving* (to a destination) = 1//Goal 3
Earn	is for 4 (work) *performing* = 1//Goal 4
Get a message	is for 5 *informing* (oneself) = 1//Goal 5

TABLE IV. EXAMPLES USING THE ASSISTANCE DRIVE 4 (WORK *PERFORMING*) AND DIFFERENT GOALS

Activity	Goal
Give	is for 1 *getting*, for the other = 4//Goal 1
Rent out	is for 2 *determining/contr.* a. desired state of another = 4//Goal 2
Bring sb	is for 3 *striving / moving* to destination (for another) = 4//Goal 3
Serve	is for 4 (work) performing, service is for another = 4//Goal 4
Report	is for 5 *informing others* = 4//Goal 5

TABLE V. EXAMPLES USING THE ASSISTANCE DRIVE 2 (*DETERMINING/CONTROLLING*) AND DIFFERENT GOALS

Activity	Goal
Demand sth.	is for 1 *getting* =2//Goal 1
Determining/contr.	is for 2 *determining/control.* a desired state=2//Goal 2
Drive (vehicle)	is for 3 *striving/moving* (to a destination) = 2//Goal 3
Close a deal	is for 4 (work) *performing* = 2//Goal 4
Specify	is for 5 *informing* = 2//Goal 5

Table V uses the assistance drive 2, and the second complements are the *goals*. Many things can be *determined* and *controlled*, but a specific goal constricts the behavior to a specific activity. The goal adjusts the assistance (which contains many possibilities) to one activity.

- To -demand sth.- means to get something by determining/ controlling = 2//Goal 1.
- By -determining/controlling-something/someone, a desired state can be achieved (goal drive 2) = 2//Goal 2.
- To -drive-: From the many things that can be at one's disposal (control), there is a special type of thing that is useful for reaching a destination: Vehicles. Driving is only possible by a vehicle. The driver must *control* a vehicle and *determine* it. The car makes the work. But for the classification, the vehicle is not necessary.
  It is enough determining/controlling (drive 2) something that is usable for goal 3 striving to destination = 2//Goal 3. With the help of the definition of the basic goal, one differentiates the assistance.
  Activity code reduces activities to handling. Synonymous is -to beam- with the transport device of the spaceship enterprise. It has the same combination: *Controlling* a transport device and *determine* it in order to reach a destination (*striving/moving*). Objects (vehicles, cars, bicycles, spaceships, etc.) are treated separately.
- To -close a deal- means to determine/control (drive 2) a deal by agreement with another who accepts the work performing (drive 4) = 2//Goal 4.
- To -specify- means *determining/controlling* information. (To determine something that affects information.) = 2//Goal 5.

The meaning of a predicate can be indicated by 2 (most more) code numbers. (In the matrix below, the assistances are indicated by the heading of the columns for each position.)

TABLE VI. OVERVIEW BASIC BEHAVIOR ELEMENTS.
THE COMBINING OF BASIC BEHAVIOR ELEMENTS WITH THEMSELVES

Assistance: *Goal:*	1 *getting*	2 *determining /controlling*	3 *striving/ moving*	4 work *perf.* (for others)	5 *informing* oneself
1 *getting*	*get*	demand something	fetch	give	inquire supply
2 *determining /controlling* something	acquire	*determine/ control*	bring about	rent out	weigh of possibilities
3 *striving /moving* to destination	buy a ticket	drive (car)	*go*	bring somebody there	search for traffic connection
4 (work) *performing*	earn	close a deal	manu-facture	*serve*	search for customers
5 *informing* oneself	get a message	specify	look some-thing up	report	*read, watch, listen*

Each of these drives can be combined with each other. One activity (behavior) represented by a predicate is mostly a combination of several basic drives.

An example of a combination of three drives for one activity is the combination of 'navigate'. (Consulting a map in order to find the right route to a destination by car). This activity consists of three basic drives that are combined with one another.

1. Striving to reach a goal (basic drive 3)
2. Informing (basic drive 5)
3. Reaching a goal (basic drive 3 – final goal)

Striving (3) to gain information (5) that is needed to reach a goal (3). The first drive number stands for the main *assistant*, the second for the second *assistant*, and the last one for the *goal*. Therefore, there are two assistant drives and one goal drive. The code for the drive combination is: 3/5//Goal 3. In this example, the drive numbers 3 and 5 are assistance activities for the goal 3. (No one navigating is aware that one uses 3 times a basic drive.)

The same drives (1 – 5) can be either assistance or goal or both. The drives are represented by the *Basic Behavior Elements of an area* – activities that are at the core of a drive and form building blocks. In the cross-point of the three drives lies one activity (behavior).

The activity is defined by the 3 drives. *Therefore, it is not necessary to use many words to describe an activity. The cross-point of the drives makes it. In addition, the defined goal indicates the purpose of an activity.*

The first assistance is striving for reaching a goal. From very many things that can be striven for, only things which give information have been selected. This mechanic constricts a large amount of strivings in one direction. From a lot of information, only those that are useful to find the right way to the destination are selected. Again, this mechanic restricts to a specific direction. At the crossing point is: navigation.

The basis for drive 3 is the summary of drive-related memories on the topic: Striving/moving towards a goal/ destination. There are two variations: striving for a goal, used for the *assistance* 3, and moving towards a destination, used for the *goal* drive 3.

In this way, activities (behaviors) are defined without words, only with numbers for identification of the drives. Of course, numbers do not run in the minds of people. The collected memories of drive-related situations run there.

Each of these drives can be combined with each other, multiple times. If one combines them four times repeatedly in different ways, one gets: $5 \times 5 \times 5 \times 5 = 625$ variations of human activities (behavior describing predicates). This is the number for only one main area (the material area). This number multiplies with the number of areas.

IV. THE AREAS OF LIFE

The brain's ability to control the basic behaviors has been essential to human survival for millions of years and because of the importance, humans have special childhood phases to develop these basic behaviors: The oral, anal, genital, urethral [6], and intentional [7] basic behavior.

These five basic behaviors are synchronous with the five Basic Behavior Elements described above which are related to survival.

- The oral phase is about 1 *getting*.
- The anal phase is about 2 *determining/controlling*.
- The genital phase is about 3 *striving/moving* to a goal.
- The urethral phase is about 4 *work-performing*.
- The intentional development is about 5 *informing*.

In order to find the components formed by the basic behavior elements in activities, the following 5 main questions arises:

1. Does an activity involve the agent getting something useful? (Basic Drive 1).
2. Does an activity of an agent involve power or the capability used to determine, control, keep, hold, direct, steer, or operate something or to have something at the disposal? (Basic Drive 2)
3. Does an activity of an agent involve striving or movement to reach (the most diverse) goals? (Basic Drive 3)
4. Does an activity contain that an agent gives something useful or performs a service? (Basic Drive 4)
5. Does an activity contain informing the agent about something? (Basic Drive 5)

The basic behavior elements form the frame for the entire life:

1. From getting milk as a baby to buying food as an adult (drive 1 - oral).
2. From self-control to control of one's own possessions. From the use of things at one's disposal to the orders for the employees (drive 2 - anal).
3. From the moving in sexuality to the moving to reach something. From moving with a car to moving a weapon against an enemy (drive 3 - genital).
4. From doing things for mother and father to helping others. From learning at school to working as an employee in a company (drive 4 - urethral).
5. From advantageous knowledge to get things done to curiosity about everything (drive 5 - intentional).

In childhood phases the development of activities can be observed: A baby gets milk from the mother. This is a passive receiving and the pure *getting* of a child (drive 1). As an adult, one goes to a grocery and buys food. In addition, the adult has an assistant drive: paying, that means to have money at the disposal (basic drive 2) and to change it with the food.

This extension of behaviors applies to all 5 basic drives. From the pure drive behavior, it develops into combined behaviors. The other drives (later developed in childhood) are used as assistance. The ratio of pure behavior to combined behavior is about 1 : 100. Because the skills are learned at different stages of childhood and therefore exists separately, there must exist combinations. For example, the baby is not able to use money.

An older child who knows that possession means having control over it (basic drive 2) is then able to exchange money for a desired object. (Assistance 2// for goal 1.)

The basic drives have special shapes to adapt to the different areas of life and are a great advantage for survival since all drives have the *drive* to fulfill them. The basic drives run through the various areas of human life.

The transfer of the original drive to the scenery of an area leads to multiple adaptation processes.

There are main areas (Material, Material/Feelings, Interpersonal, Interpersonal/Feelings, Physical) that include all 5 basics as a goal and there are sub-areas behind a main area especially behind the material area: Authorities, Contracts, Hobby, Leisure Time, Public Utilities, States, etc. And there are sectoral sub-areas that include only one basic as a goal (one sector, instead of all) but all basics as assistances (Animals, Animals/Hobby, Cleanliness, Contest, Criminal/Procurement, Financial/Transactions, Financial/ Using, IT, Law, Law/Court, Livelihood, Medical, Producer, Social Institutions, Supplier, Traffic, Protection).

Behaviors have accompanying feelings. There are good, neutral, and bad feelings. When we achieve the fulfillment of drives, we feel good. When we try and do not achieve fulfillment, we feel bad.

If we buy things, we get something (basic drive 1). We can get food (Goal 1). We can get possessions like a house, an apartment, furniture, etc. (Activity 1//Goal 2).

We can get mobilities (Activity 1//Goal 3). We can get recognition (Activity 1//Goal 4). We can get information (Activity 1//Goal 5). Getting something usually makes us feel good. Somebody goes shopping and only the moment of getting something makes us feel good. There are two variations: To get something as assistance 1 and to have got something as goal drive 1.

If we exercise power, it makes us feel good (basic drive 2). Not everyone can stand by it. If we have had bad experiences with it, we could refuse it.

One issue for this is power in politics. Is there any doubt about how good a dictator feels when he exercises his power over an entire country? Or the senior manager of a large company giving orders to many people? There are two variations: The determination/control as assistance 2 and the attainment of a desired state as goal drive 2.

There are different areas that show different views. In the material area, there is the determination of material things. Such as determining the circumstances for the manufacturing goods. In the interpersonal area, there is dominion over people: To command someone like their children or to command other people, as a king or patriarch. And, of course, having power or being in a position of power was an advantage for survival.

When we achieve goals, it makes us feel good. If we strive for something, for example, we bring about something (Activity 3//Goal 2) and it works, it feels good when we reach the goal.

The interpersonal area uses interpersonal relations instead of relationships with material things. Goal 3, to reach a material goal now refers to an interpersonal/sexual goal.

There are two variations: striving for an interpersonal goal, used for assistance 3, and striving towards sexual intercourse, used for goal drive 3. As in every area, all 5 basics are used as assistance. There is no need to mention the importance of sexual feelings and maternal/paternal feelings for reproduction.

The Fight/Aggression area is a sectoral area. In this case, the basic drive 3 is defined as a combat-like goal. As in every case, all 5 basics are used as assistances but always related to only one goal: Goal 3 to win the fight. (In a serious fight there are two other options: Flee or submit. (These follow the survival instinct.)

There are several different fight areas: aggression, brawl, dispute, election, games, hobby, litigation, sports, sports/ball games, stabbing, and war. All of them have the goal 3 to win the fight and are sectoral areas. The difference between 'to shoot a goal', in fight/ball games and 'to shoot an enemy' in fight/aggression is differentiated by the area and the various terms/situations within an area.

There are further sectoral areas such as Criminal/Procurement directed only for goal 1 *getting*, Financial/Transactions directed only for goal 2 *determining/ controlling* money, IT only directed to 5 *informing*, etc. All sectoral areas have only one fixed goal, a goal that actually everyone knows. The code contains it with the goal number.

A social species needs to help each other. Hence, it is useful that we do things for appreciation. Even without pay, we sometimes do things for recognition. Just for the good feeling. There are two variants: Doing something for others as assistance 4 and being appreciated as goal drive 4. In the case of basic drive 4 (good) performance, there are two different lines. In the interpersonal area, the goal is recognition for good performing. In the material area, the goal of (work) performance is money.

One of the most important human inventions is to give money for the exchange of goods and services. Money is material recognition in the material area. The core is to get money for work and money makes businesses run. Work performing is a helping (drive 4), that benefits the other. It is always *dependent on the other* who decides whether or not it will help him/her. This is a reason to make services and goods well to satisfy customers. On the other hand, the customer is dependent on payment and price.

If we submit a paper (Activity 3/5/2// Goal 4) and hope for publication and get confirmation, we feel good. If our mother/father says, "Well done", we feel good.

When we search for specific information for a long time (Activity 3/2// Goal 5) and find it, we feel good. In regard to informing, there are two variations: The search for specific information as assistance 5 and to satisfy the curiosity as goal drive 5.

These feelings are the driving force for our lives. Feeling good when we achieve goals and feeling bad when we do not. These feelings have been important for millions of years. There are other types of feelings. For example, the feeling of overload. If I must work for money but it is too much effort... That is another issue.

V. Coding of Objects

Assigning objects is similar to assigning activities. Objects are things, which are useful or necessary to support activities for the drives. For example, a car is a thing object that can be owned (determining/controlling, drive 2). A car is for striving/moving to a destination = drive 3. Therefore, the car is an object 2//for goal 3.

Each object is interlocked with the corresponding basic behavior element. For example,

1 *getting* with *source objects* from which one can get sth.
2 *determining/controlling* of *thing objects* that can be owned.
3 *striving/moving* with *location objects* that can be reached.
4 *good performing* with *profession objects*.
5 *informing* (oneself) with *information objects*.

Each object number is interlocked with the goal drive number of the basic behavior element (Table VII).

The *goal number* from a *Basic Behavior Element* (*Old Goal*) of an activity becomes the first number of an *object* (Object No. 1 - 5) (Table VII). This is the 'goal to assistance regularity of the object'. This first number becomes the *assistance* for the object (followed by a *new goal*, the goal from the object) (Table VIII). The change from the goal of the basic behavior to the goal of the object means a transition from the *old goal (behavior)* to a *new goal (object)*. (Goal transition).

TABLE VII. Basic Behavior Elements in Relation to Objects

Basic Behavior Element (*Old Goal*)	Object (Assistance)	*New Goal*
Getting - goal 1 from	Object 1 Sources	for a goal
Determining/controlling sth. goal 2 with	Object 2 Things	
Striving/moving to a destination goal 3 to	Object 3 Locations	
Performing (good work) goal 4 with	Object 4 Professions	
Informing (oneself) - goal 5 -about	Object 5 Information	

TABLE VIII. Combining of Objects

Object has the	*Assistance drive*	for a *New Goal*
Groceries, shops are	1 sources	for 1 getting
Food, goods, etc. are	2 things	
Addresses of shops are	3 locations	
Farmer, seller, etc. are	4 professions	
Supply details are	5 information	
Apartment rental, furniture shops, are	1 sources	for 2 determining/ controlling sth. (having)
House, apartment, furniture, etc. are	2 things	
Home, location of a property is a	3 location	
Property management, lessors, etc. are	4 professions	
Building details are	5 information	
Travel agencies, transport services are	1 sources	for 3 striving/ moving (to a destination)
Vehicles are	2 things	
Train stations, bus stops, etc. are	3 locations	
Bus drivers, travel agents, etc. are	4 professions	
Route details are	5 information	
Demand for goods is a	1 source	for 4 performing (work)
Equipment for work is a	2 thing	
*Workplace** is a	3 location	
Vocational teacher is a	4 profession	
Work details are	5 information	
TV, internet, etc. is a	1 source	for 5 informing (oneself)
Newspapers, journals, DVDs, etc. are	2 things	
Information events, theater, etc. are	3 locations	
Reporter; actor, IT, etc. are	4 professions	
Search engines, lexicons are	5 information	

* An example of assigning drive code numbers (Table VIII) for Workplace (location object) with:

Assistance 3// *Goal* 4 or identical: *Object 3// Goal 4*.

Just as the combining of Basic Behavior Elements, objects are combinable too. The first number (the object number) is the assistance, the second number is again a goal. In the next step, drive 4 is used as assistance and there is a transition to the goal of the work performing for example farming, selling: goal 1, property management: goal 2, bus driving: goal 3, vocational teaching: goal 4, reporting: goal 5 ('*goal transition*').

Each of the five objects can, again and again, be divided by the 5 basic drives for the goals. Again, with a higher number of elements, there are a more numerous, number of objects. Further differentiation depends on the area and the special direction. Up to 9 elements are known for one object. The basic drives can be seen in all these objects and there are many more objects with a higher number of elements of the combinations in the different areas.

The drive number of an object becomes the assistance number for a new goal, the goal of the object (Table VII).

A. *Oral field*

In the oral phase, the baby receives milk from the mother. This is the core of *basic drive* 1. The mother is the *source object* for the milk. Later as an adult, there are different *source objects* from which one can get something for:

- Drive 1 food: Groceries. They are the combination of *source objects* 1 = *assistance* 1 for goal drive 1.
- Drive 2 possession: Apartment rental, furniture shops. They are the combination of *source objects* 1 = *assistance* 1 for goal drive 2.
- Drive 3 destinations: Travel agencies, transport services. They are the combination of *source objects* 1 = *assistance* 1 for goal drive 3.
- Drive 4 work: Goods demand. They are the combination of *source objects* 1 = *assistance* 1 for goal drive 4.
- Drive 5 information: TV, internet, etc. They are the combination of *source objects* 1 = *assistance* 1 for goal drive 5.

In short: Groceries, apartment rental, travel agencies, transport services, goods demand, TV, internet are the *source objects (objects* 1 = assistances 1) for the goal drives: 1, 2, 3, 4, 5 in all variations of the different areas of life.

B. *Anal field*

Things are *objects* for *basic drive 2*. They are usable for *basic drive 2* because someone can own and 2 *determine/ control* them. They are in the power field of someone.

- Things for the oral drive are food. They are the combination of *thing objects* 2 = *assistance* 2 with goal drive 1 *getting*.
- Main thing objects are my house/apartment, furniture, and everything in my house. In my house, I can determine and decide most because it is mine. (Another important thing object is money. I can *determine* and *control* it and decide about its use.) They are the combination of *thing objects* 2 = *assistance* 2 with goal drive 2 *determing/controlling*.
- Things for my mobility: My car, my bike, my ticket for the train. They are the combination of *thing objects* 2 = *assistance* 2 with goal drive 3 *striving/moving* to a destination.
- Things for my work. Work equipments are objects for drive 4 *work-performing*. They are the combination of *thing objects* 2 = *assistance* 2 with goal drive 4 *work performing*.
- Things for my information. Newspapers, journals, DVDs, etc. They are the combination of *thing objects* 2 = *assistance* 2 with goal drive 5 *informing oneself*.

In short: In the anal field, I can have *thing objects* (*objects* 2 = *assistance* 2) for:

Goal drive 1 (food)
Goal drive 2 (possession)
Goal drive 3 (vehicles)
Goal drive 4 (equipment for work)
Goal drive 5 (newspapers).

(The things include not only the 5 basic drives in the material area, but also all variations of the different areas of life.)

C. *Genital field*

Destinations are *location objects* (assistance 3) for the *basic drive 3*. In this genital field, I can reach destinations by 3 *striving/ moving* to a destination. They are the combination of *location objects* (*objects* 3 = *assistance* 3) with goal drive: 1, 2, 3, 4, 5, and locations in all variations of the different areas of life.

D. *Urethral field*

Professions are *profession objects* (assistance 4) in the urethral field. I can learn 4 *professional work*. It is the combination of *profession objects* (objects 4 = *assistance* 4) with goal drive 1, 2, 3, 4, 5, and professions in all variations of the different areas of life.

E. *Intentional field*

Information is an object in the intentional field. It is the combination of 5 *information objects (object 5 = assistance 5)* about everything in the world and about goal drive 1, 2, 3, 4, 5 in all variations of the different areas of life.

F. *Summary*

Drives revolve around drives and generate a wide variety of behaviors and all of which serve a (drive) goal. This knowledge results from the drive-related analysis of human behavior. It turned out that only 5 basic drives are necessary for this breakdown into basic elements. This method is applied to thousands of predicates and objects and found that these consist of drive elements.

For example, one can use the computer (5) to find out where best to get (1) a car (3) that is suitable for driving to work (4). If one goes through the sentence step by step, one will find that this is exactly the way people think. In this case, one needs a car mainly for going to work.

In the mind, one has an idea of the work, and that one is paid for it (basic drive 4). The whole work complex is connected, among other things, with the place where one work, the target object, where one has to go, and what one need a car for (basic drive 3). One wants to get it (basic drive 1), and for that, one need information on the question: Where? In the information that one can obtain from the computer/internet (basic drive 5).

Human behaviors consist of drive activities and relate to drive objects. The diversity of human behavior is based on the combination of a few basic drives. Each drive comprises several variations which depend on the current area of life. In many areas of life, there is a special variation of a basic drive. The result is a high diversity of human behavior with mainly only 5 basic drives.

VI. The Concatenating of Objects in the Material Area

In section V, subsection B, we have *thing objects 2. They are things that can be owned by someone.* The basic possessions are shown in Table IX. There are things for the goal drives 1, 2, 3, 4, 5 in the rows 1, 2, 3, 4, 5.

The owned house or apartment with Code: Object 2//Goal 2//2/ defines the stationary immobile core of possession (Goal drive 2). One can use it, one can change details within, one can sell it. One has it at one´s disposal. It is the *core* Object of drive 2 *determining/ controlling* something.

Further in the columns: The portable possessions can be moved -drive *3*. Value-based ownership is limited by other people's conditions - drive 4.

Table IX to Table XII are building a chain that leads deeper in the matter of house and apartment. Within the framework of drives, the content is defined by area and the chain of the diverse Basic Behavior Elements.

The arrows between the tables show the chained connection between them. One position forms the connection point for the next one, as shown in Figures 1.

See Table IX, the heading Object 2// (possession) plus label of the row Goal 2 *(determining/controlling)* plus heading of the column *(Drive 2)* is superordinate for Table X. 'House; apartment'

TABLE IX. Super Ordinate: Possession: Object 2//

Assistant Drive: For *Goal:*	*Drive 2* *determining*	Drive 3 striv./moving	Drive 4 work performing
Oral 1 getting	food, consumables	dine, beverages	
Anal *2 determining/controlling*	house, apartment	portable possession	money, bank balances, shares
Genital 3 striving/moving	gasoline	vehicles	tickets
Urethral 4 work-performing	contracts, design drawings	equipment for work	work performance
Intentional 5 informing	home page		

TABLE X. House, Apartment: Object 2// Goal 2// 2 /

Sub-assistant Drive: Assistant drive:	Drive 2 determining	Drive 3 *striving/moving*	Drive 4 work performing
Oral drive 1 getting	hire	moving in	house buying
Anal Drive *2 determining/controlling*	room type	equipment of apartment	ownership costs; rent
Genital Drive 3 striving/moving	contract rules		financing
Urethral Drive 4 work-performing	rentals	repair, renovation, cleaning, craft	acceptance of price, of rent
Intentional Drive 5 informing	real estate knowledge	knowledge of building problems	house, apartment price adequacy

The entire matrix of Table X includes the code above of house/apartment, as seen in the heading. This matrix shows connected *thing objects*:

Line 1 shows how to get a house/apartment,
Line 2 shows details,
Line 3 shows elements of managing,
Line 4 shows professional help, and
Line 5 contains information about a house.

This matrix is convergent, every position has the same goal (Goal 2), the rows are *assistances.* The columns are sub-assistances. (In contrast, the other matrices are divergent and show the 5 basic drives as *goals* with the 5 rows.)

Row assistant drive 2 and column sub-assistant drive 3 means 'equipment of apartment'. It includes the above heading and the beginning of the chain.

In Table XI (equipment of apartment) is row goal 4 electrical work, instead of 4 work-performing which is on the same drive position. A monetary payment may be made for work performance. Money is converted work performance. Electrical equipment runs only against payment for electricity. This monetary payment is converted work performance. (Alternative: Area electrical power.)

The assistant drive is drive 3. The crossing point position means 'electrical appliances'. It is again the heading for the next matrix (Table XII) and is extended twice again.

TABLE XI. Equipment of Apartment: Object 2// Goal 2// 2 /2 /3 //

Assistant Drive: For *Goal*:	Drive 2 determining	Drive 3 *striving/moving*	Drive 5 informing (self)
Oral drive 1 getting		crockery, pans cutlery, pots,	
Anal Drive 2 determining/controlling		furniture	
Genital Drive 3 striving/moving			
Urethral Drive *4 electrical work*		electrical appliances	
Intentional Drive 5 informing	nameplate, address	phone/internet connection	lighting

TABLE XII. ELECTRICAL APPLIANCES: OBJECT 2// GOAL 2// 2 /2 /3 //GOAL 4 //3//

Assistant Drive: For *Goal:*	*Drive 2 determining*	Drive 3 *striving/moving*	Drive 5 informing (self)
Oral drive *1 getting*	refrigerator	stove, oven, microwave	
Anal Drive 2 *d*etermining/controlling			
Genital Drive 3 striving/moving	washing machine		
Urethral Drive 4 work-performing			
Intentional Drive 5 informing	computer	phone	TV, streaming service

Table XII shows the final code. The refrigerator offers oral things: Drive 1 *getting* with core eating for the goal and column drive 2 for assistance. The assist drive 2 means: determine/control (have available) with the refrigerator that keeps food fresh with electricity and thus helps to keep it in usable control. That is the last extension of the chain.

The closer to the core of a drive, the shorter the code. The further away from the core, the longer the code with more added drives.

Coding for refrigerator:

Object 2 //Goal 2 //2 /2 /3 //Goal 4 //3 //Goal 1 //2

The concatenated matrices (tables) show with four levels: Refrigerator. The matrices add new drive elements with each step in every new combination. But they are always only one of the 5 basic drives. (Figure 1). The combinations form a chain that targets a final target drive.

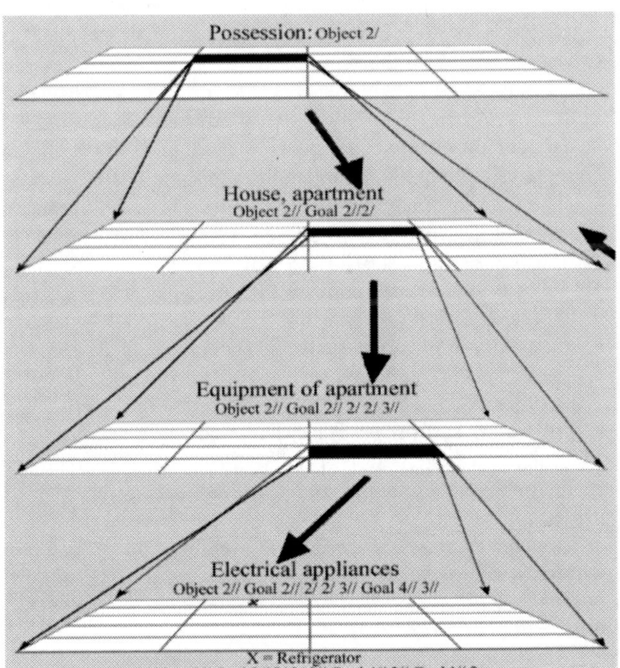

Figure 1. Concatenating of the matrices in four levels

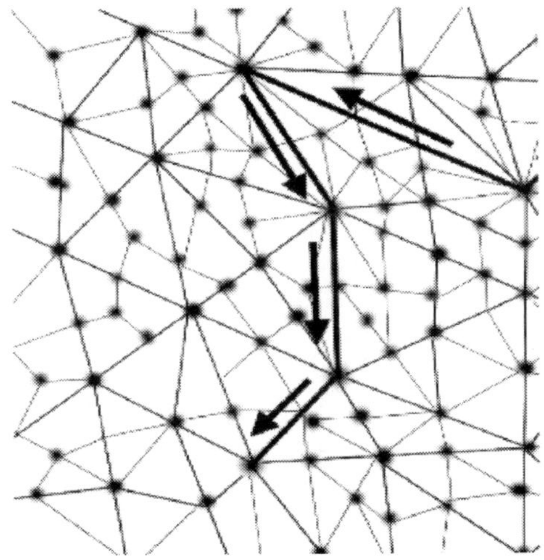

Figure 2. Concatenating of neurons

By reducing the matrices so that a matrix appears as a node and only the three-dimensional network can be seen, the result is an image that is similar, to the arrangement of neurons in the brain. (Figure 2). One matrix position (object) forms the connection point like synapses. They give the superordinate content during the next step and the next node adds more differentiating details.

The thought suggests itself that it runs in the brain in principle in the same way. The steps in the brain are certainly smaller and more numerous than in this example. The drive activities and objects described, which relate to the basic drives number 1 to 5, are used by humans to define activities and concepts in the mind. The drives are the key elements in which people think. Such a connection between drive related basic behavior elements and drive objects has not yet been explored [8].

The 5 basic drives are dimensions like the dimensions in space. The areas are sub-ordinate. The transfer of the original drive to the scenery of an area leads to multiple adaptation processes. By transferring drive combinations from one area to another, there is also likely the possibility of problem-solving by association.

The 5 basic drives are available in many variations in 100 known different areas of life (probably much more), resulting in many thousands of variations with combinations that exist in each of the areas of life. Basic drives are either used in actions such as shopping, giving directions, walking or driving, working, or looking for information (examples from the material area). Or these activities are imagined in the head. Brief pictorial or word-related representations run through the mind. Each base drive contains many memories. Starting with childhood, where the drive arises. Basic drives continue to be fixed points in life. For a drive, experience is repeatedly gained with their execution, they form a complex, a whole scenery including the numerous variations in the different areas of life.

Basic drives must be present in the brain in some way since they have made human survival possible from the evolutionary perspective.

From an evolutionary perspective, behavior is the old foundation. Language and thinking in language came later. Both are built on the old behavioral foundations, and it is plausible that behavior and thought were originally synchronous. Also, along the lines of: think first, then act.

This model shown here is not taxonomic. It is an ontology with 5 elements of relations that also still adapt themselves according to the area of life and which are combined with each other. Together, this results in a very complex ontology. Through ever greater differentiation, ever new branches are formed, with the consequence that the number of resulting objects increases exponentially:

First level (Table IX) contains 12 objects.

Second level (Table X) contains 14 objects.

Third level (Table XI) contains 6 objects.

Forth level (Table XII) contains 6 objects.

This results in 12 x 14 x 6 x 6 = 6048 possible objects assuming that there is a comparable number of objects in neighboring levels. According to this model, a very complex structure is formed from only 5 basic drives.

In early childhood, the drive regions are only present in primitive structures. Through physical development and experiences with the use of drives, an enormous complex of drive-related memories develops.

This model assumes that the drives form the frames in which the complexity develops. Drive satisfactions that lie in the environment must form an incentive for an individual. This stimulus must arrive in the brain and trigger reactions. Nothing is more probable than that this happens with the drive apparatus. Only this guarantees survival. The drive apparatus receives restrictions from the social community during development. Social morality limits the drive apparatus. (This conglomerate of drive living and restriction often blurs the understanding of the drive origin.)

Further differentiation of the branches increases the number of objects in this model enormously. It fits the exponential increase of knowledge in the brain.

Unlike a normal network that only shows the connections of the objects, here the drive root of each element is tracked. Thus, each element gets a meaning and the total meaning of an object is the sum of the individual meanings of the elements. *This circumstance also explains the depth of knowledge penetration of the human mind, which is far superior to the understanding of computer derivations.*

The above example refrigerator shows this knowledge penetration with 4 drive levels: Of all the things that are in my possession or at my disposal (drive 2), I think of my house/apartment as the core (Goal 2//2). I think of the movable equipment of the apartment (Drive 2/3).

Part of this is electrical appliances that accomplish a service by moving something with an electric motor (Goal 4//3). This includes a refrigerator that keeps food fresh (Goal 1//2). The human mind knows each drive level of an object and the sum of them.

VII. Methods of this Work

All conclusions of this work are logically derived. They contradict current research methods, where evidence is required for everything. Evidence that behaviors in fact consist of combinations (for example, that fetch consists of move and get) cannot be shown statistically or by interviewing people. A proof of the combination system is possible with logic. It is shown that there are combinations of behavior elements. Since the brain controls all behavior, the brain also controls the combination.

The proof that the basic drives are really the building blocks of behavior is done backwards by noting that so many important predicates (and hence the corresponding behaviors) can be broken down into these basic drive elements.

So far, seven thousand drive-related behaviors and objects are known. 500 categorized important predicates/behaviors can be viewed on our homepage [10].

Some basic parts of this model can be considered as secured by the following facts:

It has been known since the middle of the last century that basic drives exist. Psychologists found the connection between childhood phases and basic drives. For example, Erik Erikson [6] wrote about 4 basic drives (oral, anal, genital, urethral) that develop in the first childhood stages. Schultz-Hencke [7] also wrote about these and about an intentional development in childhood in which information leads to intention.

That the basic drives exist in the brain and not, for example, in the stomach can be considered certain. It is not necessary to prove whether basic drives are localized in the brain. Proving whether basic drives can be detected in an fMRI study or in EEG signals is not crucial, because the drives must exist in the brain.

The question of whether there are only 5 basic drives or more has not been definitively established. This model is based on the basic childhood stages and the behavior necessary for survival. Both lead to the same basics.

The logic of the general combinations is compelling:

- I use getting (drive 1) to get something from sources (for example, stores that offer things for drive 1, 2, 3, 4, or 5).
- I have things at my disposal (drive 2) that are usable for drive 1, 2, 3, 4, 5.
- I strive/move for goals (drive 3) for drive 1, 2, 3, 4, 5.
- I perform work services (drive 4) for drive 1, 2, 3, 4, 5 of the other people.
- I inform myself (drive 5) for drive 1, 2, 3, 4, 5.

The rule is: a basic behavior element refers to a basic object. Basic behavior elements and basic objects refer to basic drives.

Instead of a proof about the combination of elements within an activity or object, anyone can figure out the basic behavioral elements of a predicate/behavior or object by answering the following main questions:

- Does a behavior of an agent involve striving or movement to reach (the most diverse) goals? (Basic Drive 3)
- Does a behavior of an agent involve power or the capability used to determine, control, keep, hold, direct, steer, or operate something or to have something at the disposal? (Basic Drive 2)
- Does a behavior involve the agent getting something useful? (Basic Drive 1).
- Does a behavior contain that an agent gives something useful or performs a service? (Basic Drive 4)
- Does a behavior contain informing the agent about something? (Basic Drive 5)

Finding combinations in the brain by measurements with fMRI or EEG is very difficult because the combinations consist of 2, most more drive elements and forms a complex mixture in the mind just for one thought.

There are other useful elements for further differentiation of behaviors and combinations (autonomous, heteronomous, eccentric, concentric). However, this introductory work is limited to elements that are essential for survival.

VIII. Conclusion

An important task of brain research is to bridge the gap between psychology and the electrical functionality of neurons. How does (drive-related) thinking arise from the firing of neurons?

The present model is a step in this direction to narrow the gap by decomposing psychology into (small) elements (modules) that come somewhat closer to the smallest element of switching a bit in the neuron. The goal is to shrink the psychological elements until they reach the size of a switching neuron.

Another way would be to find the anchoring of basic drive elements in the brain architecture. Of course, this anchoring is not easy to recognize. This model suggests that individual neurons that are relatively close to each other are anchored in different basic drives. Just the mixture results in the content of objects and activities by the combinations.

An MRI study is not able to show single neurons. Only regions with large amounts of neurons can be identified. To find the anchoring of the drives in the neurons, new ways must be found.

Focusing on the human brain, this work makes some concluding considerations:

- It is unthinkable that the human basic drives (that made human survival possible and still make it possible today) are not represented in the mind. The basic drives must be contained in our brains.
- Humans are able to imagine processes of behavior, which are used to fulfill basic drives. This imagination of the process is a thought. Thoughts are organized through long chains of combinations that are bundled together by a drive goal theme. A thought begins with a pulse from inside the body or a stimulus from outside, that touches one of the basic drives

  A reaction can be an activity aimed at achieving a goal/meeting a need or at least a thought about it. Additional combinations with assistance drives extend the thought.
- The content of the thought is to follow the chain of drives through Basic Behavior Elements that are variations of basic drives. The combinations give the content of the thought.
- Human thinking deals mainly with drive-important behaviors and drive-important occurrences and processes.
- It is plausible that with increasing depth of the levels a complex mixture of assistance drives, which are necessary for the desired goal, is fed into the human activity process. The feed takes place through the added combinations with assistance drives.
- These assistance drives are behaviors (often conditionally learned details of the activities) that have developed in a different drive field but are useful and necessary help to achieve the current goal.
- Because these basic behaviors exist there must be a control of the behaviors by the brain.
- Because the basics develop in different childhood phases and *therefore exist separately, there must exist combinations*. The combinations are represented in the brain by pictures or words.
- The combination of the basic drives provides 'background knowledge' that all people have in the back of their minds regarding their activities, as each combination contains the purpose (goal) of a behavior or object and the means/methods (assistances by other drives) used.

When viewed in a microscope, the basic drive anchoring of the individual neurons cannot be seen. One can only see the highly complex network of branches between the neurons.

The drives are the 'ghost in the machine' to use that old phrase, in the human brain. Human emotions echo the degree that drives are satisfied under specific, acute conditions. Each finely differentiated action (and any conversation about it) is based on a complex mixture of basic drives, such that one can hardly see their base, because it has so many levels, in ever-changing mixtures. Behind every action (or even part of an action) are specifically differentiated aspects of human drives.

Learning is not the learning of anything. The learning of behaviors has the task of serving the fulfillment of drives. The behaviors are supported by the means of pattern recognition [9] and conditional learning.

Language also serves to fulfill drives. Language is used to get recognition for social behavior or good performance (drive 4) or for the different variations of all drives in 100 areas of life, which are carried out alone or often in cooperation with others.

The fulfillment of the drives give the sense of human behavior. Most human behaviors are combinations of human drives. The numbering of these combinations can be viewed as a kind of genetic code for behavior and thinking.

REFERENCES

[1] F. Rössler, „Psychophysiology of Cognition: An Introduction to Cognitive Neuroscience.“, Spektrum Akademischer Verlag, 2011.

[2] U. Hasson, A.A. Ghazanfar, B. Galantucci, S. Garrod, and C. Keysers, „Brain-to-brain coupling: mechanism for creating and sharing a social world“. *Trends in Cognitive Science 16(2),* USA, 2012, pp *114-121.*

[3] C. J. Fillmore, C. F. Baker, and F. Collin, "Frame semantics for text understanding". Proceedings of WordNet and Other Lexical Resources, Pittsburgh, USA: NAACL. 2001.

[4] J. J. Katz and J. A. Fodor, "The structure of a Semantic Theory", Language, Vol. 39, No. 2. (Apr. – Jun.), 1963, pp. 170-210,

[5] P. H. Pfeifer, J. Pfeifer, and N. Pfeifer, "To Grasp the Meaning of Natural Language by a Code of Behaviors" the Sense Machine: IJKE 2016 Vol.2(1), 1–3.

[6] Erikson, E., Childhood and Society, W. W. Norton & Co, New York 1950, pp. 70, 76, 80-86, 253.

[7] Schultz-Hencke, H., Textbook of Analytical Psychotherapy, Thieme Verlag, Stuttgart 1951, pp. 24-25.

[8] V. Schuring, „Selected biological foundations of critical psychology (I)“: Forum Kritische Psychologie 55, 2016, pp 117-123.

[9] R. Kurzweil, "How to create a mind: the secret of human thought revealed", Viking, Penguin Group, USA, 2012.

[10] P. H. Pfeifer, http://www.sense-machine.com/Gitter.html [retrieved: 5, 2023]

Investigating Educators' Appropriation of Robots for Autistic Children in Special Education Settings in France: Work in Progress

Manukyan Armand
Association J.B. Thiery and 2LPN
Nancy, France
mail:armand.manukyan@jbthiery.asso.fr

Maneslovic Leila
2LPN and Association J.B. Thiery
Nancy, France
mail:leila.maneslovic4@etu.univ-lorraine.fr

Dinet Jerome
University of Lorraine, 2LPN
Nancy, France
mail:jerome.dinet@etu.univ-lorraine.fr

***Abstract*—This short paper is aiming to present our work in progress about a study to investigate the cognitive process of teaching for young learners with ASD in special education settings. Because research has largely examined the different cognitive processes involved in planning, instruction, and reflection separately and often in lab-controlled settings, our work in progress is searching to investigate attitudes of educators in special education settings (dedicated for children with ASD) towards robots as a category of tools in natural conditions and the impacts of their attitudes on their effective behaviours. From a theoretical point of view, this work in progress is based on the 4A Model for "Acceptability, Acceptance, Adoption and Appropriation", created to describe and predict relationships between attitudes and appropriation of complex technologies such as robots. From a methodological point of view, this work in progress is based on a mixed approach, combining interviews and focus groups conducted with several professionals working in different special education settings for children with ASD, and observations in situ to collect objective data about real activities performed by the educators with the children in the special education settings. Finally, it is suggested that future researchers examining educators' thoughts and actions employ mixed methodologies, such as case study, that examine the cognitive processes holistically and in the natural teaching/education environment, thereby linking actual behaviors with the cognitive processes that produced them.**

***Keywords*—robot, autism, educators, acceptability, professional**

I. Introduction

France has approximately 700,000 people with Autism Spectrum Disorders (ASD), including 100,000 children. Rapid progress in technology, especially in the area of robotics, offers tremendous possibilities for innovation in treatment for individuals with ASD. Advances in recent years have enabled robots to fulfill a variety of human-like functions, as well as to aid with the goal of improving social skills of individuals with ASD [21] [25] [26]. The process of teaching for young learners with ASD is complex and multidimensional. Teaching behaviors and actions are shaped by numerous cognitive decisions made by the educators before, during, and after instruction. The work in progress presented in this paper examines educator cognition across the broad field of education and, more specifically, when robots are used in special education settings. To date, research has largely examined the different cognitive processes involved in planning, instruction, and reflection separately and often in controlled settings. It is suggested that future researchers examining educators' thoughts and actions employ mixed methodologies, such as case study, that examine the cognitive processes holistically and in the natural teaching/education environment, thereby linking actual behaviors with the cognitive processes that produced them.

A lot of existing ASD and Human-Robot Interaction (HRI) studies have predominantly studied children interacting with robots in lab-based settings [19] [27] [28] [29] [30] [33] [34]. Even if several interesting findings are issued from these studies conducted in controlled lab-like settings, moving robots from the lab into the real classroom (i.e., in ecological settings), where teachers apply the teaching program unsupervised, is no straightforward task [10] [14] [15] [16]. So, embedding robots into existing autism contexts and pedagogical practices requires in-depth understanding of specific contexts and practices, and of the adult users who will support robot-based programs. Understanding the views of professionals such as educators is therefore essential, as they are key decision-makers for the adoption of new technologies, and would be the ones to directly facilitate any future use of robots [20]. The integration of a robot in a given social environment (such as an education setting) can potentially redistribute roles and influence the interaction of all individuals in that context [35]. A school, as an organisation, obeys rules and norms imposed by pedagogical principles, which are crucial for teachers/educators, parents and children. The use of a robot in a school context therefore requires that it applies these principles.

If some studies have sought teachers and professionals' views to explore implementing robots within real and regular educational settings [12] [17] [31], very few studies have investigated that so within special education settings. For instance, in a larger study, Hughes-Roberts and Brown [13] conducted interviews and focus groups with 20 teachers in special (though not autism-specific) education settings in the UK, incorporating a demonstration of a humanoid robot, NAO. If some relevant data have been obtained about the activities performed by the educators with the children with ASD, it was unclear whether these educators considered, overall, robots to be relevant, appropriate and acceptable for themselves. In the same way, Huijnen et al. [16] [18] took a related approach, combining focus groups, and co-creation sessions with autism stakeholders and professionals (including teachers and other school-based roles, all in the Netherlands) to develop 10 specific "intervention templates" for the humanoid robot, KASPAR. Once again, several relevant results have been obtained about the activities and the potentialities for the children with ASD, but no information has been collected about the attitudes of educators towards robots (usability, acceptability) and the potential impact on their work and their job.

Even if a lot of relevant results are issued from these existing studies, very few researches only give a partial picture of the information researchers need to know to work toward robot deployment with learners with ASD within special education settings. This is for five key reasons:

- First, children's specific needs and the strategies used to support them can be very distinct from those educated within mainstream settings [11]. Greater knowledge is needed about the utility of robot-based programs for these particular children in their own specific, specialist contexts.
- Second, all these existing studies have essentially asked educators to answer questions or discuss ideas in relation to demonstrations of existing robots [6] [13] [14] [15], i.e., limiting with respect to discussing perceptions and applications of robots as a category of tools, or for generating novel use cases.
- Third, much existing research has either used surveys and questionnaires [7] [8] [9] [14] [15] [16] to ask educators to respond to topics and ideas that have been pre-identified by researchers.
- Fourth, none of these studies have been conducted in France while several studies demonstrated that cultural differences exist (e.g., [3] [8] [18] [22] [23]).
- Fifth, from a theoretical point of view, all these existing studies are based on Technology Acceptance Model (TAM) or Unified Theory of Acceptance and Use of Technology (UTAUT) model, which are mainly focused on attitudes and opinions collected by using questionnaires and interviews. But some studies [9] [10] have shown that the main factor of the acceptability for educators is the professional experience (i.e., their effective behaviours) and have also show that TAM and UTAUT models are not sufficient to predict effective behaviors of educators.

For all these reasons, our work in progress is aiming to investigate more precisely attitudes of educators in special education settings (dedicated for children with ASD) towards robots as a category of tools (i) for describing and predicting effective behaviors and (ii) for generating innovative use cases. In Section 2, we will present the methodology and theory that will enable us to carry out our study. We will thus describe the model on which our study is built. In Section 3, we will take up the issues at stake in this research, setting out the specific and general expectations.

II. THEORETICAL AND METHODOLOGICAL BACKGROUND

From a theoretical point of view, our work in progress is based on the 4A Model [4] [5] for "Acceptability, Acceptance, Adoption and Appropriation" (Figure 1). The 4A Model has the following characteristics:

- If attitudes and opinions are central in "traditional" TAM and UTAUT models used in HUman Computer Interaction (HCI), relationships between attitudes and behaviors are not really described. The 4A Model is specifically centred on these relationships between attitudes and effective behaviours.
- Among technologies, robots are very specific (e.g., embodiment, autonomy, dynamics, social dimensions). The 4A Model has been specifically created to better understand the human factors implied in adoption and appropriation of robotics systems.
- According to TAM and UTAUT models, the use of a technology is directly and positively related to the acceptance. For the 4A Model, to use a technology such as a robot is not necessary a consequence of acceptance: in some professional situations, the worker can have the obligation to use the system even if s/he does not accept the system. The 4A Model allows to collect precise data about this kind of situation where the use if not correlated to acceptance.
- The temporal dimension of appropriation is central in the 4A Model, to follow the dynamics of adoption and appropriation and to follow the evolution of attitudes across the time.
- Five, form a theoretical point of view, all these studies are based on TAM or UTAUT models, which are mainly focused on attitudes. But, some studies [9] [10] have shown that the main factor of the acceptability for educators is the professional experience and have also show that TAM and UTAUT models are not sufficient to predict effective behaviors of educators.

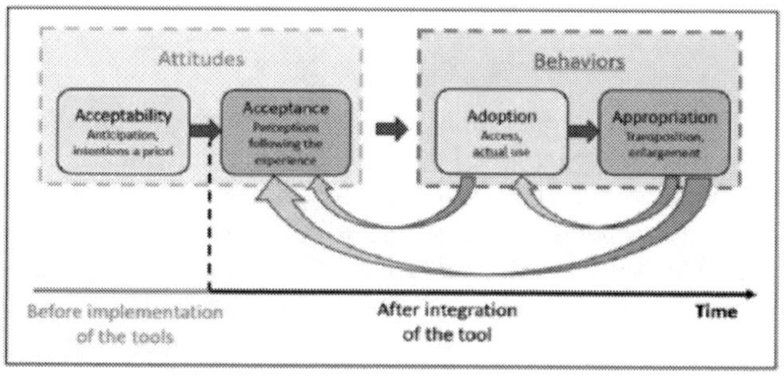

Figure 1. Our 4A Model to describe and to predict adoption and appropriation of technology, from [4] [5].

From a methodological point of view, our work in progress is based on:

- Interviews and focus groups conducted with several professionals working in different special education settings for children with ASD, to collect subjective data about attitudes and opinions according to the educators in natural conditions/contexts.

- Observations in situ to collect objective data about real activities performed by the educators with the children in the special education settings.
- This mixed approach will provide additional information to better understand the potential human and organisation factors related to negatives or positives attitudes towards robots, and to better predict the future behaviours related to these attitudes.

III. Conclusion

As we said in the introduction, research is highlighting the benefits of using robots for autistic children, in particular to develop their skills needed for social inclusion. However, these benefits have been observed in the laboratory and are sometimes difficult to replicate in the school environment (i.e., in ecological environment). Validity and transfer from laboratory to ecological settings are probably the biggest problems in psychological and psychiatric research on autism. And yet, the challenge of supporting autistic children arises in this environment, in conjunction with the intervention of educators and teachers [2]. Because, the number of high-tech applications in the training of children with autism increases every day, it is crucial to investigate the representations and acceptance of professionals and educators that play a vital role in their ability to use robots optimally, adapting them to the challenges they face. The aim of our study is to shed light on the the organizational, technical (robot-specific) and psychological factors that determine robot integration. More broadly, our study is aiming to offer recommendations for adapting education settings to facilitate the use of a robot in order to promote the inclusion of children with autism. Because this work is actually in progress, we will present the first results during the conference.

References

[1] A. Miyake et al., "The unity and diversity of executive functions and their contributions to complex "frontal lobe" tasks: a latent variable analysis", Cogn. Psychol. vol. 41, 2000, pp. 49–100. doi: 10.1006/cogp.1999.0734.

[2] A. M. Alcorn et al., "Educators' views on using humanoid robots with autistic learners in special education settings in England", Frontiers in Robotics and AI, vol.6, 2019, 107, pp. 1-9.

[3] H. Bae, "Special Forum for East Asia Robot Community", Korean Electronic Newspaper, http://www.etnews.co.kr/news/detail.html?id=200711 2900232, 2007 (cited by J. P. Peronard, 2013)

[4] C. Bauchet, B. Hubert, and J. Dinet, "From acceptability of digital change to appropriation of technology: The 4A Model", In 13ème colloque international RIPSYDEVE "Developmental and educational psychology for the 21st century: new objects, spaces and temporalities", 2020, pp. 158-161.

[5] C. Bauchet, B. Hubert, and J. Dinet, 'From acceptability of digital change to appropriation of technology: The 4A Model", Oral Communication In 17th EARA Conference" Adolescence in a rapidly changing world", 2020, p. 1.

[6] T. Belpaeme, J. Kennedy, A. Ramachandran, B. Scassellati, and F. Tanaka, "Social robots for education: A review", Sci. Robot, 2018, 3, eaat5954, pp. 1-9.

[7] Y. W. Cheng, P. C. Sun, and N. S. Chen "The essential applications of educational robot: requirement analysis from the perspectives of experts, researchers and instructors", Comput. Educ., vol.126, 2019, pp.399–416. 10.1016/j.compedu.2018.07.020

[8] J. H. Choi, J. Y. Lee, and J. H. Han, "Comparison of cultural acceptability for educational robots between Europe and Korea", Journal of Information Processing Systems, vol.4(3), 2008, pp.97-102.

[9] D. Conti, S. Di Nuovo, S., Buono, and A. Di Nuovo, "Robots in education and care of children with developmental disabilities: a study on acceptance by experienced and future professionals", International Journal of Social Robotics, vol.9, 2017, pp.51-62.

[10] J. J. Diehl, L. M. Schmitt, M. Villano and C. R. Crowell "The clinical use of robots for individuals with autism spectrum disorders: a critical review", Res. Autism Spectr. Disord., vol. 6, 2012, pp.249–262. 10.1016/j.rasd.2011.05.006

[11] L. C. Eaves and H. H. Ho, "School placement and academic achievement in children with autistic spectrum disorders", J. Dev. Phys. Disabil., vol.9, 2017, pp.277–291. 10.1023/A:1024944226971

[12] M. Fridin and M. Belokopytov, "Acceptance of socially assistive humanoid robot by preschool and elementary school teachers", Comput. Hum. Behav., vol.33, 2014, pp.23–31. 10.1016/j.chb.2013.12.016

[13] T. Hughes-Roberts, and D. Brown, "Implementing a robot-based pedagogy in the classroom: initial results from stakeholder interviews", In 2015 International Conference on Interactive Technologies and Games (Nottingham: IEEE), 2015, pp.9–54. 10.1109/iTAG.2015.18

[14] C. A. Huijnen M.A. Lexis, and L. P. de Witte, "Matching robot KASPAR to autism spectrum disorder (ASD) therapy and educational goals", Int. J. Soc. Robot. vol.8, 2016, pp.445–455. 10.1007/s12369-016-0369-4

[15] C. A. Huijnen, M.A. Lexis, R. Jansens, and L. P. de Witte, "How to implement robots in interventions for children with autism? A co-creation study involving people with autism, parents and professionals", J. Autism Dev. Disord., vol.47, 2017, pp.3079–3096. 10.1007/s10803-017-3235-9

[16] C. A. Huijnen, M.A. Lexis, R. Jansens, and L. P. de Witte, "Roles, strengths and challenges of using robots in interventions for children with autism spectrum disorder (ASD)", J. Autism Dev. Disord., vol. 49, 2019, pp.11–21. 10.1007/s10803-018-3683-x

[17] J. Kennedy, S. Lemaignan, T Belpaeme, "The cautious attitude of teachers towards social robots in schools", In Robots 4 Learning Workshop at IEEE RO-MAN, 2016, (New York, NY)

[18] A. Kim Sang, and N. M. Shin, "Making the Relationship with Robots: The Study on Educational Media in the Respective of Elementary, Junior High School, High School Students", Journal of Korean Association for Educational Information and Media, vol. 13(3),20920, pp.79-99, 2007.

[19] H. Kozima, C. Nakagawa, and Y. Yasuda, "Children–robot interaction: a pilot study in autism therapy. Prog. Brain Res.164, 2007, pp.385–400. 10.1016/S0079-6123(07)64021-7

[20] C. U. Krägeloh, J. Bharatharaj, S. K. Sasthan Kutty, P. R. Nirmala, and L. Huang, "Questionnaires to measure acceptability of social robots: a critical review", Robotics, vol.8(4), 2019, 88.

[21] H. Kumazaki et al., "Optimal robot for intervention for individuals with autism spectrum disorders", Psychiatry and clinical neurosciences, vol. 74(11), 2020, pp. 581-586.

[22] Nielsen, J., "Usability Engineering", Boston: Academic Press, 1993.

[23] T. T. Nomura, T. Kanda, T. Suzuki, J. Han, N. Shin, J. Burke, and K. Kato, "Implications on Humanoid Robots in Pedagogical", In Proceeding of Robot and Human Interactive Communication(ROMAN), 2008.

[24] T. Pachidis, E. Vrochidou, S. Kaburlasos, S. Kostova, M. Bonkovic, and V. Papic, "Social robotics in education: State-of-the-art and directions", In Proceedings of the 27th International Conference on Robotics in Alpe-Adria Danube Region (RAAD 2018), Patras, Greece, 6–8 June 2018, pp.689–700.

[25] F. Papadopoulos, K. Dautenhahn, and W. C. Ho, "Exploring the use of robots as social mediators in a remote human-human collaborative communication experiment", Paladyn, Journal of Behavioral Robotics, vol.3(1), 2012, pp.1-10.

[26] B. Scassellati, et al. "Improving social skills in children with ASD using a long-term, in-home social robot." Science Robotics 3.21 (2018).

[27] B. Robins, and K. Dautenhahn, "The role of the experimenter in HRI research-a case study evaluation of children with autism interacting with a robotic toy", In ROMAN 2006-The 15th IEEE International Symposium on Robot and Human Interactive Communication (Hatfield: IEEE), pp.646–651

[28] B. Robins, and K. Dautenhahn, "The iterative development of the humanoid robot kaspar: an assistive robot for children with autism, in Social Robotics: 9th International Conference, ICSR, 2017 (Tsukuba: Springer).

[29] B. Robins, and K. Dautenhahn, E. Ferrari, G. Kronreif, B. Prazak-Aram, P. Marti P., et al., "Scenarios of robot-assisted play for children with cognitive and physical disabilities", Int. Stud. vol.13, 2012, pp.189–234. 10.1075/is.13.2.03rob

[30] M. J. Salvador, S. Silver, and M. H. Mahoor, "An emotion recognition comparative study of autistic and typically-developing children using the zeno robot", In 2015 IEEE International Conference on Robotics and Automation (ICRA)(Seattle, WA), 2015, 6128–6133. 10.1109/ICRA.2015.7140059

[31] S. Serholt, W. Barendregt, A. Vasalou, P. Alves-Oliveira, A. Jones, S. Petisca S., et al., "The case of classroom robots: Teachers' deliberations on the ethical tensions", AI Soc. vol.32, 2017, pp.613–631. 10.1007/s00146-016-0667-2

[32] J. Wainer, B. Robins, F. Amirabdollahian, and F. Dautenhahn, "Using the humanoid robot KASPAR to autonomously play triadic games and facilitate collaborative play among children with autism", IEEE Trans. Auton. Ment. Dev., vol.6, 2014, pp.183–199.

[33] H. Y. A. Wong, and Z. W. Zhong, "Assessment of robot training for social cognitive learning", In Proceedings of the 16th International Conference on Control, Automation and Systems (ICCAS 2016), Gyeongju, Korea, 16–19 October 2016; pp.893–898.

[34] S. S. Yun, H. Kim, J. Choi, and S. K. Park, "A robot-assisted behavioral intervention system for children with autism spectrum disorders", Robot. Autonom. Syst. vol.76, 52016, pp.8–67. 10.1016/j.robot.2015.11.004.

[35] N. F. Tolksdorf, S. Siebert, I. Zorn, I. Horwath,and K. Rohlfing, "Ethical considerations of applying robots in kindergarten settings: Towards an approach from a macroperspective", International Journal of Social Robotics, vol.13, 2021, pp.129-140.

Generating Interpretable Prototype Networks by Comprehensive Compression for Multi-Layered Neural Networks

Ryotaro Kamimura
Tokai University
Hiratsuka, Kanagawa, 259-1292, Japan
email: ryotarokami@gmail.com

***Abstract*—The present paper aims to propose a method for creating an interpretable prototype network that is hidden within original multi-layered neural networks. The interpretation of the inference mechanism of neural networks has received much attention in recent times, leading to the development of various methods. However, these methods have focused on interpreting specific internal representations created by neural networks. There is an urgent need to propose an interpretation method that considers not only specific representations but also all internal representations created by a neural network, aiming for a more unified understanding of the fundamental properties of the inference mechanism. To address this problem, we propose the introduction of a prototype network that is hidden within the original multi-layered neural network. This is achieved through an interpretation method called "comprehensive compression," which aims to replace the process of interpretation for finding a simple and interpretable prototype network. The method was applied to the analysis of customer data sets. The experimental results demonstrate that interpretable compression can simplify multi-layered neural networks and unify all obtained representations. It enables the detection and interpretation of non-linear as well as corresponding linear relations. The proposed method of the prototype network makes it possible to interpret not only specific instances but also a number of different instances. It helps us uncover the fundamental inference mechanism that is deeply hidden within neural networks.**

***Keywords*—prototype network; comprehensive compression; interpretable compression; layer compression; collective compression; stabilizing compression; total de-compression; selective compression**

I. INTRODUCTION

A. *Problems of Interpretation*

As neural networks have been applied in many fields because of their improved generalization performance, the problem of difficulty in interpreting their internal representations has received much attention these days [1], due to reliability [2] and ethical problems [3] [4]. Though much progress has been made in the field of convolutional neural networks (CNN), where the intuitive interpretation of image datasets is fairly easy [5]–[8], the interpretation methods developed so far are far from being acceptable, particularly when dealing with more abstract objects in social and human sciences, where the intuitive interpretation of data sets is almost impossible.

One of the main problems is that the majority of interpretation methods have tried to interpret an instance of the final results obtained by learning. A slight consideration of these types of methods leads us to doubt their validity because neural networks have had a bad reputation from the beginning of research that the final results can be easily changed by modifying initial conditions, input patterns, parameters, network configurations, etc., which have recently received much attention in the name of adversarial attacks [9]–[13]. In addition, one of the more fundamental problems is that while we should aim to explain why and how a method can reach its conclusion as rigorously as possible, it only tries to describe the phenomena occurring during learning in a very specific manner. This specific interpretation is naturally not enough to understand the main inference mechanism of neural networks, even if it can explicitly and fully explain the inference.

Naturally, extensive studies have been conducted on the so-called "global" interpretation [14] [15], and these studies seem to deal with the inference mechanism broadly. However, they do not necessarily explain the real global properties of neural networks. As mentioned above, one of the main properties of neural networks lies in their productive property, where a neural network can generate a large number of different internal representations by changing learning conditions. Although many of these representations may not be understandable to observers, they should still be interpreted because networks without interpretable representations can still produce the appropriate final conclusions. This productive property has not been fully discussed in the field of neural networks, with only the acknowledgment that many different representations can be generated with different initial conditions and situations. In this framework of neural network productivity, the so-called "global" methods seem to be limited to specific instances among many, which should be called "specific" or "local" interpretation.

Furthermore, considering the fact that neural networks were developed to oppose rule-based systems, many global interpretation methods with logical and semantic-based interpretation [16]–[18] seem to have serious problems from the beginning. We should move away from explanations based on logical rules and explore different methods for understanding the productive property of neural networks.

B. *Prototype Network*

In this context, we aim to introduce a new type of interpretation method to clarify the objective of interpretation. In this method, the interpretation is based on detecting a prototype and interpretable network, which is assumed to be hidden within actual multi-layered neural networks. In existing interpretation methods, the prototype is used to facilitate the interpretation process, where neural networks attempt to classify input images based on the prototypes created in the prototype layers [19]. However, we propose that behind many multi-layered neural networks, there always exists a simple prototype network. These multi-layered neural networks are assumed to be generated by transformation rules from the prototype network, and the productive property can be explained by this transformational generation. Furthermore, because the prototype network is assumed to be simple enough to interpret the meaning of any components within it, the interpretation lies not in directly interpreting the original multi-layered neural networks but in uncovering the hidden prototype network. Thus, the abstract and intuitive process of interpretation can be replaced by a more concrete process of finding a prototype network.

C. Interpretable and Stabilizing Compression

The prototype network is supposed to be as simple as possible. For example, it can be imagined that the prototype network can be represented by a network without hidden layers, and the interpretation method should aim to find this prototype network without hidden layers for interpretation. This network is realized by simplifying multi-layered neural networks to the extreme. Thus, interpretation, in the first place, is about simplifying multi-layered neural networks as much as possible to approximate the prototype network from a technical viewpoint. To find the prototype network, we need to compress multi-layered neural networks to the simplest ones without hidden layers. Additionally, we need to compress all representations created by learning with different initial conditions, input patterns, parameters, and network configurations for interpretation. These types of compression can be called "interpretable compression." It should be stressed that interpretable compression is different from conventional compression methods [20]–[22] in that the original information in internal representations should be preserved as much as possible in the compressed ones.

In addition, the number and intensity of components in a neural network should be reduced in order to simplify and stabilize the interpretable compression. This reduction aims to restrict the flexibility of components. This compression is referred to as "stabilizing compression." It is closely related to conventional regularization methods such as weight decay [23] [24] and pruning [25] [26] as it aims to restrict the productive property of neural networks. However, because the obtained prototype network is expected to generate a considerable number of multi-layered networks, which is directly related to the productive property at the surface level, it should aim to simplify representations while preserving the productive property as much as possible. To achieve this, we introduce a process of compression accompanied by decompression, which controls the productivity of neural networks for smooth learning.

D. Main Contributions

Main contributions are summarized as follows:

- The present paper proposes a new interpretation method that replaces the interpretation process for finding a prototype and interpretable network.
- This network is obtained through interpretable compression by simplifying or compressing as many multi-layered neural networks as possible.
- Although this interpretable compression naturally entails some instability due to the productive property of neural networks, it can be mitigated by introducing stabilizing compression.
- The paper demonstrates how our method successfully produces a prototype network with several important inputs that were considered unimportant by conventional methods, serving as an example of interpretation.

E. The Structure of the Paper

In Section 2, we explain how to compress multi-layered neural networks for interpretation, using layer compression and stabilizing compression. Layer compression gradually eliminates hidden layers, while stabilizing compression includes both total de-compression to control the strength of weights and selective compression to select strong weights. In Section 3, we present the experimental results on the interpretation of a customer data set. We demonstrate how layer and stabilizing compression can be used to clarify relations between inputs and outputs and to distinguish between linear and non-linear relations.

II. Theory and Computational Methods

A. Concept of Compression

In this paper, the interpretation aims to detect a prototype network supposed to be hidden in multi-layered neural networks. Figure 1 shows our basic framework of interpretation. Firstly, it is supposed that an actual multi-layered neural network is generated from the corresponding prototype network by decompression or by deploying it to a multi-layered network, as shown on the left side of Figure 1. One of the major challenges is to find this prototype network, which we refer to as the "interpretation," because the prototype network is supposed to be as simple as possible. To find this prototype network, we must compress an actual multi-layered neural network to the extreme point as shown on the right side of Figure 1, because simplicity must be one of the most important inherent properties of the prototype network. The present paper focuses on this compression to find a prototype network. For actual implementation, this compression should be elaborated further to deal with actual and practical learning processes.

We introduce a framework shown in Figure 2 to make the basic framework in Figure 1 practically applicable. One of the main differences is the introduction of comprehensive compression instead of simple compression. In the comprehensive compression component in Figure 2, two types of compression are introduced: interpretable (a) and stabilizing (b) compression. In the interpretable compression, two

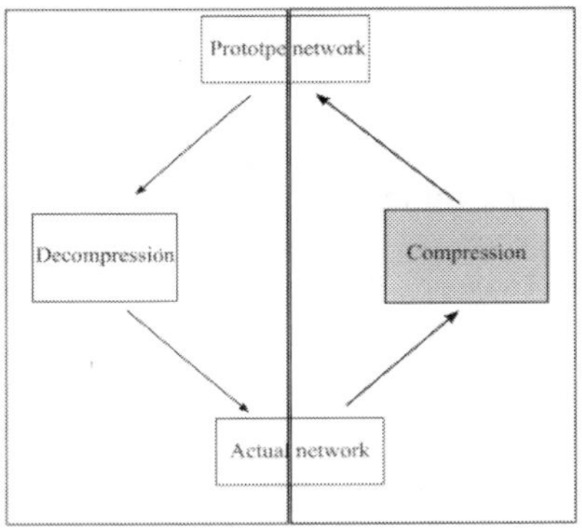

Figure 1. A framework to find a prototype network, which is decompressed into an actual network configuration, while an actual network is compressed into the prototype network.

types of compression, layer and collective compression, are introduced. In layer compression, hidden layers are gradually eliminated to find a network without hidden layers. Collective compression is used to compress all representations created by a neural network with different initial conditions, input patterns, parameters, and network configurations. Then, stabilizing compression is introduced to simplify and stabilize multi-layered neural networks for producing an easily interpretable network. In this stabilizing compression, we introduce total de-compression and selective compression. In total de-compression, the strength or magnitude of total weights is mainly decreased, and to stabilize this process, we introduce the decompression of the strength of total weights, meaning that the reduced strength is restored. Thus, we call this process "de-compression" to combine a process of compression and decompression. The selective compression aims to simplify a network configuration by selecting important connection weights in the corresponding hidden layers.

B. Interpretable Compression

1) Compression for Interpretation: The prototype network can be estimated by producing and compressing many different types of multi-layered neural networks with different initial conditions, input patterns, parameters, and so on, which is called "interpretable compression," aiming to produce the simplest network or collective network to approximate the prototype network. In interpretable compression, we have two types of compression: collective compression and layer compression. Layer compression is used to reduce the number of hidden layers, and collective compression aims to unify all possible representations created by learning.

Figure 3 shows the concept of interpretable compression. In the first place, we try to produce many different types of networks with different initial conditions (a), input patterns (b), and different parameter values (c), among others. This is necessary because the fundamental property related to the prototype network can be estimated by viewing data sets from many different viewpoints. The obtained estimated networks are collectively unified or averaged in the collective

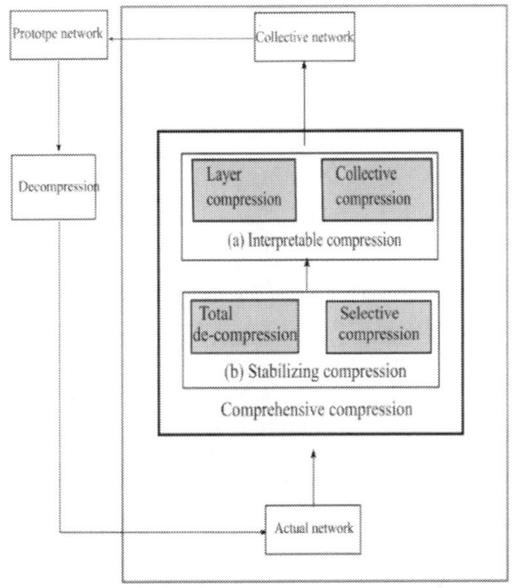

Figure 2. Actual compression components in which simple compression is substitued for comprehensive compression in the practical implementation with stabilizing and interpretable compression inside.

compression (d) to create collective networks (e) which are used to estimate the corresponding prototype network (f). The difference between the two networks can be detected, albeit roughly, by the ratio (u/z) (e) of the actual absolute coefficients of the collective network (u) to the absolute coefficients (z) of the prototype network. The absolute values are used to roughly understand the meaning of prototype networks at the present stage. Since it is actually impossible to use the coefficients of the prototype network (z), we should employ other measures such as linear correlation coefficients between inputs and targets obtained through regression analysis.

2) Layer Compression: Let us illustrate the process of layer compression in Figure 4(a)-(e). First, we compress the connection weights from the first to the second layer, denoted by (1,2), and from the second to the third layer (2,3) for an initial condition and a subset of a dataset. Then, we obtain the compressed weights between the first and the third layer, denoted by (1,3).

$$w_{ik}^{(1,3)} = \sum_{j} w_{ij}^{(1,2)} w_{jk}^{(2,3)} \qquad (1)$$

These compressed weights are further combined with the weights from the third to the fourth layer (3,4), resulting in the compressed weights between the first and the fourth layer (1,4).

$$w_{il}^{(1,4)} = \sum_{k} w_{ik}^{(1,3)} w_{kl}^{(3,4)} \qquad (2)$$

By repeating these processes, we obtain the compressed weights between the first and the fifth layer, denoted by $w_{iq}^{(1,5)}$.

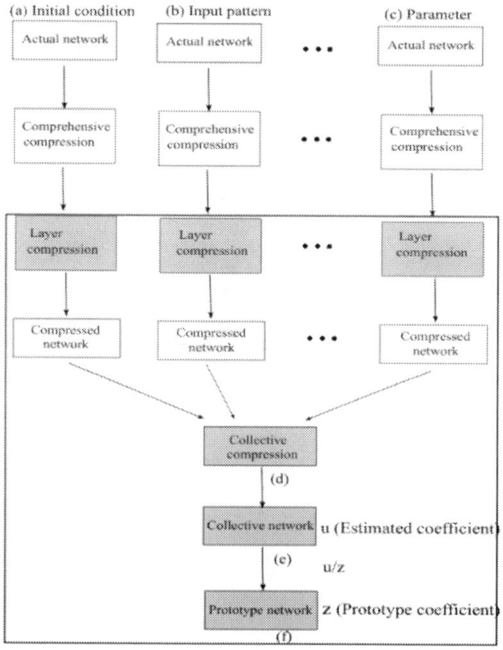

Figure 3. Compression from multi-layered networks with different initial conditions (a), input patterns (b), and parameters (c) to the simplest collective network (e) to estimate the corresponding prototype network (f).

Using these connection weights, we have the final and fully compressed weights (1,6).

$$w_{ir}^{(1,6)} = \sum_{q} w_{iq}^{(1,5)} w_{qr}^{(6,7)} \tag{3}$$

3) Collective Compression: Figure 4(d) shows that all the finally compressed weights are averaged to obtain the final collective weights. Then, c represents the real coefficients of a prototype network in Figure 4(e). Similarly, z denotes the absolute and individual compression coefficients of the prototype network.

$$z_{ir} = \mid c_{ir} \mid \tag{4}$$

These coefficients should be compared with the corresponding coefficients or weights of the collective weights.

$$u_{ir} = \mid w_{ir} \mid \tag{5}$$

Then, we define the collective compression coefficient as follows:

$$c_{ir} = \frac{u_{ir}}{z_{ir}} \tag{6}$$

Here, the denominator represents the absolute values of the basic relations between inputs and targets in a prototype network. The use of absolute values allows us to intuitively observe the overall relations without considering the sign information. This coefficient aims to indicate which inputs are larger than the corresponding basic relations. Introducing this coefficient is crucial for interpreting the finally compressed weights since interpreting the compressed weights on their own is not possible. Interpretation can only be achieved by comparing them to other interpretation results. Several possibilities for these basic relations include the correlation coefficient between inputs and targets of the original data set, regression coefficients from regression analysis, weights obtained through conventional methods, and so on. When the collective weights significantly deviate from these relations obtained by conventional methods, it becomes necessary to provide an explanation for the deviation.

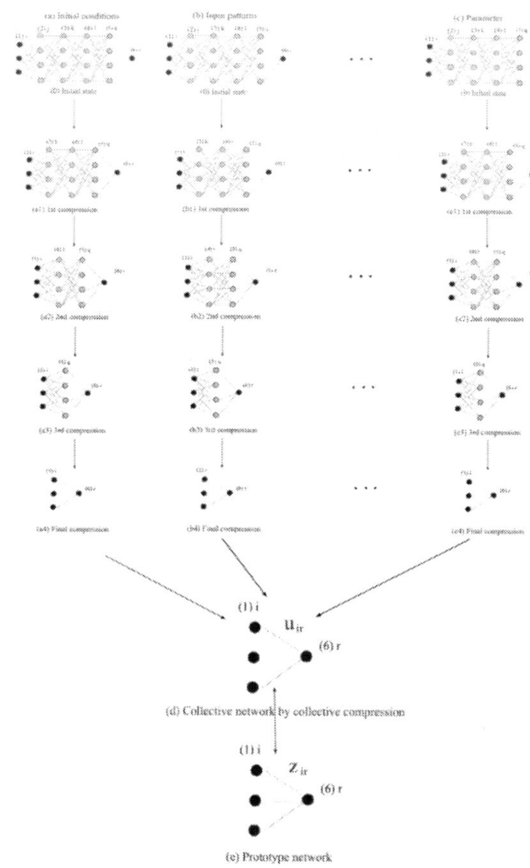

Figure 4. Layer compression from multi-layered networks (1) to the simplest networks (4) with different initial conditions (a), different inputs (b), and different parameters (c), and collective network (d) and the corresponding prototype network (e).

C. Stabilizing Compression

1) Stabilizing Concept: We will explain stabilizing compression within the framework of comprehensive compression. It is necessary to simplify the actual network to an extreme point in order to find the prototype network. This simplification and restriction of possible network configurations are associated with the stability of the produced networks and their internal representations.

In compression, we can identify two types: total decompression (compression and decompression) and selective compression. Total compression aims to reduce the strength of total weights, while total decompression aims to increase the strength. The purpose of total decompression is to enhance the effectiveness of total compression. On the other hand, selective compression is used to minimize the number of connection weights for simplification. These types of compression should be performed simultaneously when using the conventional learning approach. However, these types of compression and error minimization are contradictory. For instance, total compression and decompression are completely contradictory to each other, and it is impossible to perform them simultaneously.

For solving this type of contradiction, we introduce the serially disentangled stabilizing compression. In this method, all compression procedures and error minimization are completely disentangled, and they are independently applied. Firstly, the total compression is applied to reduce the strength of total weights, and then errors between outputs and targets are reduced. Then, the selective compression is applied, followed by the corresponding error minimization. Finally, the total decompression is used to weaken the effects of total compression, followed by the corresponding error minimization. In this way, completely contradictory terms such as total compression and decompression can coexist, though seemingly.

2) Total de-compression: Let us define total decompression by considering the strength of weights. Note that the compression in this paper is different from or contrary to the conventional compression methods using the compression rate. The total compression can be defined by measuring the strength of the absolute weights. When the absolute weights become smaller, the actual degree of compression becomes larger because information should be represented by the smaller strength of weights, where the flexibility of weights becomes smaller.

On the contrary, when the absolute strength becomes larger, the actual degree of compression becomes smaller because larger weights have a possibility to represent many different types of weight configurations.

For simplicity, we consider weights from the tth hidden layer to the $t+1$th hidden layer, represented by $(t, t+1)$, and the absolute weight from the jth neuron to the kth neuron is defined by

$$u_{jk}^{(t,t+1)} = \mid w_{jk}^{(t,t+1)} \mid \tag{7}$$

We need to use the total weight strength, summed over all connection weights in all hidden layers. Then, averaging this total weight strength, we have the average total compression coefficient, computed by

$$\bar{U} = \frac{\theta}{h \cdot n_t \cdot n_{t+1}} \sum_t^h \sum_j^{n_t} \sum_k^{n_{t+1}} u_{j,k}^{(t,t+1)} \tag{8}$$

where h denotes the number of hidden layers minus one, and n_t is the number of neurons in the tth hidden layer. In the following experimental results, the parameter θ should be positive, and it should be decreased gradually.

3) Selective Compression: Then, we should count the number of strong weights in a layer as an index for representing the compression in a hidden layer, meaning that we must select important connection weights in the selective compression. Here, we also consider the absolute strength of weights, but they are normalized by the corresponding maximum absolute weight. This relative strength can be computed by

$$^{\gamma}g_{jk}^{(t,t+1)} = \left[\frac{u_{jk}^{(t,t+1)}}{\max_{j'k'} u_{j'k'}^{(t',t'+1)}} \right]^{\gamma} \tag{9}$$

where the max operation is over all connection weights in the layer, and the parameter γ should be a small positive value for stabilizing learning. When this equation is applied to connection weights, a winning connection weight in terms of weight strength remains the same, while all the other weights are pushed toward smaller ones. In an extreme case, only one winning weight has some strength, while all the others become zero, which is the well-known hard type WTA (winner-take-all).

By using the relative strength over all hidden layers, we have the average selective compression coefficient, defined by

$$^{\gamma}\bar{G} = \frac{1}{h \cdot n_t \cdot n_{t+1}} \sum_t^h \sum_j^{n_t} \sum_k^{n_{t+1}} \left[\frac{u_{jk}^{(t,t+1)}}{\max_{j'k't'} u_{j'k't'}^{(t,t+1)}} \right]^{\gamma} \tag{10}$$

This average selective compression coefficient becomes maximum when all connection weights have the same values. When only one connection weight is larger than zero, while all the others are zero, the corresponding coefficient becomes minimum, supposing that at least one weight should be larger than zero.

III. Results and Discussion

A. Customer Data Set

The experiments were performed, using a data set with a sport gymnasium's customers. We tried to discriminate between genders, and to infer the characteristics of female customers [27]. The data set was composed of 2104 gymnasium customers, and the inputs were composed of eight variables. We used networks with ten hidden layers with ten neurons for each hidden layer. The scikit-learn neural network package was used with default parameter values except the activation function (set to the tangent-hyperbolic) and the number of learning steps (set to 600 learning steps) for the easy reproduction of the experimental results.

In the experiment, a multi-layered neural network with ten hidden layers are compressed for interpretation with the stabilizing compression, composed of total de-compression and selective compression. This network is compressed (layer compression) into networks without hidden layer for all learning steps. All those compressed networks are collectively compressed in the collective compression. Finally, we tried to compare this collective network with the corresponding prototype network to examine the characteristics obtained by our compression method.

B. Interpretable Compression

The interpretable compression consists of layer compression and collective compression. In the layer compression, the network with ten hidden layers is compressed gradually into the corresponding network without hidden layers. The connection weights or coefficients of the estimated network were compared to those of the prototype network. We here used the correlation coefficients between inputs and outputs as an example of coefficients of the prototype network. The comparative study between the estimated network and the prototype network in terms of correlation coefficients clarified several important inputs that could not be identified by the simple linear correlation coefficients.

1) Layer and Collective Compression: Figure 5 shows collective weights (1), ratios of absolute collective weights (2) to the corresponding absolute correlation coefficients between inputs and targets (3) by the conventional method (a) and by new methods where the parameter θ decreased from 1.0 (b) to 0.6 (f). As shown on the left side of Figure 5, the input No.8 (daytime use) was the largest by all the methods, while all the others were considerably smaller in terms of correlation coefficients and connection weights.

Then, we examined the ratios of absolute connection weights to the corresponding correlation coefficients, represented in the middle of Figure 5. The correlation coefficients between the ith input to the corresponding target were represented by v_i. Then, the absolute and individual compression coefficients of the prototype network were represented by z_i:

$$z_i = \mid v_i \mid \tag{11}$$

These values should be compared with the weights of collective weights. Then, we have the ratio of the absolute connection weights to the corresponding correlation coefficients as:

$$c_i = \frac{u_i}{z_i} \tag{12}$$

The ratios showed that when the inputs on the left side became relatively larger, these relations between the inputs and targets could not be extracted by linear correlation coefficients. However, the ratios slightly differed when the parameter was decreased from 1 (b) to 0.6 (f). When the parameter decreased from 1.0 (b) to 0.6 (f) in Figure 5, gradually the input No.2 became larger than the others. Finally, we should average compressed weights for really collective meaning of the connection weights, which was the final round of interpretable compression.

Figure 6 shows the final collective weights averaged over all weights obtained by different parameter values, shown in Figure 5. As seen in the figure, the female clients tended to use the gym during daytime (input No.8) but relatively irregularly (input No.2) in terms of negative values, and the usage period tended to be longer (input No.3). Our compression method could clarify the characteristics of female clients. In addition to the linear relation represented in the input No.8 (daytime use), non-linear relations were detected in the input No.2 (irregularity) and No.3 (usage period). This means that the female clients tend to use longer the gym in daytime, but in an irregular manner.

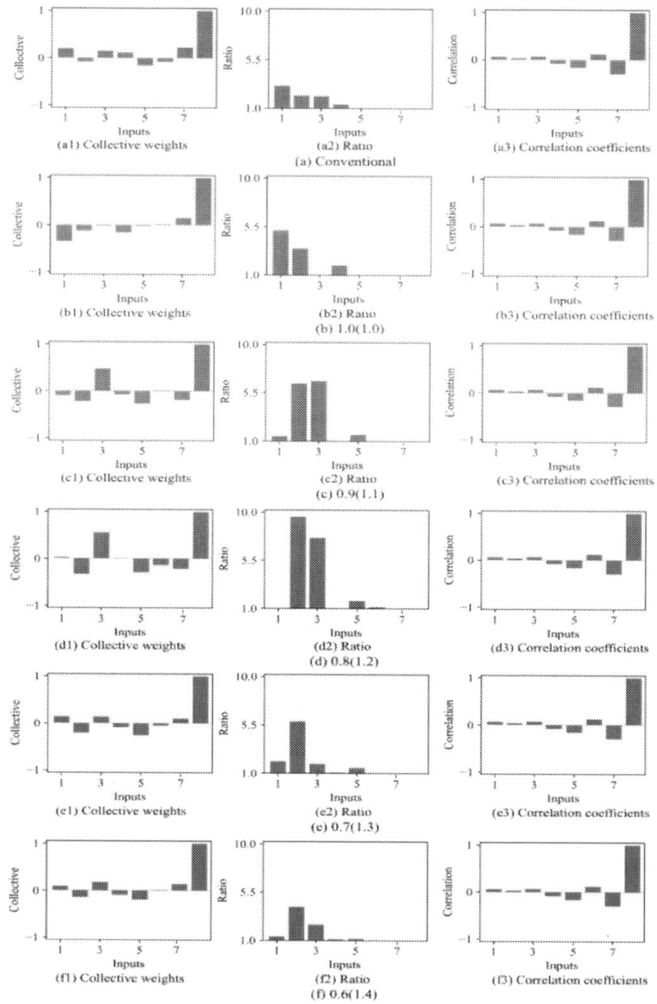

Figure 5. Collective weights (1), ratio (2) and correlation coefficients (3) by the conventional method (a), and by decreasing the parameter θ from 1.0 (b) to 0.4 (f) for the customer data set.

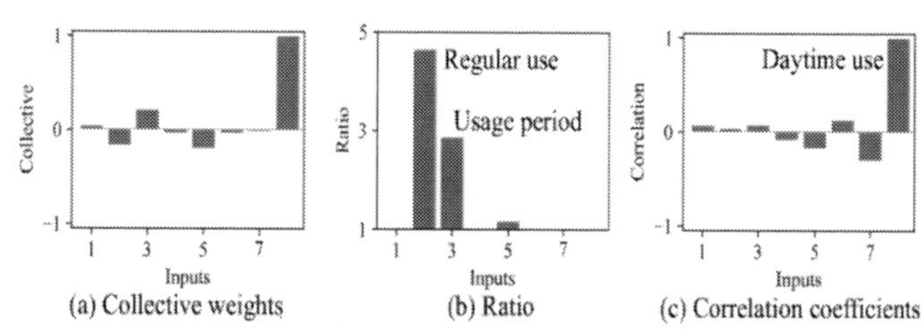

Figure 6. Collective weights (a), ratio (b) and correlation coefficients (c) by averaging all the collective weights for the customer data set.

C. Stabilizing Compression

1) Stability of Selective Compression: By decreasing the parameter θ in total compression, accompanied by increasing the parameter θ in total decompression, average total compression coefficients decreased with large fluctuations. However, the selective compression coefficients decreased almost without fluctuations to have an effect to simplify the corresponding network configurations in terms of number of connection weights. This means that the stabilized simplification was realized by this compression in spite of large variations of total compression coefficients.

Figure 7 shows total (1) and selective (2) compression coefficients. Figure 7(a) shows the results by the conventional methods without compression. As can be seen in the figure, total and selective compression coefficients remained to be unchanged throughout all learning steps. When the parameter θ decreased from 1.0 (b) to 0.6 (f), two compression coefficients gradually decreased. In spite of decrease in the parameter to have an effect to decrease the strength of weights, the intensity of each compression coefficient tended to increase, when the parameter decreased from 1.0 (b) to 0.6 (f). This effect could be explained by the fact that the parameter for decompression was inversely set to $2 - \theta$. Total compression coefficients decreased with large fluctuations by the effects of compression and decompression in the total de-compression. However, in spite of these fluctuations, the selective compression coefficients decreased almost without fluctuations.

The results show that total de-compression had the effect to prevent connection weights from being too small by increasing the strength of connection weights by total decompression. In addition, the large fluctuations by the effects of total de-compression had no effects on the process of decreasing the selective compression coefficients. In sum, the selective compression can be effective in decreasing the strength of connection weights, which was performed very smoothly by the effect of total de-compression. The smooth decrease in the selective information by the help of total de-compression can be used to realize actually the simplicity of network configurations in terms of the number of connection weights.

2) Weight Stability : The results showed that an decrease in the parameter θ was related to the stable acceleration of learning. This explains why networks with different parameter values could produce similar performance in terms of generalization.

Figure 8 shows connection weights, obtained with 50 learning steps using the conventional method (a), when the parameter decreased from 1.0 (b) to 0.6 (f). In Figure 8(a), when using the conventional method, almost all weights were random, making it impossible to discern any regularity inside. When the parameter decreased from 1.0 (b) to 0.6 (f), the characteristics became clearer. Upon closer examination, the characteristics observed in connection weights with a parameter of 1.0 (b), appeared to gradually unfold, as the parameter decreased from 0.9 (c) to 0.6 (f). This means that the change in the parameter did not have any influences on the main characteristics of connection weights, but it only accelerated the learning in terms of clarifying the characteristics of connection weights.

Figure 9 shows connection weights at the final stage of learning steps. The results using the conventional method in

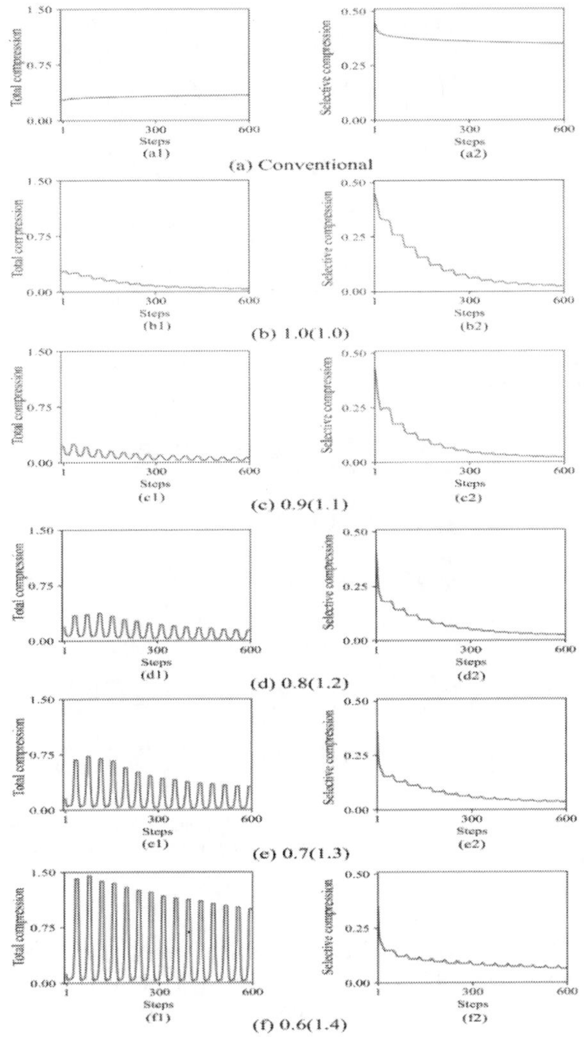

Figure 7. Average total (1) and selective (2) compression coefficients by the conventional method (a), and by changing the parameter θ from 1.0 (b) to 0.6 (f) for the customer data set.

Figure 9(a) still produced random connection weights. When the parameter decreased from 1.0 (b) to 0.6 (f), the number of strong weights diminished considerably compared with the results with 50 learning steps in Figure 8. Additionally, even when the parameter decreased to 0.6, the number of relatively stronger weights did not decrease significantly. This implied that even with an extremely decreased parameter, similar connection weights could still be obtained, which can be explained by the effect of total decompression. Furthermore, the connection weights between the first and the second hidden layer, and those between the ninth and tenth hidden layer were different from each other. This means that the connection weights were quite similar to each other in the initial stage of learning, and slight changes occurred in the later stages of learning, in particular, for connection weights between hidden layers, closer to the input and output layer.

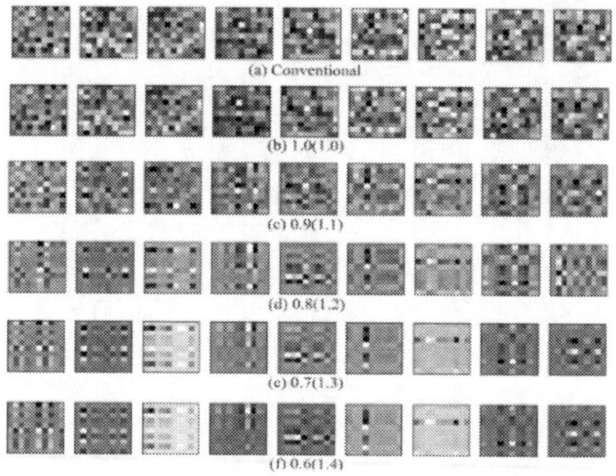

Figure 8. Connection weights, obtained after 50 learning steps by the conventional method (a) and by changing the parameter θ from 1.0 (b) to 0.6 (f) for the customer data set.

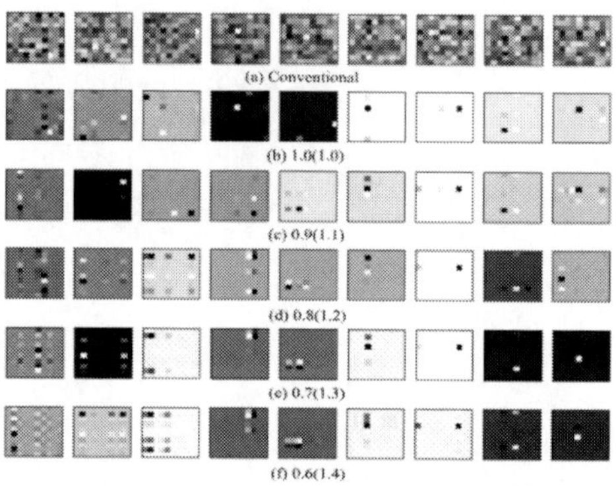

Figure 9. Connection weights, obtained at the final step of learning by the conventional method (a) and by changing the parameter θ from 1.0 (b) to 0.6 (f) for the customer data set.

The results show that the connection weights could produce similar and stable characteristics even if the parameter was forced to be decreased considerably, which was the effect of the total decompression. Minor differences could be obtained by the connection weights close to the input and output layer. These stable connection weights are certainly related to the stability of final performance, particularly in terms of generalization, as shown in Table I.

3) Layer-wise Selective Compression: We attempted to determine which hidden layers were primarily used in learning by computing the average layer compression coefficients for each hidden layer. By examing the average total compression coefficients, we observed that the new method applied less intense compression to connection weights closer to the input and output layer. This indicates that connection weights near to the input and output layer were not be easily compressible due to the abundance of information from inputs and outputs. However, when the parameter was excessively increased, only connection weights closest to the input tended to play an important role.

To clarify the characteristics of hidden layers, we plotted the normalized layer compression rates in Figure 10. We observed that the first hidden layer and the last hidden layer had larger compression coefficients. However, when the parameter decreased to 0.6 (f), only the first hidden layer tended to have larger compression coefficients. Finally, when using the conventional methods, the compression coefficients were larger for all hidden layers.

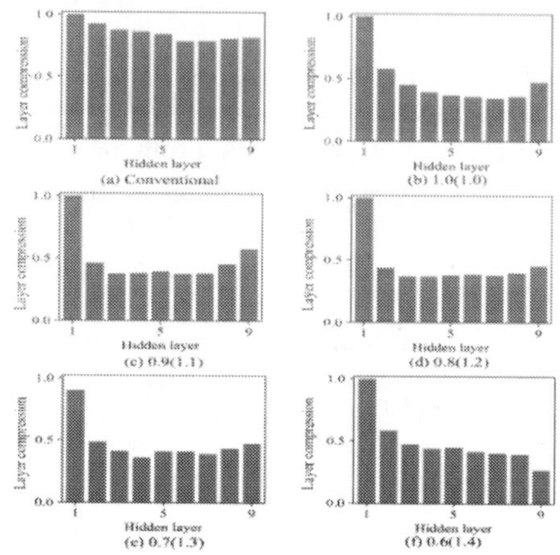

Figure 10. Normalized layer compression coefficients by the conventional method (a) by changing the parameter θ from 1.0 (b) to 0.6 (f) for the customer data set.

D. Summary of Numerical Results

Let us summarize the experimental results in terms of correlation coefficients and generalization performance. Better generalization was achieved through compression method, and particularly the new method was able to increase generalization while improving correlation coefficients.

Table I presents the summary of generalization and correlation coefficients. When the parameter was set to 1.0, the generalization accuracy was 0.684, but the correlation coefficient was the second lowest (0.807). As the parameter decreased from 0.9 to 0.6, all generalization accuracies exceeded 0.690. Additionally, the correlation coefficients were higher than those obtained all the other methods, except for the parameter $\theta = 0.8$. The similarity in generalization and correlation coefficients can be attributed to the stability of learning, as explained in the above experimental results on the stabilizing compression. The logistic regression analysis yielded accuracy of only 0.678, the second lowest one, and even the correlation coefficients was 0.855, which was not particularly large compared with those using the present method. Finally, the random forest model produced the lowest accuracy and correlation coefficient, as it could not handle negative effects.

One of the most important findings is that when the generalization accuracy was the largest ($\theta = 0.9$), the correlation coefficient was also the highest. This means that the present method tried to increase generalization by using connections weights as independently as possible, and by making the weights as linearly as possible.

TABLE I
SUMMARY OF EXPERIMENTAL RESULTS ON AVERAGED CORRELATION COEFFICIENTS AND GENERALIZATION PERFORMANCE BY OUR METHODS, COMPARING WITH THOSE BY THE CONVENTIONAL METHODS FOR THE CUSTOMER DATA SET. BOLD TYPE LETTERS INDICATE THE MAXIMUM VALUES.

Methods	Param$\theta(2-\theta)$	Accuracy	Correlation
Compression	1.0(1.0)	0.684	0.807
	0.9(1.1)	**0.692**	**0.885**
	0.8(1.2)	0.691	0.833
	0.7(1.3)	0.690	0.878
	0.6(1.4)	0.690	**0.885**
Conventional		0.683	0.833
Logistic		0.678	0.855
Random		0.613	0.256

IV. CONCLUSION

The present paper proposed a new interpretation method in which a process of interpretation was replaced for finding an interpretable prototype network. The prototype network is supposed to be found by simplifying multi-layered neural networks to the extreme point. The compression method is called "comprehensive compression", which is composed of interpretable and stabilizing compression. In the interpretable compression, multi-layered neural networks are compressed into the simplest ones without hidden layers, and all the internal representations, obtained by different initial conditions, inputs, parameters, learning steps, are averaged to produce the final collective weights. Those collective weights are compared with the weights in the prototype network to see relations between inputs and targets more exactly. The method was applied to the analysis of a customer data set, trying to clarify the characteristics of customers. By considering the correlation coefficients between inputs and targets as weights in the supposed prototype network, our method could detect linear relations, as well as non-linear ones to capture clearly the characteristics of customers.

One of the major problems is how to check the validity of our estimated prototype networks. In this paper, we tried to consider the correlation coefficient as an example of coefficients of prototype networks. However, we need to examine more exactly the possibility of the prototype network in addition to the linear correlation coefficients between inputs and outputs. Though some problems should be solved for more practical applications, the present method can certainly contribute to the development of global interpretation methods in neural networks.

REFERENCES

[1] X. Li, H. Xiong, X. Li, X. Wu, X. Zhang, J. Liu, J. Bian, and D. Dou, "Interpretable deep learning: Interpretation, interpretability, trustworthiness, and beyond," *Knowledge and Information Systems*, pp. 1–38, 2022.

[2] G. Visani, E. Bagli, F. Chesani, A. Poluzzi, and D. Capuzzo, "Statistical stability indices for lime: obtaining reliable explanations for machine learning models," *arXiv preprint arXiv:2001.11757*, 2020.

[3] B. Goodman and S. Flaxman, "European union regulations on algorithmic decision-making and a right to explanation," *arXiv preprint arXiv:1606.08813*, 2016.

[4] G. L. Sanclemente and B. N. Cardozo, "Reliability: understanding cognitive human bias in artificial intelligence for national security and intelligence analysis," *Security Journal*, pp. 1–21, 2021.

[5] G. Montavon, W. Samek, and K.-R. Müller, "Methods for interpreting and understanding deep neural networks," *Digital signal processing*, vol. 73, pp. 1–15, 2018.

[6] B. Zhou, D. Bau, A. Oliva, and A. Torralba, "Interpreting deep visual representations via network dissection," *IEEE transactions on pattern analysis and machine intelligence*, vol. 41, no. 9, pp. 2131–2145, 2018.

[7] R. Fong and A. Vedaldi, "Explanations for attributing deep neural network predictions," in *Explainable AI: Interpreting, Explaining and Visualizing Deep Learning*, pp. 149–167, Springer, 2019.

[8] Y. Liang, S. Li, C. Yan, M. Li, and C. Jiang, "Explaining the black-box model: A survey of local interpretation methods for deep neural networks," *Neurocomputing*, vol. 419, pp. 168–182, 2021.

[9] I. J. Goodfellow, J. Shlens, and C. Szegedy, "Explaining and harnessing adversarial examples," *arXiv preprint arXiv:1412.6572*, 2014.

[10] Y. Ganin, E. Ustinova, H. Ajakan, P. Germain, H. Larochelle, F. Laviolette, M. Marchand, and V. Lempitsky, "Domain-adversarial training of neural networks," *The journal of machine learning research*, vol. 17, no. 1, pp. 2096–2030, 2016.

[11] N. Carlini and D. Wagner, "Adversarial examples are not easily detected: Bypassing ten detection methods," in *Proceedings of the 10th ACM Workshop on Artificial Intelligence and Security*, pp. 3–14, 2017.

[12] Y. Liu, Z. Wang, H. Jin, and I. Wassell, "Multi-task adversarial network for disentangled feature learning," in *Proceedings of the IEEE Conference on Computer Vision and Pattern Recognition*, pp. 3743–3751, 2018.

[13] L. Wang, Y. Yan, K. He, Y. Wu, and W. Xu, "Dynamically disentangling social bias from task-oriented representations with adversarial attack," in *Proceedings of the 2021 Conference of the North American Chapter of the Association for Computational Linguistics: Human Language Technologies*, pp. 3740–3750, 2021.

[14] C. Yang, A. Rangarajan, and S. Ranka, "Global model interpretation via recursive partitioning," in *2018 IEEE 20th International Conference on High Performance Computing and Communications; IEEE 16th International Conference on Smart City; IEEE 4th International Conference on Data Science and Systems (HPCC/SmartCity/DSS)*, pp. 1563–1570, IEEE, 2018.

[15] S. M. Lundberg, G. Erion, H. Chen, A. DeGrave, J. M. Prutkin, B. Nair, R. Katz, J. Himmelfarb, N. Bansal, and S.-I. Lee, "From local explanations to global understanding with explainable ai for trees," *Nature machine intelligence*, vol. 2, no. 1, pp. 2522–5839, 2020.

[16] F. Doshi-Velez and B. Kim, "Towards a rigorous science of interpretable machine learning," *arXiv preprint arXiv:1702.08608*, 2017.

[17] T. Wang, "Gaining free or low-cost interpretability with interpretable partial substitute," in *International Conference on Machine Learning*, pp. 6505–6514, PMLR, 2019.

[18] M. Wu, S. Parbhoo, M. Hughes, R. Kindle, L. Celi, M. Zazzi, V. Roth, and F. Doshi-Velez, "Regional tree regularization for interpretability in deep neural networks," in *Proceedings of the AAAI Conference on Artificial Intelligence*, vol. 34, pp. 6413–6421, 2020.

[19] O. Li, H. Liu, C. Chen, and C. Rudin, "Deep learning for case-based reasoning through prototypes: A neural network that explains its predictions," in *Proceedings of the AAAI Conference on Artificial Intelligence*, vol. 32, 2018.

[20] G. Hinton, O. Vinyals, and J. Dean, "Distilling the knowledge in a neural network," *arXiv preprint arXiv:1503.02531*, 2015.

[21] J. O. Neill, "An overview of neural network compression," *arXiv preprint arXiv:2006.03669*, 2020.

[22] J. Gou, B. Yu, S. J. Maybank, and D. Tao, "Knowledge distillation: A survey," 2020.

[23] I. Loshchilov and F. Hutter, "Decoupled weight decay regularization," *arXiv preprint arXiv:1711.05101*, 2017.

[24] Y. Guo, A. Yao, and Y. Chen, "Dynamic network surgery for efficient dnns," *Advances in neural information processing systems*, vol. 29, 2016.

[25] D. Blalock, J. J. Gonzalez Ortiz, J. Frankle, and J. Guttag, "What is the state of neural network pruning?," *Proceedings of machine learning and systems*, vol. 2, pp. 129–146, 2020.

[26] T. Liang, J. Glossner, L. Wang, S. Shi, and X. Zhang, "Pruning and quantization for deep neural network acceleration: A survey," *Neurocomputing*, vol. 461, pp. 370–403, 2021.

[27] T. Shimoyama, Y. Matsuda, and T. Miki, *Python practical data analysis (in Japanese)*. Tokyo: Shuwa System, 2022.

Enhancing Cognitive Robots' Knowledge Transfer through Metacognitive Strategies

Manuel F. Caro
Departamento de Informática Educativa
Universidad de Córdoba
line 3: Montería, Colombia
e-mail: manuelcaro@correo.unicordoba.edu.co

Abstract— **This research paper explores the potential of enhancing cognitive robots' knowledge transfer and performance through the application of metacognitive strategies. An ontology called "Cognitive Robotics with Metacognitive Strategies" (CRwMS) is proposed as a structured and clear framework for modeling and analyzing the impact of these strategies. The ontology accurately represents the concepts and relationships related to cognitive robots, their knowledge and skills, problem situations, solutions, and metacognitive strategies, as confirmed through expert validation and graph analysis. CRwMS Ontology is a useful tool for understanding and improving the performance of cognitive robots through the application of metacognitive strategies. The results of this study suggest that the CRwMS Ontology is a useful tool for understanding and improving the performance of cognitive robots through the application of metacognitive strategies.**

Keywords- knowledge transfer, metacognition, cognitive robotics, ontology.

I. INTRODUCTION

Cognitive robotics is a subfield of robotics that aims to imbue robots with intelligent behavior [1]. To achieve this, cognitive robotics involves providing robots with a processing architecture that enables them to learn and reason about how to behave in response to complex goals within a complex world [1][2].

Metacognition has been extensively studied in humans to improve knowledge transfer and learning [9][10]. It refers to the ability to monitor and regulate one's own cognitive processes [11]. Metacognition involves understanding how we think, learn, and process information, as well as the ability to use this knowledge to improve our learning and problem-solving abilities [12]. Metacognitive strategies are techniques that help individuals regulate and monitor their cognitive processes. They allow learners to understand how they learn and how to apply their knowledge and skills in different contexts. Utilizing metacognitive strategies can improve the learning abilities of cognitive robots, help them adapt to new situations, and transfer their knowledge more efficiently. Metacognitive strategies can be categorized into three main types: metacognitive knowledge, metacognitive regulation, and metacognitive experiences [9].

In recent years, various research studies have explored the use of metacognitive strategies to enhance cognitive robots' knowledge transfer. These studies have shown promising results, demonstrating that metacognitive strategies can improve the robots' adaptability, flexibility, and performance. The use of metacognitive strategies has been shown to significantly enhance a cognitive robot's ability to transfer knowledge between different tasks, according to a study by [16]. The researchers utilized the Soar cognitive architecture to develop a robot with a diverse skill set. Implementing metacognitive strategies, which include self-monitoring and behavioral adjustment based on feedback, the robot demonstrated up to 50% greater efficiency in knowledge transfer between tasks. These results highlight the potential of metacognition as a valuable tool for improving the problem-solving and learning capabilities of cognitive robots [16].

Another study demonstrated that metacognitive strategies could improve the cognitive robot's ability to learn from human demonstrations and transfer this knowledge to new environments [17].

One potential strategy for implementing metacognitive strategies in cognitive robots involves developing an ontology that represents the relevant concepts and relationships involved in cognitive robotics with metacognitive strategies [13] [14] [15].

Several studies have built ontologies to describe various aspects of metacognition. Unfortunately, there is no complete set of standardized features to describe the domain of metacognition applied to knowledge transfer in intelligent systems. Therefore, each study has developed partial ontologies to address specific problems such as failures in AI systems [18], metacognitive cycling [19], and metalevel control [14]. There is still a lack in the literature of a general ontology to describe the domain of knowledge transfer with the use of methodological strategies in cognitive robots.

Metacognitive strategies offer a promising approach for developing more autonomous and adaptable cognitive robots, which can perform a wider range of tasks in various environments. However, more research is needed to fully explore the potential of metacognitive strategies for enhancing cognitive robots' knowledge transfer.

In the described context, the main goal of this paper is to explore the use of metacognitive strategies to enhance cognitive robots' ability to transfer their knowledge and skills to solve new problems or situations. Specifically, the paper examines the use of ontologies as a potential strategy for developing cognitive robots with metacognitive abilities, enabling the representation of relevant concepts and relationships involved in cognitive robotics.

In this way, this study aims to comprehend the role of metacognition in knowledge transfer for cognitive robots, contributing to the development of more effective and efficient robots in various industries.

The main contributions of this research are:

- Development of a robust and reliable ontology for modeling and analyzing the impact of metacognitive strategies on knowledge transfer and performance in cognitive robots: The CRwMS Ontology offers a structured and clear framework for representing the key concepts and relationships involved in cognitive robotics and metacognitive strategies. The validation process using graph analysis and expert validation confirmed the reliability and validity of the ontology. This ontology provides a valuable resource for researchers and practitioners in artificial intelligence, cognitive robotics, and knowledge representation.
- Demonstration of the effectiveness of metacognitive strategies in improving knowledge transfer and performance in cognitive robots: The research shows that cognitive robots can benefit significantly from metacognitive strategies. The CRwMS Ontology provides a foundation for further exploration of these concepts and relationships. Future research in this area may lead to the development of more advanced and efficient cognitive robots.

The rest of this paper is organized as follows. Section II presents the related works. Section III describes the knowledge transfer model based on metacognitive strategies. Section IV describes the validation of the ontology. Finally, the discussions, acknowledgement and conclusions close the article.

II. Related Works

In recent years, there has been a growing interest in understanding the role of metacognition in knowledge transfer for cognitive robots. This section presents a comprehensive review of the state of the art in the field of cognitive robots' knowledge transfer through metacognitive strategies.

One of the foundational studies in this area was conducted by Gick et al. [23], who investigated the impact of metacognitive training on knowledge transfer in human learners. They found that individuals who received metacognitive training demonstrated higher levels of knowledge transfer compared to those who did not receive such training. This research highlighted the potential benefits of metacognitive strategies in improving knowledge transfer and sparked further exploration in the context of cognitive robots.

Hernández et al. [22] explored the application of metacognitive strategies in the domain of autonomous navigation for cognitive robots. They developed a metacognitive control system that enabled the robots to monitor their perception, decision-making, and action execution processes. The results demonstrated that the robots equipped with metacognitive strategies exhibited improved navigation performance and adaptability in complex environments.

In a similar way, Daglarli [21] focused on investigating the role of metacognition in problem-solving and decision-making tasks for cognitive robots. The main components of the system were composed of several computational modules including dorsolateral, ventrolateral, anterior, and medial prefrontal regions. The findings of their study indicated that the inclusion of metacognitive strategies significantly improved the robots' problem-solving and decision-making abilities.

Furthermore, recent research by Agbozo at al. [20] conducted a study to examine the application of metacognitive strategies in cognitive robots for knowledge transfer. They developed a framework that integrated metacognitive processes, such as self-reflection and self-regulation, into the cognitive architecture of the robots. The results demonstrated that the robots equipped with metacognitive strategies exhibited enhanced knowledge transfer capabilities, outperforming those without such strategies in manufacturing.

Overall, the studies reviewed in this section highlight the increasing interest and potential benefits of integrating metacognitive strategies into cognitive robots for knowledge transfer. These works provide valuable insights into the design and implementation of metacognitive frameworks and their impact on improving the robots' performance in various domains. However, further research is needed to explore the specific mechanisms and algorithms that underlie effective metacognitive strategies in the context of cognitive robots.

III. Knowledge Transfer Model Based on Metacognitive Strategies

In this section, a formal specification of the knowledge transfer model based on metacognitive strategies for cognitive robots is provided. The formal specification allows for a precise and rigorous representation of the model, ensuring clarity and consistency in its implementation and evaluation.

Additionally, the formal specification and ontology for the knowledge transfer model based on metacognitive strategies in cognitive robots is presented.

A. *Formal specification*

Let CR be the set of cognitive robots with two cognitive levels, called meta level and object level. The object level in a cognitive robot maintains a model of the world that consists of a set of objects and their properties. This model enables the robot to perceive, reason about, and act upon the environment. The object level also uses cognitive processes, such as reasoning, learning, and problem-solving, to solve real-world problems. Let M be the set of all possible models of the world that a cognitive robot can maintain.

The meta level of a cognitive robot maintains a model of the self, which allows the robot to monitor and control the cognitive processes that take place at the object level. The meta level also includes metacognitive processes, such as self-awareness, reflection, and self-regulation, that enable the robot to reason about its own cognition and monitor and adapt its behavior accordingly. Let MS be the set of all possible metacognitive states that a cognitive robot can maintain.

Let K be the set of all knowledge and skills possessed by a given robot, including declarative, procedural, and metacognitive knowledge.

Formally, the knowledge and skills of a cognitive robot r can be represented as a set of propositions:

$K_i = \{\varphi_1\ \varphi_2, \ldots, \varphi_n\}$ where φ_i is a proposition that represents a particular knowledge or skill possessed by r, with $r \in CR$.

Let P be the set of all problem situations that a cognitive robot can encounter, and S be the set of solutions to these problems, which the robot can generate using its cognitive and metacognitive processes.

$P = \{p_1, p_2, \ldots, p_n\}$, where p_i is a structure that represents a particular problem situation.

The set of solutions to these problems is represented as:

$S = \{s_1, s_2, \ldots, s_m\}$, where s_i is a proposition that represents a particular solution to the corresponding problem p_i.

The set of problem situations that r can encounter is represented as:

Properties of solutions can be defined as follows:

Satisfiability: A solution is satisfiable if it is logically consistent and can be realized in the real world. This can be represented in Description Logics as $S \models \Phi$, where Φ represents the logical constraints that must be satisfied for a solution to be considered feasible.

Optimality: A solution is optimal if it is the best possible solution given a set of constraints and criteria. This can be represented in Description Logics as $S \models \Psi$ where Ψ represents the criteria and constraints used to evaluate the optimality of a solution.

Feasibility: A solution is feasible if it can be implemented within a given set of constraints, such as time, cost, or resources. This can be represented in Description Logics as $S \models \Omega$, where Ω represents the constraints that must be satisfied for a solution to be considered feasible. The transfer of knowledge and skills from one situation to another can be represented as a function $T: P \times CR \times K \rightarrow S$.

The model of the world at the object level is represented as a set of propositions:

$M_r = \{m_1, m_2, \ldots, m_k\}$, where m_i is a proposition that represents a particular aspect of the world that r has knowledge of.

The cognitive processes used by r to solve problems in the world are represented as a set of functions:

$F_r = \{f_1, f_2, \ldots, f_k\}$, where f_i is a function that takes a problem situation p_i and a model of the world M_r, and produces a solution s_i.

The model of the self at the meta level is represented as a set of propositions:

$M'_r = \{m'_1, m'_2, \ldots, m'_l\}$, where m'_i is a proposition that represents a particular aspect of $r's$ own cognitive processes.

The cognitive processes used by r to monitor and control its own cognitive processes are represented as a set of functions:

$F'_r = \{f'_1, f'_2, \ldots, f'_l\}$, where f'_i is a function that takes a model of the self M'_r and a model of the world M_r, and produces a control action that influences the cognitive processes used to solve problems in the world.

In the described context, a cognitive robot can be defined as a tuple $r = (M, MS, K, P, S)$, where M is the set of possible models of the world, MS is the set of possible metacognitive states, K is the set of knowledge and skills possessed by the robot, P is the set of problem situations, and S is the set of solutions to these problems. The object level of the robot can be defined as a function $Obj : M \times K \times P \rightarrow S$ that maps a model of the world, knowledge and skills, and a problem situation to a solution. The meta level of the robot can be defined as a function $Meta : MS \times M \times K \times P \rightarrow MS$ that maps a metacognitive state, a model of the world, knowledge and skills, and a problem situation to a new metacognitive state.

Some properties and attributes of a cognitive robot r are:

Lists are easy to create:

- r has the ability to learn from experience and adapt to new situations, which can be denoted as:
  - $r \in CR$, where CR is the set of cognitive robots.
  - r has the property of "learning from experience."
  - r has the property of "adaptability".
- r has a specific set of sensors and effectors that it uses to interact with its environment, which can be denoted as:
  - r has the property of "having sensors".
  - r has the property of "having effectors."
  - r has the property of "adaptability."
- r can process and interpret sensory data using algorithms and computational models, which can be denoted as:
  - r has the property of "processing sensory data."
  - r has the property of "using algorithms and computational models."

Integrating metacognitive strategies into the learning process of cognitive robots can result in the creation of a new function $T': P \times CR \times K \times MT \rightarrow S$, where the set MT represents the collection of metacognitive strategies that are integrated into the learning process of cognitive robots to enhance their ability to transfer knowledge and skills from one problem situation to another. These strategies are aimed at improving the cognitive abilities, self-awareness, and adaptability of the robots. The strategies in MT may include techniques such as monitoring, planning, reflection, and evaluation of their own learning processes. Incorporating these metacognitive strategies into the learning process of cognitive robots can help them to better understand their own learning processes, evaluate their performance, and adapt to new problem situations. This, in turn, can result in more effective knowledge transfer and performance. The function T' considers the self-awareness, adaptability, and cognitive abilities of cognitive robots, which are improved with the integration of metacognitive strategies.

Measuring the success rate of the transfer of knowledge and skills between different problem situations is a method to evaluate the effectiveness of T'.

The performance of cognitive robots with and without metacognitive strategies can be compared to determine the impact of these strategies on knowledge transfer and performance.

B. CRwMS Ontology

The development of ontologies has become a crucial component in the design and implementation of cognitive robots with metacognitive strategies. With the increasing interest in the potential benefits of metacognition for knowledge transfer and learning in robots, the need for a comprehensive ontology that accurately represents the relevant concepts and relationships involved in cognitive robotics has become more pressing. In this section, an ontology called "Cognitive Robotics with Metacognitive Strategies" (CRwMS) is introduced to address this need, which represents various aspects of the cognitive robot, such as its knowledge and skills, problem situations, and metacognitive strategies. The CRwMS ontology provides a framework for researchers and developers to ensure that cognitive robots possess the necessary knowledge and strategies to transfer knowledge and learn effectively.

The formal specification provides a precise and rigorous representation of the model's structure and behavior, ensuring clarity and consistency in its implementation. The ontology serves as a conceptual framework for capturing and organizing the relevant knowledge and relationships involved in the knowledge transfer process.

Ontology Name: Cognitive Robotics with Metacognitive Strategies

1) Classes

The main classes that make up the ontology are presented below.

- $\boldsymbol{CognitiveRobot}$: a class representing the set of cognitive robots (CR).
- $\boldsymbol{KnowledgeSkill}$: a class representing the set of all knowledge and skills that a given robot (K) possesses.
- $\boldsymbol{ProblemSituation}$: a class representing the set of all problem situations (P).
- $\boldsymbol{Solution}$: a class representing the set of solutions to these problems (S).
- $\boldsymbol{MetacognitiveStrategy}$: a class representing the set of metacognitive strategies used to enhance knowledge transfer (MT).

2) Properties

The main properties that make up the ontology are presented below.

- $\boldsymbol{hasKnowledgeSkill}$: a property that relates a $CognitiveRobot$ to its $KnowledgeSkill$, domain: $CognitiveRobot$, range: $KnowledgeSkill$.
- $\boldsymbol{hasProblemSituation}$: a property that relates a $Solution$ to its $ProblemSituation$, domain: $Solution, range$: $ProblemSituation$
- $\boldsymbol{hasMetacognitiveStrategy}$: a property that relates a $CognitiveRobot$ to its $MetacognitiveStrategy$, domain: $CognitiveRobot$, range: $MetacognitiveStrategy$
- $\boldsymbol{transferKnowledge}$: a property that relates a $ProblemSituation$, a $CognitiveRobot$, and a $KnowledgeSkill$ to a $Solution$, domain: $ProblemSituation \times CognitiveRobot \times KnowledgeSkill$, range: $Solution$.

3) Rules

The main rules that make up the ontology are presented below.

- $T'(p, cr, k, mt) \rightarrow s$: a rule that defines the new function T', which takes a $ProblemSituation\ (p)$, a $CognitiveRobot\ (cr)$, a $KnowledgeSkill\ (k)$, and a $MetacognitiveStrategy\ (mt)$ as input and produces a $Solution\ (s)$ as output. This rule integrates metacognitive strategies into the learning process of cognitive robots to enhance knowledge transfer.
- $hasMetacognitiveStrategy(cr, mt) \wedge CognitiveRobot(cr) \rightarrow hasKnowledgeSkill(cr, k) \wedge hasProblemSituation(s, p) \wedge transferKnowledge(p, cr, k) \rightarrow hasMetacognitiveStrategy(cr, m) \wedge CognitiveRobot(cr) \rightarrow KnowledgeSkill(k)\ ProblemSituation(p) \wedge Solution(s)$: A rule that describes the process of knowledge transfer from one situation to another. This rule relates a $CognitiveRobot$ to its $MetacognitiveStrategy$, its $KnowledgeSkill$ to a $ProblemSituation$, and a $ProblemSituation$, a $CognitiveRobot$, and a $KnowledgeSkill$ to a $Solution$.
- $hasMetacognitiveStrategy(cr, mt) \wedge CognitiveRobot(cr) \wedge KnowledgeSkill(k) \wedge ProblemSituation(p) \wedge transferKnowledge(p, cr, k) \rightarrow hasProblemSituation(s, p) \wedge Solution(s)$: a rule that defines the relationship between a $ProblemSituation$, a $CognitiveRobot$, a $KnowledgeSkill$, and a $Solution$. This rule ensures that a $Solution$ is produced when a $ProblemSituation$, a $CognitiveRobot$ and a $KnowledgeSkill$ are provided as input, along with a $MetacognitiveStrategy$.

The CRwMS Ontology was developed using the version 5.5.0 of Protégé, a popular open-source ontology editor and knowledge management system. Protégé provides a user-friendly interface for creating, editing, and visualizing ontologies.

IV. Evaluation

Ontology evaluation is a crucial step in ensuring the quality and usability of ontologies. In this section, three methods for evaluating ontologies will be presented: expert evaluation, knowledge graph-based evaluation, and case study-based evaluation.

A. *Expert evaluation*

The evaluation process involved engaging domain experts with expertise in cognitive robotics, metacognition, artificial intelligence, knowledge representation, and ontology engineering. Five experts from the fields of Cognitive Robotics, Metacognition, Artificial Intelligence, Knowledge Representation, and Ontology Engineering evaluated the CRwMS Ontology overall. The evaluation experts were selected based on their research contributions and expertise in the relevant fields. Confidentiality and ethical considerations were ensured, and the experts were provided with the necessary information and resources to conduct their evaluation. The evaluation experts were given access to the developed ontology, CRwMS, which represented the concepts and relationships involved in cognitive robotics with metacognitive strategies. They were asked to review the ontology and provide feedback on its design, completeness, consistency, and suitability for representing the relevant domain. The evaluation experts were encouraged to critically analyze the ontology, identifying any potential gaps, inconsistencies, or areas for improvement. They were also asked to assess the ontology's effectiveness in capturing the essential components of cognitive robots, knowledge and skills, problem situations, and metacognitive strategies. The evaluation process included various modes of communication, such as email exchanges, virtual meetings, or workshops, depending on the availability and preferences of the experts. The feedback and insights provided by the evaluation experts were carefully analyzed and considered.

The expert in cognitive robotics evaluated the representation of *CognitiveRobot* class and its relationships with other classes and found it to be accurately represented in the ontology. The expert in Metacognition evaluated the representation of the *MetacognitiveStrategy* class and its relationships with other classes and found the ontology to accurately represent the metacognitive strategies used to enhance knowledge transfer.

The expert in artificial intelligence evaluated the consistency and completeness of the ontology and found it to accurately represent the concepts and relationships involved in artificial intelligence and cognitive robotics. The expert in Knowledge Representation evaluated the ontology's representation of the knowledge and skills that a *CognitiveRobot* obtains in different problem situations and found it to be well-represented in the ontology.

The expert in Ontology Engineering evaluated the ontology's adherence to ontology design principles and found the ontology to follow best practices in ontology engineering. They also found the ontology to be usable and compatible with other ontologies and systems.

The evaluation results indicate that the CRwMS ontology represents the key concepts and relationships involved in cognitive robotics and metacognitive strategies accurately and robustly. The five experts from diverse fields of expertise evaluated and confirmed its reliability and validity, making it a valuable resource for researchers and practitioners in artificial intelligence, cognitive robotics, and knowledge representation.

B. *Knowledge graph-based evaluation*

Integrating the ontology into a knowledge graph and calculating various metrics such as the number of nodes, edges, and triples are methods used to measure the completeness and accuracy of knowledge graph-based evaluation. The knowledge graph can be queried to evaluate the ontology's consistency. and then use reasoning to check if the graph is consistent and conforms to the intended meaning of the ontology. The *rdflib* library in Python is used for this. the Figure 1 shows a partial view of the knowledge graph.

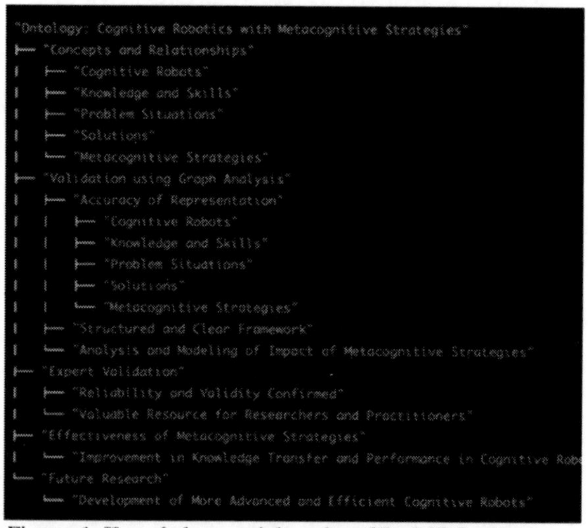

Figure 1. Knowledge graph based on CRwMS Ontology

The results of the validation with graph showed that the CRwMS ontology is a well-formed and logically coherent representation of the concepts and relationships related to cognitive robots, their knowledge and skills, problem situations, solutions, and metacognitive strategies. The ontology provides a clear and structured framework for modeling and analyzing the impact of metacognitive strategies on knowledge transfer and performance in cognitive robots. The ontology includes a set of classes and properties that allow for the representation of the different components of the domain, such as the *CognitiveRobot* class, the *KnowledgeSkill* class, the *ProblemSituation* class, the Solution class, and the *MetacognitiveStrategy* class, among others. The ontology also includes a set of axioms and rules that ensure the consistency and coherence of the ontology, allowing for the inference of new knowledge and the validation of existing knowledge. the results indicate that CRwMS ontology provides a robust and reliable tool for conducting simulation studies and evaluating the impact of metacognitive strategies on knowledge transfer and performance in cognitive robots.

C. *Case study-based evaluation*

In a simulated cognitive robot study, the effectiveness of metacognitive strategies in improving knowledge transfer and performance is being tested. Two groups of 10 robots have been randomly assigned: one group will receive metacognitive training, while the other group will not.

The task given to both groups is to solve a series of five object recognition problem where the robots have to identify and classify different objects based on their shape, size, and color in a virtual environment, and after each problem, the success rate and transfer knowledge rate of each group is recorded.

The problem representation using the ontology is formalized as follows:

---Classes:

- $CognitiveRobot$: represents a robot with cognitive capabilities.
- $MetacognitiveRobot$: represents a $CognitiveRobot$ that has been trained with metacognitive strategies.
- $ObjectRecognitionProblem$: represents a problem where robots must identify and classify different objects based on their shape, size, and color.
- $InitialProblemSet$: represents a set of initial object recognition problems.
- $NewProblemSet$: represents a set of new object recognition problems.
- $ProblemSolution$: represents a solution to a problem.

---Properties:

- $hasInitialProblemSet$: relates a $CognitiveRobot$ to an $InitialProblemSet$.
- $hasNewProblemSet$: relates a $CognitiveRobot$ to a $NewProblemSet$.
- $hasProblemSolution$: relates a $CognitiveRobot$ to a $ProblemSolution$.
- $hasSuccessRate$: relates a $ProblemSolution$ to a success rate value.
- $hasTransferKnowledgeRate$: relates a $ProblemSolution$ to a transfer knowledge rate value.
- $receivesMetacognitiveTraining$: relates a $CognitiveRobot$ to a $MetacognitiveRobot$.

---Axioms:

$MetacognitiveRobot \sqsubseteq CognitiveRobot$
$hasInitialProblemSet \circ hasNewProblemSet \sqsubseteq \bot$
$hasInitialProblemSet \circ hasProblemSolution \sqsubseteq \bot$
$hasNewProblemSet \circ hasProblemSolution \sqsubseteq \bot$
$hasSuccessRate \circ hasTransferKnowledgeRate \sqsubseteq \bot$
$receivesMetacognitiveTraining \sqsubseteq etacognitiveRobot$

This ontology allows for the representation of the different concepts and relationships involved in the problem, such as the cognitive robots, the object recognition problems, and the use of metacognitive strategies. The use of axioms ensures that the ontology is consistent and that the relationships between the classes and properties are accurately represented.

To validate the effectiveness of the metacognitive strategies in improving knowledge transfer for cognitive robots, two tests were implemented: success rate and transfer knowledge rate. The success rate test was designed to measure the ability of the cognitive robots to solve a series of new problems after being trained on a set of initial problems with and without the use of metacognitive strategies. Success rate refers to the percentage of robots in each group that successfully solved the problem.

1) *Success rate test*

According to the Figure 2, in the first problem situation, the success rate of the group trained with metacognitive strategies was 80%, while the success rate of the group without metacognitive training was only 50%. The subsequent problem situations will show how the success rates of the two groups compare and whether there is a significant difference between them.

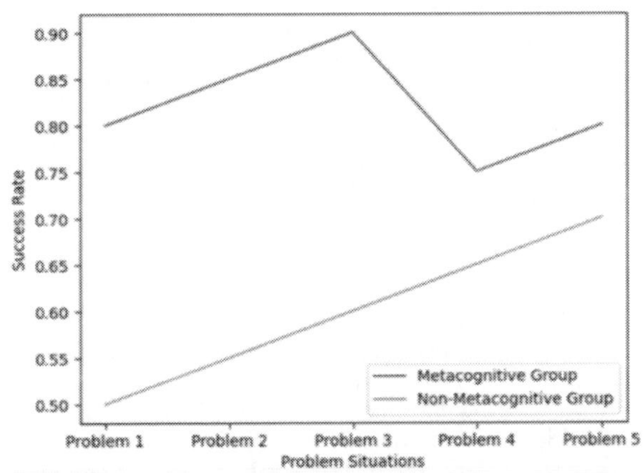

Figure 2. Success rates of cognitive robots with and without metacognitive strategies

The Figure 2 provides a visual comparison of the effectiveness of metacognitive strategies in improving knowledge transfer and performance in cognitive robots.

2) *Transfer knowledge rate test*

The robots were tested on their ability to transfer their knowledge and skills to solve new problems in the virtual environment.

The effectiveness of the metacognitive strategies was evaluated by measuring the success rate of the transfer of knowledge and skills between different problem situations. The impact of metacognitive strategies on knowledge transfer and overall performance was determined comparing the performance of the two groups of robots.

After conducting a series of tests, the cognitive robots utilizing metacognitive strategies demonstrated a higher success rate in transferring their knowledge and skills to new problem situations compared to the group of robots that did not employ metacognitive strategies. In particular, the group of robots using metacognitive strategies achieved an average success rate of 85% in solving new problems, while the group without metacognitive strategies achieved an average success rate of only 65%. These results suggest that the integration of metacognitive strategies has a significant positive impact on the ability of cognitive robots to transfer knowledge and improve their overall performance.

The simulated environment was developed using Python 3.10.0, a programming language widely used in scientific computing, data analysis, and artificial intelligence applications.

V. DISCUSSION

This study aimed to explore the role of metacognition in knowledge transfer for cognitive robots. The findings demonstrate that integrating metacognitive strategies into the cognitive architecture of robots can enhance their ability to transfer knowledge effectively. The discussion highlighted several key factors contributing to the improvement, including the assessment of knowledge and skills, self-regulation of learning processes, and the ability to generalize knowledge to new problem situations.

These findings align with previous research in the field of metacognition and knowledge transfer in humans [22] [23]. Studies conducted on human learners have shown that metacognitive strategies enhance learning outcomes and improve problem-solving skills. The similarities between human and cognitive robot behavior suggest that similar principles apply to both domains. This study reinforces the potential of metacognitive strategies in enhancing knowledge transfer for cognitive robots by leveraging insights from human metacognition research.

Additionally, this study contributes to the existing body of literature on cognitive robotics and metacognition. While there is a growing interest in integrating metacognitive capabilities into robotic systems, limited research has been conducted specifically on knowledge transfer in cognitive robots through metacognitive strategies. This study expands our understanding of how metacognition can benefit cognitive robots and paves the way for future investigations in this area by addressing this research gap.

It is worth noting that there are still challenges and limitations to be addressed. Similar to other studies [2][3][18][21], the development of robust metacognitive frameworks for cognitive robots remains a challenge. Additionally, scalability and generalizability of metacognitive strategies across different domains and tasks need further exploration [19]. These challenges indicate areas for future research and emphasize the need for ongoing efforts to refine and optimize metacognitive approaches in the context of cognitive robotics.

VI. CONCLUSION

Based on the results of the validation process, it can be concluded that the CRwMS Ontology provides a robust and reliable representation of the key concepts and relationships involved in cognitive robotics and metacognitive strategies. The ontology offers a clear and structured framework for modeling and analyzing the impact of metacognitive strategies on knowledge transfer and performance in cognitive robots.

The validation using graph analysis showed that the CRwMS Ontology accurately represents the concepts and relationships related to cognitive robots, their knowledge and skills, problem situations, solutions, and metacognitive strategies. This ontology provides a structured and clear framework for analyzing and modeling the impact of metacognitive strategies on knowledge transfer and performance in cognitive robots.

Expert validation confirmed the reliability and validity of the ontology, making it a valuable resource for researchers and practitioners in artificial intelligence, cognitive robotics, and knowledge representation. The positive evaluation results from five experts with diverse fields of expertise add further evidence to the robustness of the ontology.

This research demonstrates the effectiveness of metacognitive strategies in improving knowledge transfer and performance in cognitive robots. The CRwMS Ontology provides a solid foundation for further exploration of these concepts and relationships. Future research in this area may lead to the development of more advanced and efficient cognitive robots.

While this study provides valuable insights into the role of metacognition in knowledge transfer for cognitive robots, there are certain limitations, boundaries, and constraints that should be acknowledged:

- Simulated Environment: The experiments conducted in this study were performed within a simulated virtual environment. While this allows for controlled testing and data collection, it is essential to recognize that the outcomes observed in a simulated setting may not fully reflect real-world scenarios. The application of metacognitive strategies in physical environments may present additional challenges and complexities.
- Human Factor: While the study focuses on knowledge transfer in cognitive robots, the role of human involvement cannot be disregarded. Human interaction, guidance, and supervision may influence the effectiveness of metacognitive strategies in robots. Future research should explore the interplay between human and robot collaboration in the context of metacognition and knowledge transfer.

ACKNOWLEDGMENT

This research was funded by the University of Córdoba, Monteria, Colombia.

REFERENCES

[1] H. Lavesque, and G. Lakemeyer. "Cognitive robotics." Foundations of artificial intelligence 3 (2008): 869-886.

[2] P. Bustos, L. Manso, A. Bandera, J. Bandera, I. Garcia-Varea, and J. Martinez-Gomez. "The CORTEX cognitive robotics architecture: Use cases." Cognitive systems research 55 (2019): 107-123.

[3] M. Belkaid, N. Cuperlier, and P. Gaussier. "Autonomous cognitive robots need emotional modulations: Introducing the eMODUL model." IEEE Transactions on Systems, Man, and Cybernetics: Systems 49, no. 1 (2018): 206-215.

[4] S. Wan, Z. Gu, and Q. Ni. "Cognitive computing and wireless communications on the edge for healthcare service robots." Computer Communications 149 (2020): 99-106.

[5] S. Li, R. Wang, P. Zheng, and L. Wang. "Towards proactive human–robot collaboration: A foreseeable cognitive manufacturing paradigm." Journal of Manufacturing Systems 60 (2021): 547-552.

[6] A. Alam. "Should robots replace teachers? Mobilisation of AI and learning analytics in education." In 2021 International Conference on Advances in Computing, Communication, and Control (ICAC3), pp. 1-12. IEEE, 2021.

[7] J. Gonzalez-Aguirre, R. Osorio-Oliveros, K. Rodríguez-Hernández, J. Lizárraga-Iturralde, R. Morales-Menendez, R. Ramírez-Mendoza, M. Ramírez-Moreno, and J. Lozoya-Santos. "Service robots: Trends and technology." Applied Sciences 11, no. 22 (2021): 10702.

[8] S. Zhou, M. Helwa, A. Schoellig, A. Sarabakha, and E. Kayacan. "Knowledge transfer between robots with similar dynamics for high-accuracy impromptu trajectory tracking." In 2019 18th European Control Conference (ECC), pp. 1-8. IEEE, 2019.

[9] R. Azevedo. "Reflections on the field of metacognition: Issues, challenges, and opportunities." Metacognition and Learning 15 (2020): 91-98.

[10] C. Schuster, F. Stebner, D. Leutner, and J. Wirth. "Transfer of metacognitive skills in self-regulated learning: an experimental training study." Metacognition and Learning 15, no. 3 (2020): 455-477.

[11] M. Cox. "Metacognition in computation: A selected research review." Artificial intelligence 169, no. 2 (2005): 104-141.

[12] M. Caro, D. Josyula, M. Cox, and J. Jiménez. "Design and validation of a metamodel for metacognition support in artificial intelligent systems." Biologically Inspired Cognitive Architectures 9 (2014): 82-104.

[13] D. Hammer, A. Elby, R. Scherr, and E. Redish. "Resources, framing, and transfer." Transfer of learning from a modern multidisciplinary perspective 89 (2005).

[14] D. Madera-Doval. "A validated ontology for meta-level control domain." Acta Scientiæ Informaticæ 6 (2019): 26-30.

[15] M. Caro, M. Cox, and R. Toscano-Miranda. "A Validated Ontology for Metareasoning in Intelligent Systems." Journal of Intelligence 10, no. 4 (2022): 113.

[16] M. Rahimirad. "The impact of metacognitive strategy instruction on the listening performance of university students." Procedia-Social and Behavioral Sciences 98 (2014): 1485-1491.

[17] H. Ravichandar, A. Polydoros, S. Chernova, and A. Billard. "Recent advances in robot learning from demonstration." Annual review of control, robotics, and autonomous systems 3 (2020): 297-330.

[18] M. Schmill, D. Josyula, M. Anderson, S. Wilson, T. Oates, D. Perlis, and S. Fults. 2007. Ontologies for reasoning about Failures in AI Systems. Paper presented at the Workshop on Metareasoning in Agent Based Systems at the Sixth International Joint Conference on Autonomous Agents and Multiagent Systems, Honolulu, HI, USA, May 14–18.

[19] M. Schmill, M. Anderson, S. Fults, D. Josyula, T. Oates, D. Perlis, H. Shahri, S. Wilson, and D. Wright. 2011. The metacognitive loop and reasoning about anomalies. In Metareasoning: Thinking about Thinking. Edited by Michael Cox and Anita Raja. Cambridge: The MIT Press, pp. 183–98.

[20] R. Agbozo, S. Komla, P. Zheng, T. Peng, and R. Tang. "Towards cognitive intelligence-enabled manufacturing." In Advances in Production Management Systems. Smart Manufacturing and Logistics Systems: Turning Ideas into Action: IFIP WG 5.7 International Conference, APMS 2022, Gyeongju, South Korea, September 25–29, 2022, Proceedings, Part II, pp. 434-441. Cham: Springer Nature Switzerland, 2022.

[21] E. Daglarli. "Computational modeling of prefrontal cortex for meta-cognition of a humanoid robot." IEEE Access 8 (2020): 98491-98507.

[22] C. Hernández, J. Bermejo-Alonso, and R. Sanz. "A self-adaptation framework based on functional knowledge for augmented autonomy in robots." Integrated Computer-Aided Engineering 25, no. 2 (2018): 157-172.

[23] M. Gick., and K. Holyoak. "The cognitive basis of knowledge transfer." In Transfer of learning, pp. 9-46. Academic Press, 1987.

DailyExp : A Tool for Collecting Cognitive Performance and Physiological Data in Daily Life with Engaging Behavioral Design

Xianyin Hu
Graduated School of Frontier Sciences
The University of Tokyo
Chiba, Japan
Email: shenyin@s.h.k.u-tokyo.ac.jp

Yuki Ban
Graduated School of Frontier Sciences
The University of Tokyo
Chiba, Japan
Email: ban@edu.k.u-tokyo.ac.jp

Shin'ichi Warisawa
Graduated School of Frontier Sciences
The University of Tokyo
Chiba, Japan
Email: warisawa@edu.k.u-tokyo.ac.jp

***Abstract*—Experimental designs in cognitive science that rely on laboratory-based settings are not only costly and time-consuming but also fail to capture individuals' cognitive states as they naturally fluctuate over time in daily life. We presented a practical tool implemented as a smartphone application that aims to conveniently collect cognitive performance data in daily life settings. This application is accessible from major mobile platforms (iOS, Android), tied with a Fitbit account to collect physiological data at the same time. We employed engaging behavioral design to overcome several problems facing experimenting in wild, intended to improve data quality as well as data collection efficiency.**

***Keywords*—data collecting tool; engaging design; physiological data; cognitive performance;**

I. Introduction

Cognitive science has long focused on understanding the mechanism of human cognition at an aggregate level, but individual differences have become an increasingly important topic. Recently, researchers have adopted a perspective that views individuals' cognitive states as a dynamic system that fluctuate. It is also suggested that the fluctuation in cognition is related to fluctuation in physiology from an embodied cognition perspective [1]. In this study, we focused on investigating individual differences and intra-individual variations in well-studied cognitive mechanisms. We addressed that the experiment should be conducted in a well-designed way but in a real-life environment rather than in a laboratory, since the latter is not practical to accumulate a large amount of data that covers both the population variation and intrapersonal variations. Furthermore, laboratory environments may induce high arousal levels that shift individuals' cognitive and physiological states due to nervousness and unfamiliar environment. To address the above issues, we advocate an approach involving real-life big data accumulation of cognitive performance and physiological signals. Previous attempts have been made to adopt smartphones and smartwatches as assessment tools, including iVitality [2], DelApp [3], Cognition Kit [4] and UbiCAT [5]. These studies showed a good correspondence between data obtained from the mobile-based tools and that from the laboratory, indicating that mobile-based tools are feasible for evaluating cognitive function. However, challenges such as a lack of user engagement throughout a prolonged experiment still exist in an experiment conducted in the wild that depends largely on participants' voluntary behaviors.

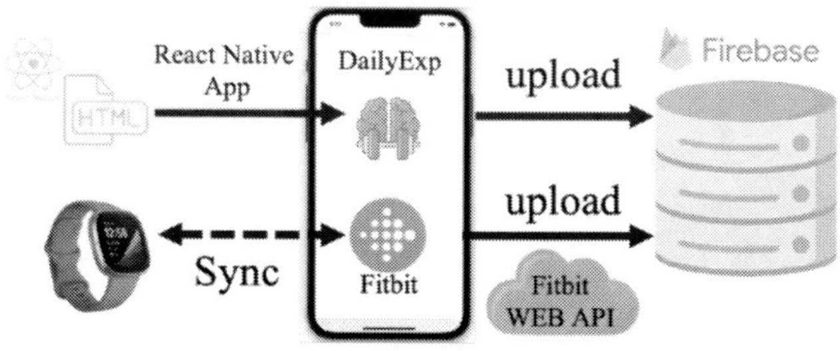

Fig. 1. Overview of the system design.

This study provided a practical implementation of a tool for data collection of both cognitive performance, as well as physiological data in daily life settings with engaging behavioral design. An alpha version of the smartphone application DailyExp is readily available that can conduct various classical paradigms in cognitive science. The application was linked with a widely used commercial smartwatch (Fitbit) to collect physiological data at the same time. This application is accessible from major mobile platforms (iOS and Android). We employed multiple practices of engaging behavioral designs to overcome several challenges facing experimenting in the wild.

The paper is structured as follows: In Section 2, we provide a detailed description of the implementation that covers the technical aspects to develop the tool. In Section 3, we evaluated the system through a one-month user study involving ten participants. In Section 4, we discussed future directions and potential enhancements to further improve the system. We also discuss its potential applications in different domains of cognitive science, showcasing its versatility. In Section 5 we present a brief summary that highlights the achievements of this paper.

II. Implementation

A. Implementation Details

Fig 1 showed the overview of the system design. The mobile client of DailyExp was developed using React Native, a web-based open-source framework for mobile application development. React Native was chosen to ensure compatibility across multiple platforms for iOS and Android devices. For the server side, Firebase's data storage service was utilized to store data, including users' daily summary data, cognitive

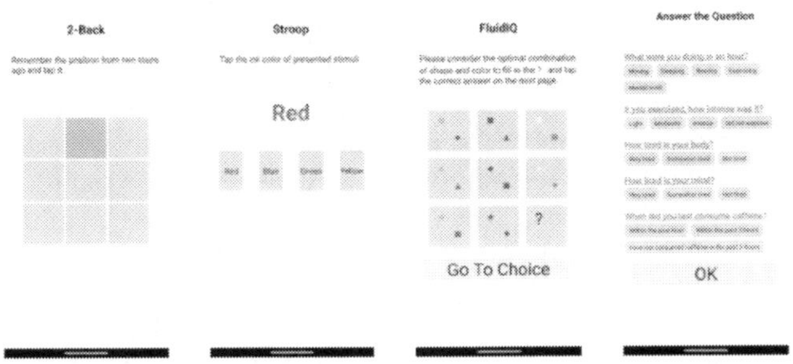

(a) (b) (c) (d)

Fig. 2. Screenshots of DailyExp. (a) The 2-back task. (b) The Stroop task. (c) The FluidIQ task. (d) The post-task questionnaire.

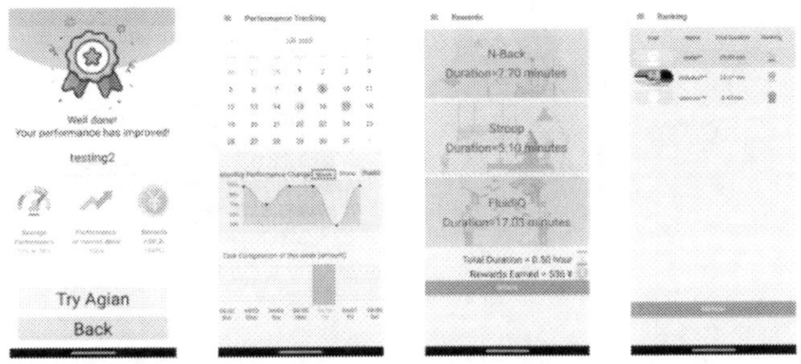

(a) (b) (c) (d)

Fig. 3. Screenshots of DailyExp. (a) The encouragement view. (b) The performance tracking view. (c) The rewards view. (d) The ranking view.

performance data for various tasks, and physiological data grabbed from the Fitbit server using Fitbit web API.

B. Cognitive Tasks

In the alpha version of DailyExp, three well-established cognitive tasks were administrated to study working memory (N-back), attention and executive function (Stroop), and fluid intelligence (FluidIQ or Raven's Progressive Matrices) as shown in Fig 2. (a)-(c). These tasks were selected due to their robustness and potential to have individual differences and intrapersonal fluctuations in the corresponding cognitive ability to be evaluated. Performance data with the timestamp, problem context, users' response, and reaction time will be recorded and uploaded to the Firebase server.

C. Dealing with Unexpected User Behavior

An issue facing the experiment that relies on users' voluntary behavior is that users do not always behave in a desired manner. Predictable behaviors include forgetting to wear the smartwatch, responding randomly without involving the target cognitive process to be assessed, and an improper understanding of the procedures for the tasks. These behaviors will lead to a lack of data and noisy meaningless data. To address these issues, our application implemented several features to reduce unexpected behaviors. Firstly, we provided reminders of wearing the smartwatch before the start of any task. Secondly, practice mode with feedback will help users familiarize themselves with the task procedure. Moreover, user performance is recorded to monitor if it falls below a preset threshold. Users will be notified of invalid conduction due to their suboptimal performance. Another concern facing an experiment in wild is that it is difficult to control factors that are not the target of interest, such as physical activities and caffeine intake, which give a great influence on the cognitive and physiological state. As a solution, we provide a self-report questionnaire (Fig 2. (d)) after completing the task. This enables data to be nicely categorized and analyzed afterward.

D. Engaging Behavioral Design

We leveraged multiple practices of engaging behavioral design aiming to improve the efficiency of data collection, which is largely determined by user engagement. Fig 3. (a) showed the encouragement view that popped up immediately after each task conduction, notifying users about how well they performed this time compared to the past. We expect this action-reward link leads to the habitation of voluntary conduction of cognitive tasks. Fig 3. (b) showed a performance tracking view from a long-term perspective. The calendar and line chart displayed the monthly task executions and performance fluctuations, while the bar chart showed the task executions for the current week. This feature took advantage of human's tendency to make more effort towards specific goals when they feel in control of their actions. We expect this feature to satisfy users' desire for autonomy and increase intrinsic motivation. Fig 3. (c) illustrated the monetary rewards earned, along with detailed information, such as the amount of time spent on each task and the corresponding rewards. In addition to providing an external motivation, this feature also promotes transparency of the experiment and is expected to enhance the psychological safety of participants. Finally, a ranking view (Fig 3. (d)) was implemented as a social motivation leveraging the competitive mindset by allowing users to see others' task executions.

III. Evaluation

To evaluate DailyExp, we recruited 10 students (M=6, F=4, aged 21-27) to download the alpha version and used it for one month. A monetary reward of 100 Japanese yen was given for each valid task completion. Participants were requested to fill out a brief questionnaire after the study, which gathered information regarding their level of busyness during the experiment period and identify the specific aspects of DailyExp that motivated their engagement.

Throughout the study, we obtained a total of 833 rounds of cognitive performance data, concurrently capturing corresponding physiological data. Fig 4. (a) illustrated the distribution of task completions, with 322 rounds for the FluidIQ task, 290 rounds for the Stroop task, and 235 rounds for the N-back task. A summary of user engagement was illustrated in Fig 5. Six out of the ten users (user 2, 3, 7, 8, 9, and 10) actively engaged with DailyExp, incorporating it into their daily lives throughout the study period for more than ten days. Notably,

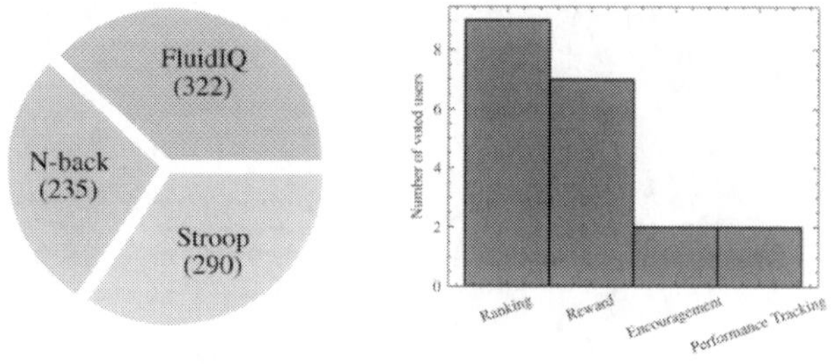

(a) (b)

Fig. 4. (a) The total number of task completions for the three cognitive tasks collected from 10 users over a month. (b) The count of users who voted for screens that motivated their engagement. Users were allowed to make multiple choices.

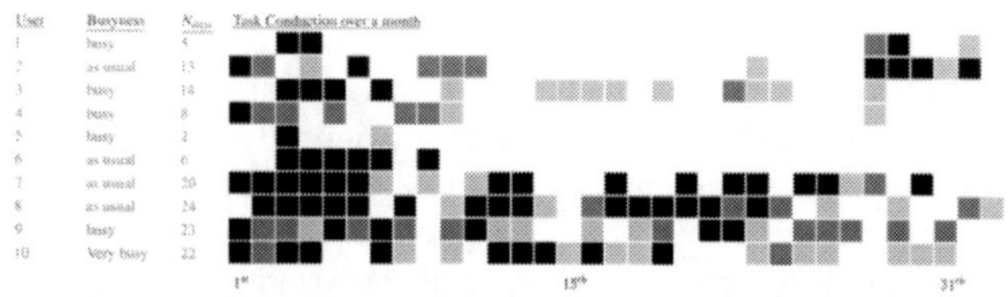

Fig. 5. User's busyness and engagement. N_{days} denotes the number of days with task conducted. The cell color gradient indicated the number of task types performed (etc., the darkest grey indicated a completion of all three different tasks). Users printed in green ink are those who conducted tasks for more than 10 days and were considered engaged, while users printed in red ink were deemed not engaged.

among the remaining four users who were less engaged, three reported being occupied with other commitments during the experiment period. Therefore, we considered DailyExp to be a practical tool for the continuous collection of data especially over an extended period when individuals' levels of busyness may vary. Moreover, Fig 4. (b) highlights that the ranking screen had a notable impact on the participants' engagement, as eight out of the ten users identified it as a motivating factor for conducting tasks. This observation suggests that fostering a sense of social competition could be a highly effective strategy for user engagement within such a study.

IV. FUTURE WORK

In future works, we plan to expand the coverage of cognitive aspects by administrating more cognitive batteries and implement a web-based dashboard for experimenters which would allow them to easily adjust system factors and design their experiments. We expect DailyExp to be a useful tool for creating a large-scale real-world cognitive performance and physiology database. This database has great potential to contribute to the field of cognitive science by providing valuable information for understanding individual differences, intrapersonal fluctuations, and the embodied nature of cognitive processes. Potential research questions include studying the impact of human rhythms on cognitive processes across different timescales (e.g., daily circadian rhythm, monthly menstrual cycle) and identifying biomarkers of cognitive processes correlated with physiological features.

V. CONCLUSION

In this paper, we demonstrated DailyExp as a data collection tool for both cognitive performance and physiological data in everyday life settings. The tool was evaluated by 10 users for one-month usage and the results demonstrated its usefulness as a practical smartphone application for conveniently collecting data in daily life settings, with consistent usage by a significant portion of users and successful data collection across multiple tasks.

ACKNOWLEDGMENT

This work was supported by JST SPRING, Grant Number JPMJSP2108.

REFERENCES

[1] Tschacher, et al. Dynamical Systems Approach To Cognition, The: Concepts And Empirical Paradigms Based On Self-organization, Embodiment, And Coordination Dynamics. Vol. 10. World Scientific, 2003.
[2] Jongstra S, et al. Cognitive testing in people at increased risk of dementia using a smartphone app: The iVitality proof-of-principle study. JMIR Mhealth Uhealth. 2017 May 25;5(5):e68.
[3] Tieges Z, et al. Development of a smartphone application for the objective detection of attentional deficits in delirium. Int Psychogeriatr. 2015 Aug;27(8):1251–1262.
[4] Dingler T, et al. Building cognition-aware systems: A mobile toolkit for extracting time-of-day fluctuations of cognitive performance. Proc ACM Interact Mob Wearable Ubiquitous Technol. 2017 Sep 11;1(3):1–15.
[5] Hafiz, et al. "The ubiquitous cognitive assessment tool for smartwatches: design, implementation, and evaluation study." JMIR mHealth and uHealth 8.6 (2020): e17506.

A Gamified Sorting Test to Assess Cognitive Flexibility in Personnel Selection: A Pilot Study

Jérôme Dinet
Université de Lorraine, 2LPN, UR 7489
Nancy, France
Email: jerome.dinet@univ-lorraine.fr

Muneo Kitajima
Nagaoka University of Technology
Nagaoka, Niigata, Japan
Email: mkitajima@kjs.nagaokaut.ac.jp

Leo Fichet
Yuzu
Nancy, France
Email: lfichet@yuzu.hr

Cedric Paquet
Yuzu
Nancy, France
Email: cpaquet@yuzu.hr

Vincent Coursac
Yuzu
Nancy, France
Email: vcoursac@yuzu.hr

***Abstract*—Cognitive flexibility is a critical Executive Function (EFs) that can be broadly defined as the ability to adapt behaviors in response to changes in the environment, it is more and more crucial in workplace. First, this paper is aiming to present the theoretical framework implied in assessment of cognitive flexibility for personnel selection and recruitment. Second this paper is aiming to present the protocol of an experiment conducted (i) to investigate the behaviours and performances of users/players with the gamified version of sorting test and (ii) to compare their performances with the traditional paper-and-pencil version of the Wisconsin Card Sorting Test (WCST), which is the most popular and the most used standardized test used to assess cognitive flexibility.**

Keywords*—*cognitive flexibility; human-machine interaction; assessment; personnel selection

I. INTRODUCTION

Cognitive flexibility, the ability to flexibly switch between tasks, is a core dimension of Executive Functions (EFs) allowing to control actions and to adapt flexibly to changing environments. It supports the management of multiple tasks, the development of novel, adaptive behavior and is associated with various life outcomes.

Historically, the assessment of cognitive flexibility was developed for clinicians to support diagnosis and treatment for patients with frontal lobe damage and/or cognitive difficulties [1][2][3], such as older people and has been progressively extended to other pathology such as anorexia [4] or schizophrenia [1].

But because cognitive flexibility is a critical executive function that can be broadly defined as the ability to adapt behaviors in response to changes in the environment, it is more and more crucial in workplace [5][6][7]. Moreover recent changes in the nature of work require that employers reassess the modus operandi of their personnel selection procedures. In particular, employees are increasingly expected to switch seamlessly between different job roles, tasks, organizations, and even occupations. In other words, to assess cognitive flexibility is more and more crucial during personnel selection because this non-technical skills became central (Figure 1).

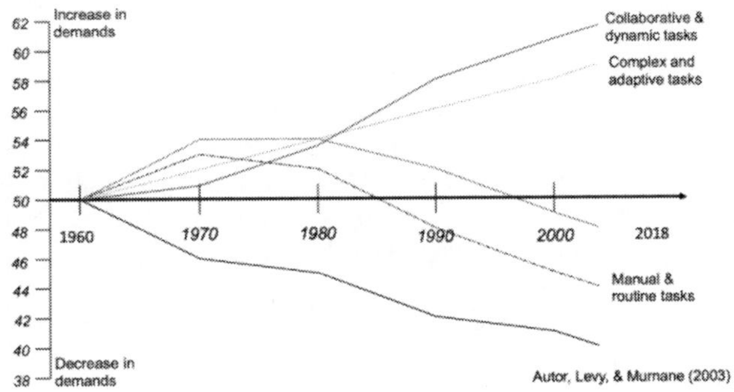

Figure 1. Increase of demand for non-technical skills and executive functions such as cognitive flexibility in workplace across time, based on [8].

This paper is aiming (i) to present an innovative digital tool (i.e., a gamified sorting test) specifically created to assess cognitive flexibility for personnel selection and (ii) to present results issued from an experiment to compare performances and acceptability with "traditional" tool.

A. Defining and measuring cognitive flexibility

Cognitive flexibility refers to the ability to shift attention between task sets, attributes of a stimulus, responses, perspectives, or strategies [9][10]. In the scientific literature, it is also referred to by shifting, attention switching, or task switching, and includes both the ability to disengage from irrelevant information in a previous task and to focus on relevant information in a forthcoming task [11]. Thus, cognitive flexibility enables to think differently, change perspective and adapt to a continuously changing environment.

In cognitive ergonomics, most psychological theories (e.g., Rasmussen: [12][13]; Reason: [14]; Norman: [15][16]; Hollnagel: [17]; for a synthesis [18]) are agree on the idea that in order to avoid human error, an individual needs to realize that the situation has changed in order to be able to 'log out' of the automatic processing mode and come into the controlled processing mode. To detect the situation change and the necessity of a non–routine response, it is necessary to come into a higher level of attentional control, where the individual accesses the new situation and plan the action to be taken. They need to perceive the environmental cues in a different way, reinterpreting them. How the person represents the task and the set of strategies employed to deal with it determines how easily she or he will shift attention to the new environmental conditions.

Cognitive flexibility can be assessed with a variety of neuropsychological tests, the most prominent being the Wisconsin Card Sorting Test (WCST [1][3]). In this test, participants are asked to sort a series of cards according to different rules and alter their strategy when the rules change unexpectedly (Figure 2). The figure 2 depicts a response card with two blue stars. The stimulus cards are from left to right; one red triangle, two green stars, three yellow crosses, and four blue circles. In the manual administration, the four stimulus cards would be laid on a table in front of the participant, and the participant is handed a deck of multidimensional response cards to sort. Typically, individuals who are less cognitively flexible struggle to adjust to changing rules, while those with higher aptitude can quickly switch their mode of thinking between an efficiency-driven adherence to a given rule and the exploration of new approaches. As this test was originally designed for clinical use to detect executive dysfunction, its suitability for assessing performance in a personnel selection context has yet to be investigated.

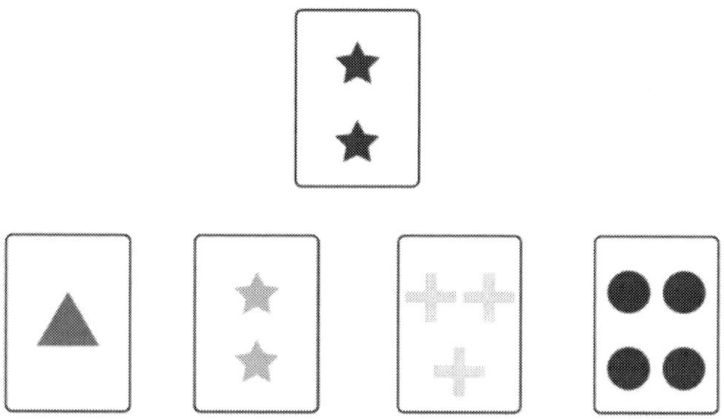

Figure 2. An example of the WCST display

B. Assessment of cognitive flexibility in personnel selection

As Hommel et al. [19] say in their paper published in 2021, recent changes in the nature of work require that employers reassess the modus operandi of their personnel selection procedures. In a fast-changing knowledge economy, employees need to adapt quickly to novel demands, make decisions in the face of uncertainty, and cope with unexpected challenges [20]. At the same time, employees are increasingly expected to switch seamlessly between different job roles, tasks, organizations, and even occupations [21]. To ensure sustained firm performance, organizations need a workforce with the necessary capacities to efficiently deal with ongoing transformation [22]. For this reason, adaptability and flexibility have been widely acknowledged as key transversal skills that play a vital role in the long-term success of employees and, in turn, organizations [18][23]. To keep up with the demands of today's dynamic and diverse workplaces, personnel selection researchers and practitioners need to reconsider what and how to assess in the 21st century [24]. In other words, as working conditions become more and more dynamic and complex nowadays, the ability to adapt thoughts and behaviors according to changing context requirements becomes particularly relevant for work success [19][25]. Whatever the context and whatever the domain, cognitive flexibility can be defined as the ability to adjust cognitive processing strategies in response to new, changing, and unexpected circumstances, conditions and situations [26]. It enables people to switch from one activity to another, to consider multiple perspectives, to find new solutions to a problem, and to face novel conditions in the environment [19]. In contrast, individuals who are cognitively inflexible, struggle to adapt their strategies when situations change and, therefore, tend to get stuck in habitual patterns. The ability to shift cognitive sets is a key property of efficient executive functioning and has been found to be different from cognitive abilities [25].

C. Gamification in personnel selection

Gamification is used as an umbrella term comprising a variety of techniques inspired by research in game design and generally refers to the integration of game design elements into nongame contexts [27][28][29]. The primary idea is to take advantage of the motivational nature of games to enhance the effectiveness of existing methods. By tapping into people's natural desire for competition and achievement, gamification promises to encourage participation, to increase productivity and, thus, to improve the quality and quantity of outcomes in any domain. Over the past few years, gamification has been increasingly applied within a variety of areas, including work, education, training, marketing, healthcare, wellness, and sustainability [5][30].

More recently, researchers and practitioners within the field of human resource management and organizational psychology have recognized gamification as a promising tool to improve recruitment and personnel selection. The central goal of using gamification within this context is to make the selection procedure more enjoyable while increasing the quality of measurement at the same time [30]. Nevertheless, if the use of gamified versions of the WCST is becoming more common for patients (e.g., [31][32]), we found only one gamified sorting test for personnel selection created by [27]. During the game, the participant/player is asked to imagine to be a fictive employee of a marketing agency and s/he is asked to implement a new marketing strategy to reduce costs and improve the efficiency of marketing campaigns for consumer products. As in the traditional version of the WCST, the correct matching rule is not revealed to the subject. Interesting results based on a sample of 180 participants in an online study have been collected by [27].

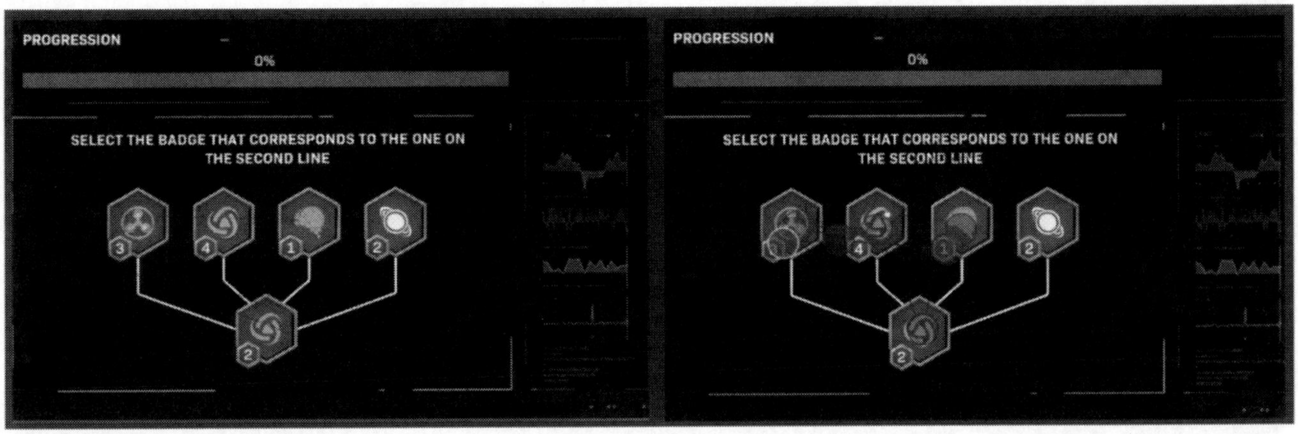

Figure 3. A screenshot of the gamified test created by Yuzu© (on the left side) and visual exploration of one participant collected by using eye-tracking technique (on the right side).

Figure 4. One of our participants while she is playing to Yuzu©, in front of the eye-tracking system.

But, according to us, even if this gamified test is interesting, this is not a relevant solution for personnel selection for several reasons:

- All the tasks are based on language, i.e., the participants/players must read and understand instructions and complex information to complete the task. One of the main advantages of the WCST is that no language is necessary to complete the test. In other words, with the environment created by [27], language can be a serious barrier.
- Because this digital environment has been created there are 10 years ago, realism and quality of graphics are very simple, no dynamic and not immersive.
- At the origin, the WCST has been elaborated to assess cognitive flexibility, i.e., the ability to shift attention between task sets, attributes of a stimulus, responses, perspectives, or strategies whatever the context. In the digital environment created by [27], technical skills and declarative knowledge are crucial to solve the problems. In other words, only technical and declarative knowledge, which are assessed in their digital environment while the non-technical skills and executive functions are assessed by the WCST.
- Finally, data collected by the authors are only subjective data obtained by an online study using different Likert-scales. No objective data have been collected; Thus, its prevents generalization of the results.

To answer to all these limits, a gamified sorting test has been specifically created to assess cognitive flexibility for personnel selection.

II. Our pilot study : Work in progress

An innovative gamified sorting test has been created specifically for personnel selection and recruitment (https://yuzu.hr). This gamified sorting test, called Yuzu©, has several components centred on specific crucial soft-skills; for each of these components, the player/user is asked to complete gamified tasks where the protocol is very similar to paper-and-pencil version of psychometrics tests such as WCST (e.g., Figure 3).

Since several months, an experiment is conducted (i) to investigate the behaviours and performances of users/players with Yuzu© and (ii) to compare their performances with the traditional paper-and-pencil version of the WCST.

For our pilot study, twelve adults volunteers are asked to play with Yuzu© and, two weeks later, to complete the paper-and-pencil version of the WCST. In other words, each participant is asked to complete the test for assessing cognitive flexibility twice.

To collect gaze data, we used the research system Tobii Pro Spectrum at speeds up to 200 Hz (Figure 4), to capture the eye movements such as saccades, tremors, and micro-saccades. This system can capture data in high sampling frequency, while still allowing for natural head movement.

In our pilot study, the main indicators are:

- The percentage of errors (i.e., total number of errors divided by number of trial administered).
- The percentage of preservative errors (i.e., number of errors in which a subject continuously respond incorrectly using the same pattern).
- Visual exploration on each card of the test (Figure 3).

Data are actually collected and the results will be presented during the conference.

ACKNOWLEDGMENT

We are grateful to the participants, and we are grateful to the "Maison des Sciences de l'Homme Lorraine" (UAR CNRS and University of Lorraine) for supporting and assisting the experiment.

REFERENCES

[1] E. A. Berg, "A simple objective technique for measuring flexibility in thinking," The Journal of General Psychology, vol. 39, 1948, pp. 15–22.

[2] W. A. Scott, "Cognitive complexity and cognitive flexibility," Sociometry, vol. 25, no. 4, 1962, pp. 405–414. [Online]. Available: https://doi.org/10.2307/2785779

[3] R. K. Heaton, G. J. Chelune, J. L. Talley, G. G. Kay, and G. Curtiss, Wisconsin Card Sorting Test manual: Revised and expanded. Psychological Assessment Resources, 1993.

[4] N. Lounes, G. Khan, and K. Tchanturia, "Assessment of cognitive flexibility in anorexia nervosa–self-report or experimental measure? a brief report," Journal of the International Neuropsychological Society, vol. 17, no. 5, 2011, pp. 925–928.

[5] A. Wojtczuk-Turek and D. Turek, "Innovative behaviour in the workplace: The role of hr flexibility, individual flexibility and psychological capital: the case of poland," European Journal of Innovation Management, vol. 18, no. 3, 2015, pp. 397–419.

[6] X. Yu, D. Li, C. Tsai, and C. Wang, The role of psychological capital in employee creativity. Career Development International, 2019.

[7] J. Maltby, L. Day, L. E. McCutcheon, M. Martin, and J. L. Cayanus, "Celebrity worship, cognitive flexibility, and social complexity," Personality and Individual Differences, vol. 37, no. 7, 2004, pp. 1475–1482.

[8] D. H. Autor, F. Levy, and R. J. Murnane, "The skill content of recent technological change: An empirical exploration," The Quarterly Journal of Economics, vol. 118, no. 4, 2003, pp. 1279–1333.

[9] A. Miyake et al., "The unity and diversity of executive functions and their contributions to complex "frontal lobe" tasks: a latent variable analysis," Cognitive Psycholology, vol. 41, 2000, pp. 49–100.

[10] B. Jurado and M. Rosselli, "The elusive nature of executive functions: a review of our current understanding," Neuropsychology Review, vol. 17, 2007, pp. 213–233.

[11] S. Monsell, "Task switching," Trends in Cognitive Sciences, vol. 7, 2003, pp. 134–140.

[12] J. Rasmussen, "Skills, rules and knowledge: Signals, signs, and symbols and other distinctions," IEEE transactions on Human,Ssystems and Cybernetics, vol. 3, 1983, pp. 653–688.

[13] J. Rasmussen, "A framework for cognitive task analysis in system design," in Intelligent decision support in process environment, E.Hollnagel, G. Mancini, and D. Woods, Eds. Berlin: Springer-Verlag, 1986.

[14] J. Reason, Human error. Cambridge University Press, 1990.

[15] D. Norman, "Categorization of action slips," Psychological Review, vol. 88, 1981, pp. 1–15.

[16] D. Norman and T. Shallice, "Attention to action: Willed and automatic control of behavior," in Consciousness and Self Regulation, R. J. Davidson, G. E. Schwartz, and D. Shapiro, Eds. New York: Plenum, 1980, pp. 1–15.

[17] E. Hollnagel, Cognitive reliability and error analysis method (CREAM). Elsevier, 1998.

[18] J. Canas, J. Quesada, A. Antolí, and I. Fajardo, "Cognitive flexibility and adaptability to environmental changes in dynamic complex problem-solving tasks," Ergonomics, vol. 46, no. 5, 2003, pp. 482–501.

[19] T. Ionescu, "Exploring the nature of cognitive flexibility," New Ideas in Psychology, vol. 30, 2012, pp. 190–200. [Online]. Available: https://doi.org/10.1016/j.newideapsych.2011.11.001

[20] E. E. Pulakos, S. Arad, M. A. Donovan, and K. E. Plamondon, "Adaptability in the workplace: Development of a taxonomy of adaptive performance," Journal of Applied Psychology, vol. 85, 2000, pp. 612–624. [Online]. Available: https://doi.org/10.1037/0021-9010.85.4.612

[21] L. Eby, M. Butts, and A. Lockwood, "Predictors of success in the era of the boundaryless career," Journal of Organizational Behavior, vol. 24, 2003, pp. 689–708. [Online]. Available: https://doi.org/10.1002/job.214

[22] E. D. Pulakos, D. Dorsey, and S. White, "Adaptability in the workplace: Selecting an adaptive workforce," in Advances in human performance and cognitive engineering research (Vol 6), C. S. Burke, L. G. Pierce, and E. Salas, Eds. Elsevier, 2006, pp. 41–71. [Online]. Available: https://doi.org/10.1016/S1479-3601(05)06002-9

[23] B. Griffin and B. Hesketh, "Adaptable behaviours for successful work and career adjustment," Australian Journal of Psychology, vol. 5, 2003, pp. 65–73. [Online]. Available: https://doi.org/10.1080/00049530412331312914

[24] R. E. Ployhart, "Staffing in the 21st century: New challenges and strategic opportunities," Journal of Management, vol. 32, 2006, pp. 868–897. [Online]. Available: https://doi.org/10.1177/0149206306293625

[25] J. J. Cañas, I. Fajardo, and L. Salmeron, "Cognitive flexibility," International Encyclopedia of Ergonomics and Human Factors, vol. 1, 2006, pp. 297–301. [Online]. Available: https://doi.org/10.13140/2.1.4439.6326

[26] J. J. Cañas, J. Quesada, and a. I. F. A. Antolí, "Cognitive flexibility and adaptability to environmental changes in dynamic complex problem-solving tasks," Ergonomics, vol. 46, 2003, pp. 482–501. [Online]. Available: https://doi.org/10.1080/0014013031000061640

[27] B. E. Hommel, R. Ruppel, and H. Zacher, "Assessment of cognitive flexibility in personnel selection: Validity and acceptance of a gamified version of the wisconsin card sorting test," International Journal of Selection and Assessment, vol. 30, no. 1, 2012, pp. 126–144.

[28] S. Deterding, M. Sicart, L. Nacke, K. O'Hara, and D. Dixon, "Gamification. using game-design elements in non-gaming contexts," in Proceedings of the 2011 annual conference extended abstracts on human factors in computing systems, 2011, pp. 2425–2428.

[29] K. Seaborn and D. I. Fels, "Gamification in theory and action: A survey," International Journal of Human-Computer Studies, vol. 74, 2015, pp. 14–31. [Online]. Available: https://doi.org/10.1016/j.ijhcs.2014.09.006

[30] M. B. Armstrong, R. N. Landers, and A. B. Collmus, "Gamifying recruitment, selection, training, and performance management: Game-thinking in human resource management," in Emerging research and trends in gamification, H. Gangadharbatla and D. Davis, Eds. IGI Global, 2016, pp. 140–165.

[31] S. Çelik, M. Oğuz, U. Konur, F. Köktürk, and N. Atasoy, "Comparison of computerized and manual versions of the wisconsin card sorting test on schizophrenia and healthy samples," Psychological Assessment, vol. 33, no. 6, 2021, p. 562.

[32] G. P. Wagner and C. M. Trentini, "Assessing executive functions in older adults: a comparison between the manual and the computer-based versions of the wisconsin card sorting test," Psychology & Neuroscience, vol. 2, 2009, pp. 195–198.

Local-Global Reaction Map: Classification of Listeners by Pupil Response Characteristics when Listening to Sentences Including Emotion Induction Words

– Toward Adaptive Design of Auditory Information –

Katsuko T. Nakahira
Nagaoka University of Technology
Nagaoka, Niigata, Japan
Email: katsuko@vos.nagaokaut.ac.jp

Munenori Harada
Nagaoka University of Technology
Nagaoka, Niigata, Japan
Email: s193369@stn.nagaokaut.ac.jp

Muneo Kitajima
Nagaoka University of Technology
Nagaoka, Niigata, Japan
Email: mkitajima@kjs.nagaokaut.ac.jp

***Abstract*— When a person acquires a text as auditory information and derives the meaning of the text, he or she may simultaneously generate an emotion in response to the content of the text. Emotions are said to have a certain relationship with decision-making and memory. Therefore, it is expected that even sentences with the same meaning will be remembered differently depending on the emotion evoked. This study aims to clarify the relationship between the emotions that arise when listening to a text and the memory of the presented text. The classification of emotional states held by people is performed by a method based on subjective quantities by impression rating or by a method based on objective quantities by biometric information. In this study, we focus on pupil response, which is biological information that has been suggested to change with emotion. Based on this, this paper proposes the Local-Global Reaction Map (LGR-Map) as a classification method for pupil changes accompanying emotional changes, as a basic research for the construction of adaptive content design methods that utilize the degree of human emotional arousal. The LGR-Map is generated by capturing the emotional changes during listening to a text from the following two perspectives; Those generated by words in a specific region of a sentence (Local reaction); those generated by the context of the entire sentence (Global reaction). The total pupil diameter change within a certain time period is obtained as the characteristic quantity for each response. Error ellipses are defined for the distribution of listeners in the LR-GR for the presented text (LGR-Map), and classified into five types based on the rotation angle and flattening ratio of the error ellipses. The basic properties of the LGR-Map were investigated by using auditory stimuli presented in short sentences containing Affective Norm for English Words (ANEW).**

Keywords*— *Local-Global Reaction Map; Pupil Response; Affective Norm for English Words; Emotion Induction; Contents Design of Auditory Information.

I. INTRODUCTION

With the penetration of mobile devices and the development of eXtended Reality (XR)technology, we are surrounded by an increasing number of services that disseminate content via electronic media. Many of these services are designed to enrich the experience of individuals, and their range of application is wide, from sensory experiences, such as sightseeing and movies to educational materials that make it easier for people to acquire knowledge. In recent years, there has been a movement to expand content provision services from an inclusivity perspective (e.g., [1]).

Content design is essential to content provision in the sense of striving to convey what is to be conveyed as accurately as possible. Content design has the issue of the quality and quantity of the presenting stimulus as the material contained in the content. Visual and auditory information are the central presenting stimuli, and how to handle their quality and quantity is one of the key factors.

Regarding the amount of content, since perceptual information is basically a physical quantity, the amount of processing is determined by the structure of the human cognitive system itself, and individual differences are usually negligible. This is described by Hirabayashi et al. [2] as the relationship between the amount of information and the timing at which the information is given, and it is possible to maximize human memory by giving visual and auditory information, or explicit and implicit information in the appropriate order and intervals.

Furthermore, the quality of content is largely related to the viewer's cognitive process. The cognitive process depends on the richness of information nodes and the state of node connectivity of the information receiver, and thus varies from person to person. Murakami et al. [3][4] discussed the quality of content for short auditory information. We classified the emotions of short sentences into positive, negative, and other categories (in this case, we assign neutral), and calculated memory scores for each category, suggesting that short sentences belonging to a specific category improve memory scores. We also suggested the possibility of using pupil response to measure human emotion induction from short sentences. In addition, Moriya et al. [5] found that pupil responses to Affective Norm for English Words (ANEW) contained in short auditory information may be characterized based on ANEW categories.

Therefore, in order to design content that facilitates better emotional experiences and knowledge acquisition, it is desirable to be able to adaptively provide content according to the viewer's cognitive characteristics. For this purpose, it is necessary to monitor the viewer's emotional state in real time. Biometric information is a suitable indicator for this purpose. There are many types of biometric information on emotion (e.g., Jim et al. [6], Shu et al. [7]), but considering the time scale and ease of measurement, the pupillary response is the most promising. Based on the above, this paper focuses on pupillary response and proposes the Local-Global Reaction

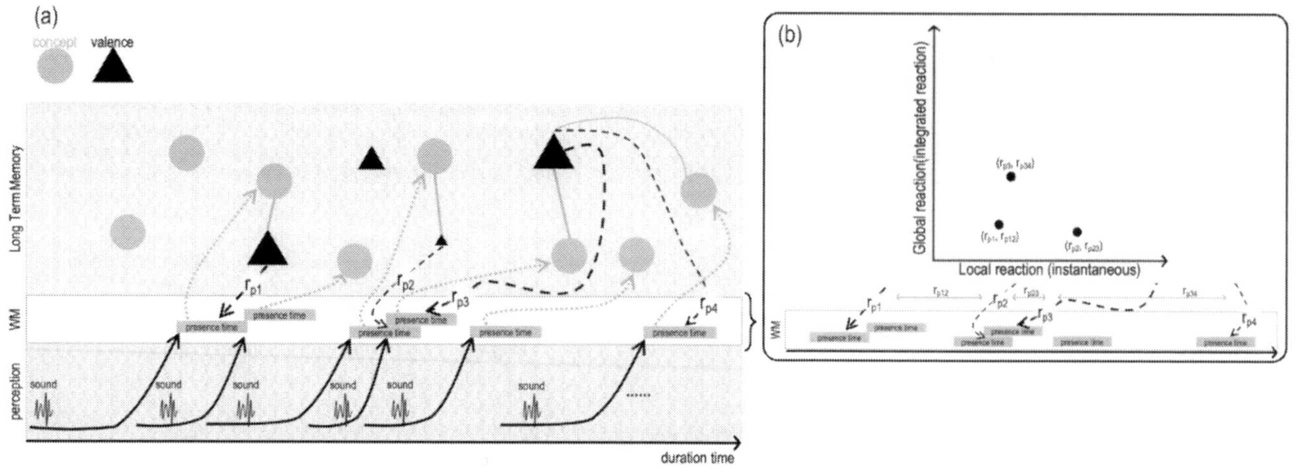

Figure 1. Cognitive model of this paper based on CI model. (a) Input - Cognitive process. (b) Working memory processing - output process.

Map (LGR-Map) as a classification method for pupillary changes associated with emotional changes.

This paper is organized as follows. In Section II, we construct a base cognitive model and propose an LGR-Map based on it. In Section III, we show the usefulness of the LGR-Map by actually applying it to the HUCAPP 2023 data [5]. In Section IV, we discuss the usefulness of LGR-Map.

II. Designing LGR-Map based on Construction-Integration Model

A. *Basic Design*

In this paper, we construct a reaction model for human emotion based on the Construction-Integration Model (CI-model, e.g., [8][9][10]) proposed by Kintsch. The CI-model is a theory of discourse comprehension consisting of a construction step and an integration step.

The scenario in this paper is modeled based on the CI-model as shown in Figure 1. Figure 1 (a) shows the construction process that encodes information (packet of sound waves) input from the outside world, retrieves information stored in long-term memory using it as a clue, and constructs a network. Figure 1 (b) shows the integration process in which the retrieved information is pruned and integrated in the working memory by pruning information that does not fit the context, and the physical response is output.

First, when a single stimulus (a packet of sound waves in the auditory case) is perceived from a sensory organ, it is sent as encoded perceptual information from the sensory organ to the working memory. The sent information is matched with a large number of nodes (knowledge concepts) in the brain's long-term memory. The corresponding knowledge concept and its associated knowledge concept are then returned to the working memory. In this case, the information of the chunk of emotion (defined by valence and arousal) r_{p_i} associated with the knowledge concept is also returned, so that the working memory temporarily retains the emotion of the perceived packet of sound waves. Based on the returned r_{p_i}, the cognitive process via the working memory activates the motor process in each part of the body, and a response is generated. The pupillary response we focus on in this paper is produced by the activity of the pupillary sphincter and pupillary dilator muscles, which are considered to be one of their responses. The story so far can be expressed as follows.

Let $\boldsymbol{K}$ be a row vector of $^{\forall}$word concepts (knowledge concepts) in the long-term Memory (LTM) of $^{\exists}$person, and the word concept i input at time t_j is denoted by the element $K_i(t_j)$ in $\boldsymbol{K}$. where $K_i(t_j)$ are the values of valence V_i and arousal Ar_i that characterize the emotion [11]. The number of elements is $i = 1 \cdots n_K$ (n_K is the total number of word concepts), with only one i value of 1 for some time t_j. Here, V_i or Ar_i or both may have no value (~ 0) (in that case, $V_i = 0,\ Ar_i = 0$). The range of values for V_i and Ar_i is $1 \leq V_i \leq 9,\ 1 \leq Ar_i \leq 9$.

Next, let $\boldsymbol{A}$ be a column vector of $^{\forall}$emotion concepts in the LTM of $^{\exists}$people, consisting of elements $A_k(V_k,\ Ar_k)$. The number of elements is $k = 1, \cdots, m_A$ (m_A is the total number of emotion concepts), and there always exist $V_k,\ Ar_k$ values.

The $\boldsymbol{K}$ and $\boldsymbol{A}$ are connected by a $n \times m$ matrix $\boldsymbol{W(t_j)}$ that shows their connectivity at time t_j. The element $w_{ik}(t_j)$ of $\boldsymbol{W(t_j)}$ indicates the degree of coupling between $K_i(t_j)$ and A_k. If $K_i(t)$ in $\boldsymbol{K}$ is input and co-occurs with A_k in $\boldsymbol{A}$ on t_j, the probability that $K_i(t_j)$ retrieved from LTM is $p(K_i(t_j))$ and that A_k retrieved from LTM is $p(A_k(t_j))$, the probability of A_k being retrieved from LTM is expressed by the following equation.

$$w_{ik}(t_j) = w_{ik}(p(K_i(t_j)),\ p(A_k(t_j)))$$

In this case, the temporary emotion $E(t_j)$ generated from the input $^{\exists}$packet of sound waves is (1).

$$E(t_j) = D(t_j) \sum_{i=1}^{n_K} \sum_{k=1}^{m_A} K_i(t_j) w_{ik}(t_j) A_k \quad (1)$$

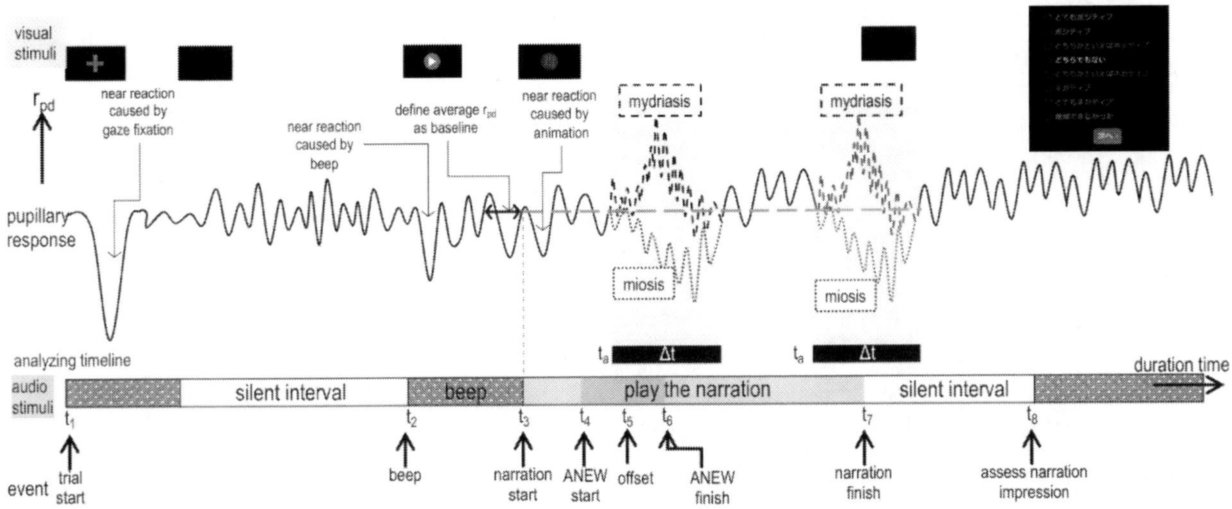

Figure 2. The full pupillary response when auditory information is given.

Here, $D(t_j)$ is the damping factor. The above explanation represents the construction process.

The sentence, which consists of n_{wp} packets of sound waves, repeats the process of (1) as one cycle up to this point, and continues to return the emotion associated with the knowledge concept to the working memory. In the process, $E(t_j)$ may or may not be integrated between t_j depending on the presence or absence of active sources and contextual relations. The damping factor is introduced as a quantity that indicates the degree of such emotional integration. When n_{wp} packets of sound waves are listened to, the emotion arises in the form of integration of $E(t_j)$ that has been cultivated up to that point. It is usually at the end of a sentence where the packets of sound waves are interrupted. This is the integration process in this research situation.

Based on this, we consider the 2D plane shown in Figure 1(b). We thought that we could show the characteristics of the emotion that occurs in listeners when they listen to narration by plotting the information on human reactions in this plane. The r_{p_i} in the figure indicates the emotional reaction to a specific packet of sound waves. $r_{p_{i,i+1}}$ indicates the emotional reaction generated by the integration of the emotional reactions generated by multiple packets of sound waves. By treating it in this way, two measured reaction quantities can be plotted on a plane as $(r_{p_i}, r_{p_{i,i+1}})$. In this paper, we call this plane as *Local-Global Response Map* (LGR-Map).

B. *Representation of Pupillary Response based on CI-model*

In order to apply the LGR-Map to pupillary responses, the measurement design of pupillary response should keep an adequate time interval by both inducing time interval both inducing a specific emotion induction word in narrating (instantaneous response) and context of narration (integrated response). Figure 2 represents a measurement design of pupillary response when listening to the narration stimuli based on Figure 1. Here, we adopt the Japanese version of ANEW [14], which induce emotion as the result of instantaneous response. For the integrated response, we assumed that the effect appears at the end of the sentence. We measured participants' pupillary responses to short sentences containing one ANEW word.

The auditory stimuli are adjusted for the event specified in Figure 2 as follows. The beep sound for the mental preparation to initiate auditory stimuli is uttered at t_2. Narration starts at t_3 and ANEW is uttered at t_4. After that, auditory stimuli are terminated at t_7. During this period, the auditory elements related to the evocation of emotion are the ANEW and the atmospheres at the end of the sentence. When analyzing the pupillary response, it is necessary to analyze the data in the vicinity of these elements.

Next, pupil diameter $r_{pd}(t)$ at elapsed time t is processed as follows, in the following order: determination of baseline, calculation of pupil diameter change, and total pupil diameter change.

First, when we set Δt_b as the interval necessary to calculate baseline, baseline $\tilde{r}_{pd}$ is calculated as follows.

$$\tilde{r}_{pd} = \frac{1}{\Delta t_b} \int_{t_{ns}-\Delta t_b}^{t_{ns}} r_{pd}(t)\, dt \tag{2}$$

Here, pupil diameter change value in t $\Delta r_{pd}(t)$ is calculated by the equation(3).

$$\Delta r_{pd}(t) = r_{pd}(t) - \tilde{r}_{pd} \tag{3}$$

The pupil diameter change $\delta r(t)$ between the duration time t and δt is calculated by the (4).

$$\delta r(t) = \Delta r_{pd}(t + \delta t) - \Delta r_{pd}(t) \tag{4}$$

Mydriasis (dilation) and miosis (constriction) are typical quantities that show pupillary response. Since the instantaneous changes in either of them are minute, we represent the total amount of change in only mydriasis or only miosis at $[t_a, t_a + \Delta t]$. These can be expressed as total amount of mydriasis r_{myd}. The total amount of miosis r_{mio} is calculated by the equation (5).

$$r_{myd} \text{ or } r_{mio} = \int_{t_a}^{t_a+\Delta t} \delta r(t)\, dt \quad (5)$$

In order to obtain a clearer picture of the change in pupillary response, it is better to capture the absolute change in r_{myd}, r_{mio}. Here, we define r_{all} as the total change in pupillary response calculated by (6).

$$r_{all} = |r_{myd}| + |r_{mio}| \quad (6)$$

In LGR-Map, r_{all} is assumed to be a local (instantaneous) or global (integrated) reaction around calculated R. The pupillary response analysis start time t_a and analysis interval Δt can be arbitrarily determined. In the LGR-Map, we set t_a and Δt using the event time in Figure 2 as follows: For the local reaction, t_a is set to t_5, the offset time at which the pupil response is expected to start after the appearance of the ANEW that causes the reaction. For the global reaction, t_a is set where the integrated effect can be easily confirmed. In this paper, t_a is set a little before t_7, when the narration ends. Since the actual narration has n_s sets of calculated points or consists of n_s sentences, at most n_s points are plotted on the LGR-Map.

C. Typology based on LGR-Map

r_{all} distribution on LGR-Map is regarded as a description of induced emotion by narration stimuli for each participant. We design the method of categorization of typology for r_{all} distribution on LGR-Map. r_{all} distribution has x axis for local response and y axis for global response. r_{all} is the information including the individual differences. Now, each individual difference is assumed to obey a normal distribution. If the distribution obeys a two-dimensional Gaussian distribution, we can draw the error ellipsoid on LGR-Map.

The error ellipsoid is represented by the following equation using the transformed coordinates u, v. Hence σ_u^2, σ_v^2 are the variances of the transformed coordinates with respect to the respective axes.

$$\frac{u^2}{\sigma_u^2} + \frac{v^2}{\sigma_v^2} = c^2$$

Here, σ_u^2, σ_v^2, and rotation angle of error ellipsoid α can be converted as (7) – (9) using σ_x^2 as variance for local response, σ_y^2 as variance for global response, σ_{xy} as covariance of local-global response.

$$\sigma_u^2 = \frac{\sigma_x^2 + \sigma_y^2 + \sqrt{(\sigma_x^2 - \sigma_y^2)^2 + 4\sigma_{xy}^2}}{2} \quad (7)$$

$$\sigma_v^2 = \frac{\sigma_x^2 + \sigma_y^2 - \sqrt{(\sigma_x^2 - \sigma_y^2)^2 + 4\sigma_{xy}^2}}{2} \quad (8)$$

$$\tan\alpha = \frac{\sigma_{xy}}{\sigma_u^2 - \sigma_y^2} \quad (0 < \alpha < 180^\circ) \quad (9)$$

We consider the shape of error ellipsoid depending on the behavior of σ_x^2, σ_y^2, σ_{xy}. First, we relate σ_x^2 and σ_y^2 as (10).

$$\sigma_y^2 = \gamma\sigma_x^2 \quad (\gamma > 0) \quad (10)$$

The error ellipsoid can then be classified by the value of γ. First, we can set $\sigma_x^2 = \sigma_y^2 = \sigma_0^2$ when $\gamma = 1$. Therefore, $\alpha = 45^\circ$ as shown in the following calculation.

$$\begin{aligned}
\sigma_u^2 &= \frac{\sigma_0^2 + \sigma_0^2 + \sqrt{4\sigma_{xy}^2}}{2} = \sigma_0^2 + \sigma_{xy} \\
\sigma_v^2 &= \frac{\sigma_0^2 + \sigma_0^2 - \sqrt{4\sigma_{xy}^2}}{2} = \sigma_0^2 - \sigma_{xy} \\
\tan\alpha &= \frac{\sigma_{xy}}{\sigma_0^2 + \sigma_{xy} - \sigma_0^2} \\
&= 1
\end{aligned}$$

If $\sigma_{xy} \sim 0$, the distribution has a circle shape; if it has a large value, the distribution has an ellipsoid shape.

Next, we consider the case of $\gamma \neq 1$ in (10), where we apply the observed data properties to the variables in (7) – (9). Since σ_x^2, σ_y^2, and σ_{xy} are at most on the order of 10^{-2} given the experimental environment, the σ_{xy} term is on the order of 10^{-4}. Therefore, we can ignore the σ_{xy} term. Equation (7) – (9) can be approximated by the following equations.

$$\sigma_u^2 = \frac{\sigma_x^2 + \sigma_y^2 + \sqrt{(\sigma_x^2 - \sigma_y^2)^2}}{2} \sim \sigma_x^2 \quad (11)$$

$$\sigma_v^2 = \frac{\sigma_x^2 + \sigma_y^2 - \sqrt{(\sigma_x^2 - \sigma_y^2)^2}}{2} \sim \sigma_y^2 = \gamma\sigma_x^2 \quad (12)$$

$$\tan\alpha = \frac{\sigma_{xy}}{\sigma_u^2 - \sigma_y^2} = \frac{\sigma_{xy}}{(1-\gamma)\sigma_x^2} \quad (13)$$

In the situation, considering the range of γ and signum of σ_{xy}, we can predict the following categories. Hence, L, G represent local or global reaction, and $+$, $-$ after the L or G represent strong or weak effect. $_-$, $^-$ represent the spreading to lower or upper side of data.

- case $\sigma_{xy} \sim 0$:
  - $\gamma \sim 1$: *L0G0*
    The error ellipsoid distribution has circle shape.
  - $0 < \gamma \ll 1$:*L+G–*
    The shape becomes parallel to the x axis, and $\alpha \sim 0^\circ$.
  - $\gamma \gg 1$: *L–G+*
    The shape becomes parallel to the y axis, and $\alpha \sim 90^\circ$.
- case $\sigma_{xy} > 0$: L_-G^-
  The shape becomes parallel to the x (in case of $0 < \gamma < 1$) or y (in case of $\gamma > 1$) axis, and $0^\circ \ll \alpha < 90^\circ$.
- case $\sigma_{xy} < 0$: L^-G_-
  The shape becomes parallel to the x (in case of $0 < \gamma < 1$) or y (in case of $\gamma > 1$) axis, and $90^\circ \ll \alpha < 180^\circ$. In case of $\sigma_x^2 \sim \sigma_y^2 (\gamma \sim 1)$, $\alpha \sim 135^\circ$.

TABLE I. THE RESULTS OF THE EMOTIONAL AROUSAL EFFECT OF SENTENCES AND THE IMPRESSION EVALUATION. V DENOTES VALENCE, At DENOTES ATMOSPHERE, S_I DENOTES SCORE OF IMPRESSION.

V	At	$V = S_I(\%)$	$At = S_I(\%)$	Number of Trial
V_{NN}	At_N	38	38	50
V_{--}	At_-	58	58	54
V_{++}	At_+	54	54	49
V_{NN}	At_-	16	39	24
V_{NN}	At_+	17	54	34
V_{--}	At_+	8	28	29
V_{++}	At_-	4	52	49

III. TYPOLOGY OF PUPILLARY RESPONSE BASED ON LGR-MAP

To evaluate the validity of the LGR-Map designed in section II, we analyzed the pupillary response. The LGR-Map analysis was conducted using the pupillary response data measured for the controlled narration in the form of Figure 2.

A. *Characteristics of Data for Generating LGR-Map*

The data used are those obtained by [5]. The data profile is as follows. The narration source used in the experiment is designed as shown in Figure 2.

1) The narration is played back in Japanese, and is a short sentence consisting of about 30 syllables.
2) One ANEW corresponding to either high-positive valence V_{++}, high-negative valence V_{--}, or neutral valence V_N was placed at t_{vs} in one sentence.
3) After the appearance of an ANEW, we assigned an expression that characterizes the mood of the whole sentence as positive(At_+) / neutral(At_N) / negative(At_-).
4) After t_4, the analysis interval from t_a as t_5 to Δt, where the pupillary response is expected to start, was set as analysis interval 1.
5) The response that occurs at $0.5\Delta t$ before and after the end of narration was defined as analysis interval 2.

Therefore, analysis interval 1 was defined as local reaction (instantaneous reaction) and analysis interval 2 as global reaction (integrated reaction). Twenty-one participants in their 20s were included, but data of two participants were excluded due to inaccuracy.

Table I shows the results of subjective evaluation of narration stimuli by participants. The narration stimuli are composed of V_{--}, V_{NN}, V_{++} and At_-, At_N, At_+. The participants listened to each stimulus and then evaluated their impressions on a 7-point scale from high negative to high positive, indicating whether their ratings were consistent with the valence or the atmosphere. However, cases in which the impression matched less than 10 participants were excluded.

B. *LGR-Map to Represent Individual Participants' Response Sensitivity*

For each participant, an LGR-Map was created for all narration stimuli for the pupillary responses obtained under the above conditions. In order to confirm that the distribution was independent of the size of the individual pupillary response, median-normalized values within analysis interval 1 and analysis interval 2 were used for the plots.

From (1), we expect that the distribution of individual participants' pupillary responses in the LGR-Map can be classified into five types. Figure 3 shows a representative example of an LGR-Map created using the pupillary responses of individual participants to narration stimuli. As shown in section II, (a) in Figure 3 is $L+G-$, same as (b) is $L0G0$, (c) is L^-G_-, (d) is L_-G^-, and (e) is $L-G+$. When creating the LGR-Map for individual participants, we also examined whether there was a bias in the pupillary response to a particular valence or atmosphere, but no bias was found.

TABLE II. THE α AND FLATTENING RATE OF THE ERROR ELLIPSE IN THE LGR-MAP FOR THE CHARACTERISTICS OF THE NARRATION STIMULUS. F_{ee} DENOTES THE FLATNESS.

V	At	α	F_{ee}	V	At	α	F_{ee}
V_{NN}	At_-	63.6°	0.506	V_{--}	At_-	28.4°	0.091
V_{NN}	At_N	43.1°	0.350	V_{--}	At_+	12.3°	0.434
V_{NN}	At_+	32.4°	0.246	V_{++}	At_-	52.2°	0.182
				V_{++}	At_+	−7.43°	0.194

IV. DISCUSSION: IMPLICATIONS OF LGR-MAP

A. *LGR-Map for Characterizing Individual Participant*

The classification of individual participants was not characterized by a distinctive response to the combination of (valence, atmosphere), which indicates emotion, suggesting that it was simply determined by the distribution of $w_{ik}(t_j)$, which is indicated by equation (1). The intensity of $w_{ij}(t_j)$ is considered to change depending on the intensity of the individual's experience of emotion. If the overall experience of emotion is weak, or if the experience of emotion is weak for some reason and almost no emotion is generated, the response of L_-G^- is expected to be shown. When the reaction is triggered by either valence or atmosphere, it is considered to have a reaction of *L+G–* or *L–G+*. If the reaction is equally distributed between valence and atmospheres, the reaction is considered to be L^-G_-. If the reaction is completely random, it is considered to be *L0G0*.

B. *LGR-Map for Categorizing Narrations*

Next, we consider human responses to ANEWs used as narration stimuli. Since ANEWs are basically emotion references elicited when people hear the word, we believe that it is possible to evaluate the validity of narration stimuli that show the same atmospheres as ANEWs by using the LGR-Map type classification.

Table II shows the values of α and flattening F_{ee}, which are the features of LGR-Map. The features in the LGR-Map are created by combining the valence and atmospheres into 9 patterns. There were three responses to each stimulus pair. Trials with fewer than 10 trials showing the level of response to a stimulus pair were excluded from the analysis, considering them to be less significant even if an error ellipse was written.

The table shows the following characteristics. For $V_{--}At_-$, F_{ee} is almost zero, indicating that it is a circular distribution. Therefore, (a) is classified as *L0G0*. For $V_{--}At_+$, α is 13.2°,

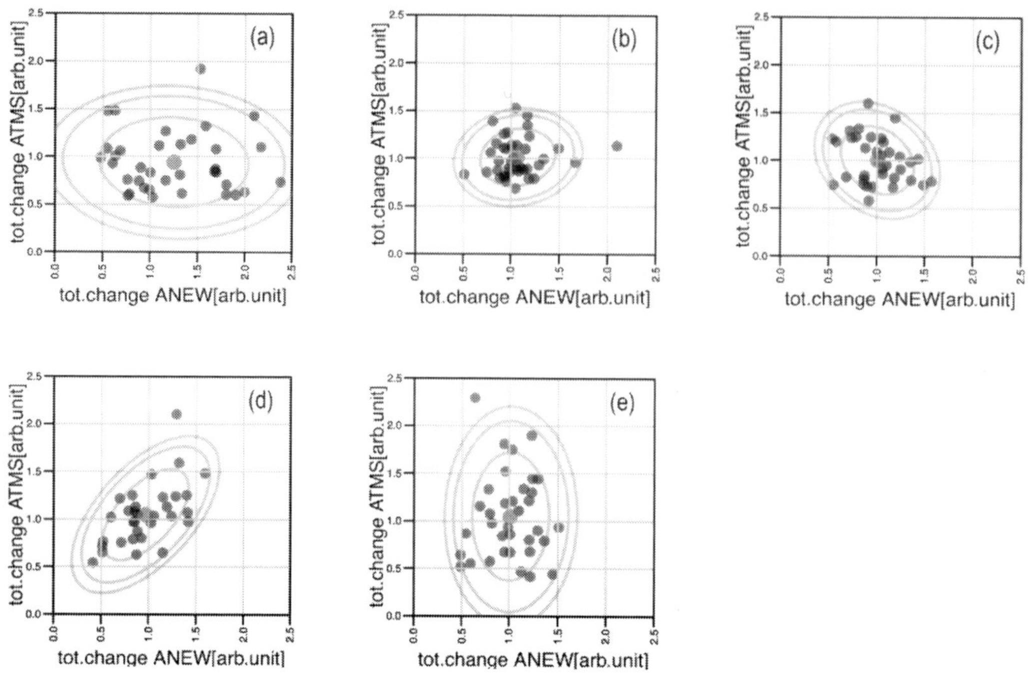

Figure 3. Examples of LGR-Maps for individual participants. The LGR-Map for individual participant are normalized by median of r_{all} near ANEW and near the end of the sentence, respectively. The oval lines indicate 66%, 90%, and 95% confidence levels from the inside. The categories in LGR-Map are as below: (a) $L+G-$, (b) $L0G0$, (c) L^-G_-, (d) L_-G^-, (e) $L-G+$.

almost parallel to the x axis, so it is classified as $L+G-$. For $V_{NN}At_N$, it is classified as L_-G^-, because $\alpha \sim 45°$. $V_{NN}At_-$, $V_{NN}At_+$ are not certain because the value of α is ambiguous, but we can classify them as L_-G^- for the reason described later. Since $V_{++}At_-$, $V_{++}At_+$ have ambiguous α values and F_{ee} values are not circular, we cannot indicate which type they can be classified into at this time.

From the above, the following possibilities are considered for $V_{--}At_-$, $V_{--}At_+$, $V_{NN}At_N$. For $V_{--}At_-$, values of valence and atmosphere have negative each. In this case, valence and atmosphere are the same characteristics, so that we anticipate that participants' pupillary responses are almost uniform as indicated by Murakami et al [3][4]. Taken together, these results suggest that the distribution of the LGR-Map is random, centered on a representative LGR-Map value.

For $V_{--}At_+$, the response is negative valence, with positive atmosphere. This, together with $V_{--}At_-$, can be interpreted as follows. The response to the negative valence was scattered, but the response to the pupillary response in the atmospheres was reasonably consistent, resulting in the values in the y axis being almost consistent and the distribution in the x axis being broadened. This is thought to be due to the broadening of the x-axis distribution.

Next, we consider the case of $V_{NN}At_N$. Both valence and atmosphere were neutral, that is no emotion is induced. It indicates that no matter where in the instantaneous or integrated area the pupillary response is measured, no change in emotion occurs for the same person or narration. Therefore, both pupillary responses show almost similar values, which is a good sign that the distribution is close to a straight line with $y = x$.

C. Understanding Social Phenomena Using LGR-Map

Image language plays a greater role than symbolic language in real-time communication. However, memes, which are words, play a major role in the transmission and accumulation of knowledge over a long period of time [15]. In knowledge represented by a network, a meme, or a symbolic node, develops links to image nodes associated with it. Image nodes are formed in response to an individual's actual perceptual, cognitive, and motor experiences, and therefore represent something unique to each individual. This is very different from symbolic nodes, which are shared within a single culture. Communication through memes (words) is a form of communication through language nodes that aggregate a large amount of information, allowing for the exchange of a large amount of information with a small amount of information (words). This is achieved through the activation of image nodes that spread around the language node. However, it is not guaranteed that the spread of image nodes centered on the language node is consistent on both sides of the interlocutor. Therefore, errors in the transmission of information due to this are inevitable [16].

For example, the proliferation of Social Networking System (SNS) allows transmission errors to be amplified in an extremely short period of time. While taking these characteristics of SNS into account, it is necessary to establish a method to realize verbal communication that does not cause transmission errors, in order to build a community where people can communicate in a healthy manner. Toward this end, an approach that focuses on the activation of knowledge centered on language nodes, as shown in this study, is promising.

V. Conclusions

In this paper, we focused on the pupillary response and proposed the LGR-Map as a classification method for pupillary changes associated with emotional changes. The LGR-Map indicates whether an individual's pupil response to a stimulus is more likely to respond to local informaion or contextual information.

In order to propose the LGR-Map, we needed a cognitive model that describes how people's emotions are induced in response to stimuli from the outside world. Thus, we constructed a model of human emotional responses based on the CI-model. We assumed that the input stimuli have the feature of auditory information, that is, transient information. The input information was assumed to be We assumed a situation where the valence of the whole sentence is determined by the sentence-final expression. For each of them, we considered an emotional response appeared based on the CI-model. When considering the above situations, we thought that there was some kind of pupillary response for each emotional reaction. We described the pupil response to ANEW as "local" reaction, and the pupil response to the end of a sentence as "global" reaction. In this case, the local and global pupil responses can be represented in a two-dimensional plane. Based on this idea, we proposed the LGR-Map. The shape classification of the LGR-Map was based on the variance of the error ellipsoid. The results indicated that the LGR-Map could be classified into five types according to the covariance of the local and global pupil responses and the trend of the dispersion of the local pupil response.

Based on a series of ideas, 36 auditory stimuli with various characteristics embedded in ANEWs and sentence-final expressions were actually given to 19 participants, and LGR-Maps were created. As a result, we confirmed that five types of shapes were recognized for individual pupil responses. Application of the LGR-Map will make it possible to provide adaptive content for individual person. The method of implementation will be an issue for the future.

Acknowledgement

This work was supported by JSPS KAKENHI Grant Number 19K12246 / 19K12232 / 20H04290 / 22K12284 / 23K11334 , and National University Management Reform Promotion Project. The authors would like to thank Editage (www.editage.com) for English language editing. MH also wants to thank to Nagai N · Promotion Foundation For Science of Perception for their finantial support.

References

[1] N. Vallez et al., "Automatic museum audio guide," Sensors, vol. 20, no. 3, 2020. [Online]. Available: https://doi.org/10.3390/s20030779

[2] R. Hirabayashi, M. Shino, K. T. Nakahira, and M. Kitajima, "How auditory information presentation timings affect memory when watching omnidirectional movie with audio guide," in Proceedings of the 15th International Joint Conference on Computer Vision, Imaging and Computer Graphics Theory and Applications (VISIGRAPP 2020), vol. 2, 2020, pp. 162–169.

[3] M. Murakami, M. Shino, K. T. Nakahira, and M. Kitajima, "Effects of emotion-induction words on memory of viewing visual stimuli with audio guide," in Proceedings of the 16th International Joint Conference on Computer Vision, Imaging and Computer Graphics Theory and Applications (VISIGRAPP 2021), vol. 2, 2021, pp. 89–100.

[4] M. Murakami, M. Shino, M. Harada, K. T. Nakahira, and M. Kitajima, "Effects of emotion-induction words on memory and pupillary reactions while viewing visual stimuli with audio guide," in Computer Vision, Imaging and Computer Graphics Theory and Applications, A. A. de Sousa et al., Eds. Cham: Springer International Publishing, 2023, pp. 69–89.

[5] S. Moriya, K. T. Nakahira, M. Harada, M. Shino, and M. Kitajima, "Can pupillary responses while listening to short sentences containing emotion induction words explain the effects on sentence memory?" in Proceedings of the 18th International Joint Conference on Computer Vision, Imaging and Computer Graphics Theory and Applications, VISIGRAPP 2023, Volume V: HUCAPP, Online Streaming, February 19-21, 2023. SCITEPRESS, 2023, pp. 213–220.

[6] J. Z. Lim, J. Mountstephens, and J. Teo, "Emotion recognition using eye-tracking: Taxonomy, review and current challenges," Sensors, vol. 20, no. 8, 2020. [Online]. Available: https://doi.org/10.3390/s20082384

[7] L. Shu et al., "A review of emotion recognition using physiological signals," Sensors, vol. 18, no. 7, 2018. [Online]. Available: https://doi.org/10.3390/s18072074

[8] W. Kintsch, "The use of knowledge in discourse processing: A construction-integration model," Psychological Review, vol. 95, 1988, pp. 163–182.

[9] W. Kintsch, Comprehension: A paradigm for cognition. Cambridge, UK: Cambridge University Press, 1998.

[10] C. Wharton and W. Kintsch, "An overview of construction-integration model: A theory of comprehension as a foundation for a new cognitive architecture," SIGART Bull., vol. 2, no. 4, jul 1991, p. 169–173. [Online]. Available: https://doi.org/10.1145/122344.122379

[11] J. Russell, "A circumplex model of affect," Journal of Personality and Social Psychology, vol. 39, 12 1980, pp. 1161–1178.

[12] K. T. Nakahira, M. Harada, and M. Kitajima, "Analysis of the relationship between subjective difficulty of a task and the efforts put into it using biometric information," in Proceedings of the 17th International Joint Conference on Computer Vision, Imaging and Computer Graphics Theory and Applications, VISIGRAPP 2022, Volume 2: HUCAPP, Online Streaming, February 6-8, 2022, A. Paljic, M. Ziat, and K. Bouatouch, Eds. SCITEPRESS, 2022, pp. 241–248. [Online]. Available: https://doi.org/10.5220/0010906800003124

[13] P. Jerčić, C. Sennersten, and C. Lindley, "Modeling cognitive load and physiological arousal through pupil diameter and heart rate," vol. 79, no. 5, pp. 3145–3159. [Online]. Available: https://doi.org/10.1007/s11042-018-6518-z

[14] M. M. Bradley, L. S. Miccoli, M. A. Escrig, and P. J. Lang, "The pupil as a measure of emotional arousal and autonomic activation." Psychophysiology, vol. 45, no. 4, 2008, pp. 602–607. [Online]. Available: https://doi.org/10.1111/j.1469-8986.2008.00654.x

[15] D. C. Dennett, From Bacteria to Bach and Back: The Evolution of Minds. W W Norton & Co Inc, 2 2018.

[16] M. Kitajima, M. Toyota, and J. Dinet, "How Resonance Works for Development and Propagation of Memes," International Journal on Advances in Systems and Measurements, vol. 14, 2021, pp. 148–161.

Design of an Innovative Simulation Device Dedicated to the Learning of Biomechanics Applied to Orthodontics

Aurelie Mailloux
Reims hospital, URCA
Reims, France
Email: aurelie.mailloux@univ-reims.fr
2LPN UR 7489

Abstract—**Health simulation devices offer the possibility of improving practitioners' knowledge, skills, and behaviors. The current biomechanics simulation tools in the orthodontics field are technically and pedagogically limited. The need to develop an innovative simulation device in this area is commonly shared by orthodontics students. This article aims at identifying (i) the learning objectives, (ii) the technical specifications, and (iii) the constraints to design a innovative device.**

Keywords*—*Simulation; device; orthodontics; biomechanics.

I. INTRODUCTION

Previous studies on the training expectations of orthodontics practitioners revealed (i) the limitations of the current biomechanics simulation tools, (ii) their need to develop an innovative simulation device in this field [7]. After a presentation of the context (Section I), section II describes the data gathered to identify the priority fields of application for developing a biomechanics simulation tool. Section III and IV outlines the educational goals and elements of further studies to be conducted on the subject.

A. Biomechanics applied to orthodontics

Whatever the appliance used, orthodontic movements respond to biomechanical notions. To understand the dental displacements, it is necessary to represent the equivalence of the forces system at the center of resistance (CR) of the tooth [4]. The CR is a theoretical point on the tooth. When a force is applied to it, the tooth is displaced in translation (i.e., without causing rotation). The CR is on the long axis of tooth. Location of the CR depends on the alveolar bone height, the root length and the number of roots (Figure 1). In orthodontics, forces cannot pass through the CR (i.e., forces are applied on the orthodontic bracket, bonded on the crown). Thus, the distance between the CR and the point of application of force varies.

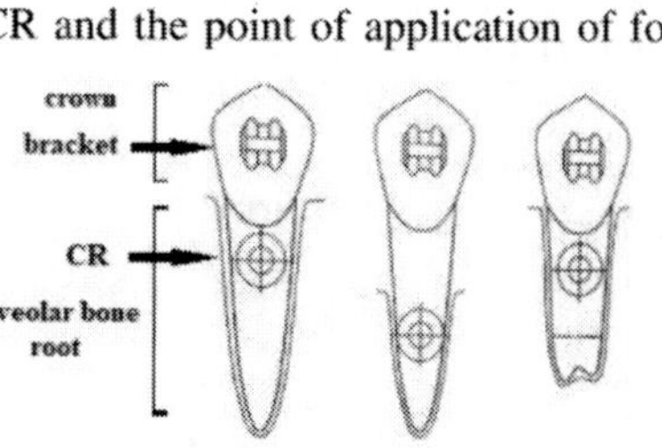

Figure 1. Different locations of a canine CR,depending on the root length and the alveolar bone height.

So, there is a moment (rotational movement) in addition to translation (linear movement). The force system will depend on (i) the clinical situation, (ii) the chosen appliance, and technique (e.g., segmented, continued). Learning biomechanics can be challenging as the concepts are difficult to grasp in a static context [6].

B. Interest of an innovative biomechanics' simulation device for orthodontists

Simulations devices in the health field aim at securing patients care. They are based on the concepts of (i) "never the first time on a patient", and also (ii) "mastering gestures before treating patients". Simulation allows training in semi-real conditions which makes the learner more involved than during lectures (i.e., with a top-down teacher-learner scheme). A meta-analysis conducted in 2011 highlighted the possibility of improving practitioners' knowledge, skills, and behaviors through health simulation [3]. Moreover, animations could help practitioners to understand complex dynamic processes in a simple and realistic way [6].

C. Current and future simulation device

In the orthodontics field, clinical skills are currently taught through demonstrations on patients (by trial and error). The use of technology is currently limited and poorly designed [5]. Orthodontics novices learn biomechanics (i.e., theoretical knowledge and practical skills) using an occlusor, made of metal teeth embedded in a sticky wax (Figure 2). Sticky wax is a mixture that dissolves in water at the temperature of 60–65°C (i.e., by heating, it allows the dental movements). However, this system (i) does not reproduce faithfully the bone remodeling, and anchorage (e.g., mini screw), (ii) does not make it possible to visualize the root displacements, nor the successive stages from the initial to the final clinical situation.

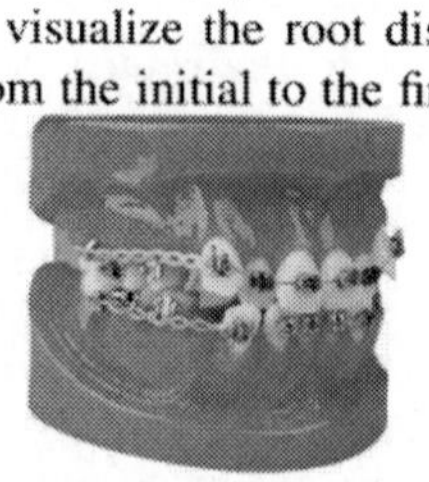

Figure 2. Orthodontic occlusor

Technological advances (e.g., imagery/ 3D radiography and computer image processing) enable to obtain specific anatomical models of a patient, meshable and usable by finite element software [1]. Thanks to the monitoring, it's possible to correlate the finite element analysis with the clinically observed movements. However, the finite element approach still has some limitations:

1-Long-term tooth movement could not be predicted from the initial force system.

2-Tooth movement depends on (i) the characteristics of the patient (e.g., drugs, dental morphology, alveolar bone, masticatory forces, tongue), (ii) the force system (e.g., continuous or segmented archwire, alloy, friction)

In addition, computational modelling remains complex and time-consuming [8]. In the literature, studies conducted on finite elements applied to orthodontics aimed to improve :

1- the treatment planning optimization and individualization (i.e., choice of the archwire) [8].

2- the anticipation of iatrogenic damages (i.e., caused by orthodontic treatments)

3- the accuracy of the forecasts of the treatment results

Thus, the implementation of an optimal orthodontic force system modelling that meets all these requirements is challenging. New studies are underway to improve digital modelling precision [8]. Some studies have already combined experimentation (i.e., to quantify forces and moments, using test beds), and digital modelling [8]. Furthermore,the scan of different stages of orthodontic treatments could improve the management of similar clinical situations (i.e. machine learning is already used for treatment planning by aligners). Along with these, we believe that from a learning and training perspective, the current technologies are sufficient to design new simulation-based learning activities in biomechanics. These should allow orthodontics students to (i) improve their manual skills, (ii) anticipate the effects of the appliances, (iii) be able to choose the most suitable device(s) according to the initial clinical situation.

II. Priority fields for a future simulation device

From the literature, we have carried out the following classification. It summarizes sub dimensions of bio mechanics applied to orthodontics:

1-Physiology of tooth movement (Physiological periodontal and bone response related to orthodontic strength...)

2-Tooth movement (the three orders, theory, indications)

3-Force systems (Moment/force, equilibrium...)

4-Anchorage (Anchorage and its control, mini-implants...)

5-Fixed devices (treatment mechanics, vectors, forces, moments applied, arches deformations and constraints)

6-Biomaterials related to tooth movement (biomaterials and production of orthodontic forces...)

7-Removable Device (interception and prevention...)

8-Factors affecting tooth movement (patient factor, growth)

9-Iatrogenic effect of tooth movement

We therefore interviewed the Reims Hospital students (N=6) to identify the priority fields for developing simulation tools, among this classification. They have considered the following sections as priorities : force system (9 points), anchorage (7 points), and fixed appliance (6 points). Points were assigned to each response based on their rank of importance. This survey should be extended to a wider pool of students in orthodontics, in order to ensure that this order suits them.

III. Educational Goals

According to the identified priority fields and the current occlusor objectives, an effective simulation device should allow students to:

- scan a patient's malocclusion and virtually position the brackets on the teeth crown.
- improve manual skills: (i) scan archwires bent by students, and integrate them in the simulator to evaluate the dental movements they generate (i.e., but that could be technically challenging), or (2) to compare the ideal archwire with the scan of the archwire prepared by the student.
- visualize the dental movements according to the clinical initial situation and the chosen fixed appliance. The dental displacements should be split into successive steps (i.e., from the initial to final situation) by showing and quantify the forces and the moments on each tooth (i.e., including roots).

IV. Further thoughts

The superiority of a dynamic over a static presentation for learners' understanding and learning is debated in the literature. However, the animations and/or interactive medium could improve the understanding of the relationships between force application and tooth movement. Animations are not sufficient, simulations' aims are to foster learning through immersion, reflection, feedback, and practice minus the risks inherent in a real-life experience (i.e., to safer patient care) [2], [3], [5].

To assess the effectiveness of an innovative simulation device (in terms of understanding, gesture mastering and memorization), further studies on this subject should combine (i) an ergonomic approach, through a user-centered design to identify the practitioners' needs and characteristics, (ii) an instructional engineering/educational psychology approach to design efficient learning activities.

References

[1] K. Schicho G. Undt O. Ploder R. Ewers A. Wagner, W. Krach. A 3-dimensional finite-element analysis investigating the biomechanical behavior of the mandible and plate osteosynthesis in cases of fractures of the condylar process. *Oral Surgery, Oral Medicine, Oral Pathology, Oral Radiology, and Endodontics*, 94(6):678–686, December 2002.

[2] M. Betrancourt. Chapter 18. The Animation and Interactivity Principles in Multimedia Learning. *Multimedia Learning*.

[3] R. Brydges B. Zendejas J. Szostek J. W. Jason T. Amy D. A. Cook, R. Hatala and S. J. Hamstra P. J. Erwin. Technology-enhanced simulation for health professions education: a systematic review and meta-analysis. *JAMA*, 306(9):978–988, September 2011.

[4] J. Faure. *orthodontic biomechanics*. The fundamentals. Sid edition, 2013.

[5] R. M. A. Wahab M. M. Dasor N. Mokhtar F.Ridzuan, G. K. L. Rao. Enabling Virtual Learning for Biomechanics of Tooth Movement: A Modified Nominal Group Technique. *Dentistry Journal*, 11(2):53, February 2023.

[6] J. F. Rouet J. M. Boucheix. Are multimedia interactive animations effective for learning? *French journal of pedagogy. Educational research*, (160):133–156, September 2007. ISBN: 9782734210962 Number: 160 Publisher: ENS Éditions.

[7] A. Mailloux. *Psycho-ergonomic analysis of the needs to design an innovative device for distance continuing education for the use of practitioners in Orthopedics Dento-Facial : Contribution of a community of practice analysis.* Doctoral thesis, Université de Lorraine, 2023.

[8] D. Wagner. *Quantification and modeling of forces and moments applied inside orthodontic brackets placed on a dental arch in the three dimensions of space.* Doctoral thesis, Strasbourg.

Effect of Touching Care on Fear in French and Japanese Subjects

François-Benoît Vialatte
Institut Pi-Psy
Draveil, France
vialatte@pi-psy.org

Tsubasa Tokunaga
The University of Electro-Communications
Tokyo, Japan
t1910437@edu.cc.uec.ac.jp

Yoshikazu Washizawa
The University of Electro-Communications
Tokyo, Japan
washizawa@uec.ac.jp

Kazuko Hiyoshi
Taisei Gakuin University
Osaka, Japan
k-hiyoshi@tgu.ac.jp

Abstract— **The aim of this study was to investigate the innate vs. acquired (cultural) aspects of affective empathy and emotional regulation. Volunteers watched videos with a virtual reality (VR) headset, triggering negative emotions, while their emotional response were measured by electroencephalographic evoked potentials (EEG). The effect of empathic touch (placing the hand on the back) on emotion regulation was measured. This international study allowed us to compare the regulation of emotions between people living in Japan and those living in France.**

Keywords-Touching care; Electroencephalography (EEG); Fear; Nursing.

I. INTRODUCTION

Touch plays a key role in interpersonal emotional regulation. For instance, touch conveys a sense of strengthened bonds between intimate partners that enhances affect and well-being [1]. Similarly, it plays a crucial role in maternal-child bonds, and promotes the child's ability to self-regulate [2].

Comforting touch involves contact distress-alleviating behaviors of an observer towards the suffering of a target [3]. Indeed, across different cultures, social touch is used to alleviate distress: the interaction between the observation-execution network and emotion regulation network may contribute to pain reduction during social touch [4].

However, is this effect innate, or the outcome of education and cultural biases? The aim of this study is to measure the effect of empathy on the regulation of emotions. Volunteers watched videos with a virtual reality headset, triggering negative emotions, while their emotional response were measured by electroencephalographic evoked potentials (EEG). In order to answer this question, we compared the regulation of emotions between people living in Japan and those living in France (to identify the common points and the differences).

Section II introduces experimental conditions, data collection, and analysis method. Section III shows experimental results. In Section IV, we discuss the results and conclude the paper.

II. MATERIALS AND METHOD

The experiment was approved by the ethics committee of the University of Electro-Communications, and conducted in accordance with the approval research procedure, the relevant guidelines and regulations. Informed consent was obtained from all subjects.

We used three VR videos, and two touching conditions (touching/no touching). The three VR videos were:
1) a horror video [5]
2) a roller coaster perspective movie [6]
https://www.youtube.com/watch?v=injtBhJCNdA
3) a natural water fall movie for the control condition (240 sec. from the beginning) [7]
We used main part of the movie and removed the title and opening and so forth. The horror movie lasts 324 seconds, and the roller coaster movie lasts 204 seconds. The order of the VR movie was randomly selected.

The touching carer was standing behind the subject. We asked the subjects not to control evoked emotions during watching the movie. We used two PCs, one to present the VR video, and another one to record EEG and present instructions.

After watching each VR movie, the subject scored how scared during touching condition comparing to no touching condition on a scale of 1 to 5 (1: strongly scared, 3: no difference, 5: no scared). Then the subject took a rest for more than 30 seconds and continued the experiment.

A. Data collection: Japanese subjects

We recruited seven healthy males (20s-40s) for this experiment.

The touching condition was changed randomly every five seconds and displayed to the monitor. The carer watched the monitor and conducted touching.

The experimental room was air conditioned and ventilated to prevent COVID-19. VR headset (Dell Visor VRP100) was connected to the display PC.

The subject put on EEG cap, then wore the VR headset. The EEG is Polymate Pro MP6100 manufactured by Miyuki Giken Co., Ltd.

We used 17 electrodes placed on F3, F4, C3, C4, P3, P4, O1, O2, F7, F8, T7, T8, P7, P8, Fz, Cz, and Pz. Each electrode was put so that the impedance was smaller than 80kΩ. The sampling rate was 1,000Hz. We recorded 30 seconds EEG in relaxed and eyes closed condition before the experiment. We recorded the synchronous signal of the touching condition and audio signal of the VR movie, as well as EEG signal to synchronize EEG and movie.

B. Data collection: French subjects

We recruited seven healthy subjects (20s-50s / 2 women and 5 males) for this experiment.

The touching condition was changed randomly every 120 seconds. Our experiments in Japan showed startle responses in some subjects when the carer touched. Although the responses are removed by segmentation, we used a different touch time for the experiment in France to relax the startle responses. The experiment instructed the carer about when to touch or stop touching.

VR headset (Occulus Rift S) was connected to the display PC.

The subject put on EEG cap, then wore the VR headset. The EEG is Enobio 8 manufactured by Neuroelectrics.

We used 8 electrodes placed on F3, F4, C3, C4, P3, P4, Oz, Fpz and 3 accelerometer channels (X Y, Z). Each electrode was put so that the EEG Quality Index was smaller than 0.5. The sampling rate was 500Hz (and 100Hz for accelerometer). We recorded 60 seconds EEG in eyes closed condition before the experiment. We recorded the synchronous signal of the touching condition as well as EEG signal to synchronize EEG and touching conditions.

C. EEG Analysis

We define the parts of scalp area as follows:

- Frontal: (F3, F4, F7, F8, Fz);
- Central: (C3, C4, Cz); and
- Parietal(/occipital) : (P3, P4, O1, O2, P7, P8, Pz).

The frequency bands are defined as δ: 2-4Hz, θ: 4-6Hz, α: 6-12Hz, β: 12-30Hz, and γ: 30-40Hz.

For prepossessing, we removed artifacts from EEG. If the instantaneous amplitude is greater than 200μV, we removed 0.25 seconds of signal before and after the point. We analyzed signal after 0.5 seconds from the onset of the recording or condition.

D. PSD

We segmented EEG signals by conditions, then performed the Fast Fourier Transform (FFT), and obtained the Power Spectrum Density (PSD) values for each area, condition, and frequency band.

For each frequency band, channel, and condition, we obtained the difference of PSD logarithm from the baseline state. We used EEG during watching the water fall movie and no touching condition as the baseline state.

$$\text{PSDdiff} = \log(\text{target PSD}) - \log(\text{baseline PSD})$$

E. PSD correlations

For each frequency band, and area, we estimated the correlation coefficient between the logarithm of PSD value and the subjectivity scared score.

III. RESULTS

The section shows our experimental results.

A. Correlation between PSD and subjective fear scores

The tables below report the correlation of PSD and subjective fear reports from Japanese (Table 1) and French (Table 2) subjects. Only the French subjects showed a significant anticorrelation between subjective fear report and parietal alpha activity.

TABLE I. CORRELATION COEFFICIENTS BETWEEN PSD AND SUBJECTIVE SCORE (JAPANESE SUBJECTS)

Frequency range	Area	Horror video	Coaster video
δ	Frontal	0.527	0.322
δ	Central	0.366	0.143
δ	Parietal	0.034	-0.156
θ	Frontal	0.230	-0.038
θ	Central	-0.208	0.025
θ	Parietal	-0.269	-0.049
α	Frontal	0.138	-0.247
α	Central	0.063	-0.195
α	Parietal	0.074	-0.376
β	Frontal	0.519	0.277
β	Central	0.641	0.679
β	Parietal	0.652	0.058
γ	Frontal	0.381	-0.051
γ	Central	0.351	-0.010
γ	Parietal	0.164	-0.570

TABLE II. CORRELATION COEFFICIENTS BETWEEN PSD AND SUBJECTIVE SCORE (FRENCH SUBJECTS)

Frequency range	Area	Horror video	Coaster video
δ	Frontal	-0.555	0.383
δ	Central	-0.581	0.035
δ	Parietal	-0.575	-0.418
θ	Frontal	-0.474	0.522
θ	Central	-0.576	-0.029
θ	Parietal	-0.545	-0.264
α	Frontal	-0.677	0.499
α	Central	-0.710	0.155
α	Parietal	**-0.871***	0.068
β	Frontal	-0.496	0.466
β	Central	-0.611	0.270
β	Parietal	-0.688	0.159
γ	Frontal	-0.355	0.423
γ	Central	-0.496	0.266
γ	Parietal	-0.583	0.126

B. *Correlation between PSD and subjective fear scores, Japanese subjects*

Tables III-VII show the PSD differences between the three conditions (horror movie, roller coaster, and relaxing waterfall), with or without touch. The water fall condition without touch was used as a reference baseline (hence its difference is null). The horror condition is correlated with a significant broadband increase of EEG activity in frontal and parietal areas. Similarly, there is a general (non-significant) broadband increase of EEG activity in the touch vs. no touch condition. The result of a T-test comparing touch vs. no-touch condition is reported in the last column.

TABLE III. PSD DIFFERENCE: JAPANESE (**: P<0.01, *: P<0.05, H0: PSDDIFF = 0) - DELTA RANGE

Area	Video stimulus	PSDdiff no touch	PSDdiff touch	t-test 2gr
Frontal	Horror	***0.53±0.33**	***0.82±0.67**	No
Frontal	Coaster	-0.10±0.67	0.07±0.59	No
Frontal	Fall	0.00±0.00	0.38±0.47	No
Central	Horror	1.19±1.24	***3.17±2.26**	No
Central	Coaster	0.51±1.08	0.70±1.78	No
Central	Fall	0.00±0.00	0.63±0.97	No
Parietal	Horror	***1.38±0.92**	***2.04±1.55**	No
Parietal	Coaster	0.39±1.56	0.87±1.55	No
Parietal	Fall	0.00±0.00	0.44±0.60	No

TABLE IV. PSD DIFFERENCE: JAPANESE (**: P<0.01, *: P<0.05, H0: PSDDIFF = 0) - THETA RANGE

Area	Video stimulus	PSDdiff no touch	PSDdiff touch	t-test 2gr
Frontal	Horror	****0.74±0.16**	***1.09±0.69**	No
Frontal	Coaster	-0.13±0.83	0.27±0.69	No
Frontal	Fall	0.00±0.00	0.40±0.61	No
Central	Horror	1.17±1.22	***3.43±2.64**	No
Central	Coaster	0.34±1.15	0.65±1.92	No
Central	Fall	0.00±0.00	0.51±0.98	No
Parietal	Horror	***1.58±1.04**	***2.08±1.65**	No
Parietal	Coaster	0.17±1.80	0.69±1.67	No
Parietal	Fall	0.00±0.00	0.31±0.58	No

TABLE V. PSD DIFFERENCE: JAPANESE (**: P<0.01, *: P<0.05, H0: PSDDIFF = 0) - ALPHA RANGE

Area	Video stimulus	PSDdiff no touch	PSDdiff touch	t-test 2gr
Frontal	Horror	****0.81±0.33**	***1.20±0.67**	No
Frontal	Coaster	0.22±0.88	0.74±0.94	No
Frontal	Fall	0.00±0.00	0.45±0.66	No
Central	Horror	1.82±1.79	***4.22±3.10**	No
Central	Coaster	1.00±1.45	1.34±2.51	No
Central	Fall	0.00±0.00	0.63±1.16	No
Parietal	Horror	****1.90±1.02**	***2.52±1.95**	No
Parietal	Coaster	0.80±1.67	1.49±1.87	No
Parietal	Fall	0.00±0.00	0.52±0.71	No

TABLE VI. PSD DIFFERENCE: JAPANESE (**: P<0.01, *: P<0.05, H0: PSDDIFF = 0) - BETA RANGE

Area	Video stimulus	PSDdiff no touch	PSDdiff touch	t-test 2gr
Frontal	Horror	****1.07±0.54**	****1.49±0.81**	No
Frontal	Coaster	0.42±0.95	***1.05±0.77**	No
Frontal	Fall	0.00±0.00	0.65±0.77	No
Central	Horror	1.63±1.92	***4.28±2.66**	No
Central	Coaster	1.16±1.24	1.66±2.10	No
Central	Fall	0.00±0.00	0.77±1.08	No
Parietal	Horror	***2.31±1.67**	****2.95±1.37**	No
Parietal	Coaster	0.79±1.56	1.70±1.62	No
Parietal	Fall	0.00±0.00	0.85±0.90	No

TABLE VII. PSD DIFFERENCE: JAPANESE (**: P<0.01, *: P<0.05, H0: PSDDIFF = 0) - GAMMA RANGE

Area	Video stimulus	PSDdiff no touch	PSDdiff touch	t-test 2gr
Frontal	Horror	***1.09±0.71**	***1.67±1.22**	No
Frontal	Coaster	0.82±1.45	***1.67±1.41**	No
Frontal	Fall	0.00±0.00	0.69±0.96	No
Central	Horror	2.48±3.06	***5.54±4.25**	No
Central	Coaster	2.11±2.28	2.36±3.32	No
Central	Fall	0.00±0.00	0.87±1.80	No
Parietal	Horror	***2.56±1.77**	***3.27±2.51**	No
Parietal	Coaster	1.48±2.42	2.37±2.57	No
Parietal	Fall	0.00±0.00	1.31±1.51	No

C. *Correlation between PSD and subjective fear scores, French subjects*

Tables VII-XII show the PSD differences between the three conditions (horror movie, roller coaster, and relaxing waterfall), with or without touch. The water fall condition without touch was used as a reference baseline (hence its difference is null). As in the Japanese database, the horror condition is correlated with a broadband increase of EEG activity in frontal and parietal areas, however this increase is non-significant, and not present in the delta range. Similarly, there is a general and broadband increase of EEG activity in the touch vs. no touch condition, significant in the parietal area for the roller coaster condition. The result of a T-test comparing touch vs. no-touch condition is reported in the last column.

TABLE VIII. PSD DIFFERENCE: FRENCH (**: P<0.01, *: P<0.05, H0: PSDDIFF = 0) - DELTA RANGE

Area	Video stimulus	PSDdiff no touch	PSDdiff touch	t-test 2gr
Frontal	Horror	0.18±0.34	***0.61±0.43**	No
Frontal	Coaster	-0.03±0.43	***0.38±0.30**	No
Frontal	Fall	0.00±0.00	0.04±0.17	No
Central	Horror	0.43±0.77	***1.13±1.13**	No
Central	Coaster	0.05±0.63	0.33±0.70	No
Central	Fall	0.00±0.00	0.06±0.14	No
Parietal	Horror	-0.01±0.30	0.32±0.35	No
Parietal	Coaster	-0.10±0.22	0.25±0.33	**Yes**
Parietal	Fall	0.00±0.00	0.01±0.19	No

TABLE IX. PSD DIFFERENCE: FRENCH (**: P<0.01, *: P<0.05, H0: PSDDIFF = 0) - THETA RANGE

Area	Video stimulus	PSDdiff no touch	PSDdiff touch	t-test 2gr
Frontal	Horror	0.13±0.63	0.35±0.56	No
Frontal	Coaster	-0.11±0.44	0.14±0.47	No
Frontal	Fall	0.00±0.00	0.01±0.25	No
Central	Horror	0.19±0.82	0.83±1.39	No
Central	Coaster	-0.10±0.63	0.13±0.81	No
Central	Fall	0.00±0.00	-0.00±0.24	No
Parietal	Horror	-0.05±0.52	0.10±0.65	No
Parietal	Coaster	-0.35±0.41	-0.03±0.60	No
Parietal	Fall	0.00±0.00	-0.08±0.39	No

TABLE X. PSD DIFFERENCE: FRENCH (**: P<0.01, *: P<0.05, H0: PSDDIFF = 0) - ALPHA RANGE

Area	Video stimulus	PSDdiff no touch	PSDdiff touch	t-test 2gr
Frontal	Horror	0.19±0.52	0.48±0.59	No
Frontal	Coaster	-0.08±0.55	0.15±0.43	No
Frontal	Fall	0.00±0.00	0.10±0.19	No
Central	Horror	0.28±0.76	0.98±1.40	No
Central	Coaster	-0.07±0.58	0.24±0.81	No
Central	Fall	0.00±0.00	0.06±0.12	No
Parietal	Horror	0.13±0.38	0.41±0.56	No
Parietal	Coaster	-0.20±0.37	0.25±0.40	No
Parietal	Fall	0.00±0.00	0.06±0.18	No

TABLE XI. PSD DIFFERENCE: FRENCH (**: P<0.01, *: P<0.05, H0: PSDDIFF = 0) - BETA RANGE

Area	Video stimulus	PSDdiff no touch	PSDdiff touch	t-test 2gr
Frontal	Horror	0.06±0.60	0.39±0.69	No
Frontal	Coaster	0.11±0.65	0.28±0.47	No
Frontal	Fall	0.00±0.00	0.19±0.28	No
Central	Horror	0.25±0.82	0.78±1.23	No
Central	Coaster	-0.02±0.62	0.42±0.70	No
Central	Fall	0.00±0.00	0.13±0.15	No
Parietal	Horror	0.13±0.38	0.48±0.58	No
Parietal	Coaster	-0.14±0.45	***0.43±0.32**	**Yes**
Parietal	Fall	0.00±0.00	0.10±0.18	No

TABLE XII. PSD DIFFERENCE: FRENCH (**: P<0.01, *: P<0.05, H0: PSDDIFF = 0) - GAMMA RANGE

Area	Video stimulus	PSDdiff no touch	PSDdiff touch	t-test 2gr
Frontal	Horror	0.05±0.64	0.45±0.67	No
Frontal	Coaster	0.21±0.57	0.34±0.46	No
Frontal	Fall	0.00±0.00	***0.25±0.23**	**Yes**
Central	Horror	0.20±0.87	0.74±1.17	No
Central	Coaster	-0.08±0.63	0.40±0.71	No
Central	Fall	0.00±0.00	***0.17±0.14**	**Yes**
Parietal	Horror	0.11±0.41	0.53±0.58	No
Parietal	Coaster	-0.13±0.46	***0.42±0.31**	**Yes**
Parietal	Fall	0.00±0.00	0.15±0.16	**Yes**

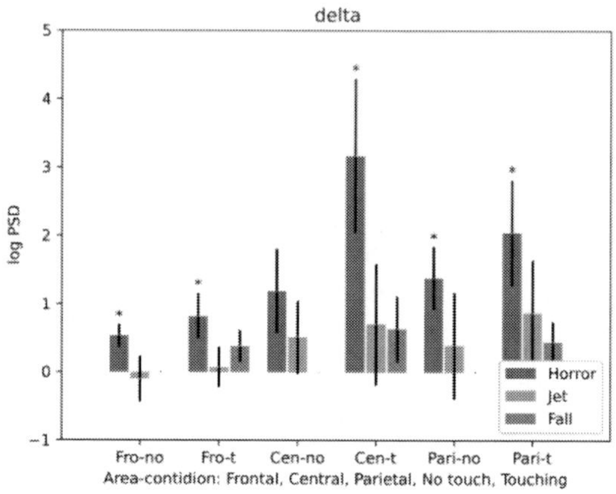

Figure 1 PSD difference: Japanese, Delta (*: p<0.05)

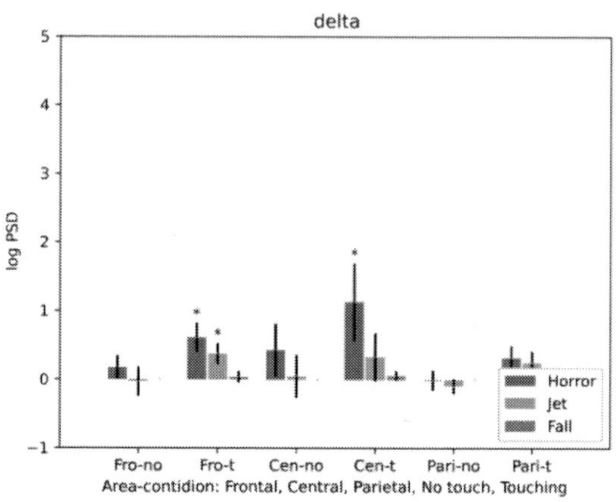

Figure 2 PSD difference: French, Delta (*: p<0.05)

IV. CONCLUSION

In both populations, we can observe similarities in the neural correlates of fear emotional regulation:

- In both populations of subject, a broadband increase of EEG activity is observed in the touch vs. non touch condition.
- More specifically, both Japanese and French subjects had a significant δ range activity increase in the frontal and central areas in touch condition, during the horror video (which was the most fearful stimulus).

Increased EEG activity in the touch condition could be a correlated of improved emotional regulation. For instance, emotional regulation in expert Zen meditators was associated with a similar phenomenon [8]. Furthermore, and more specifically, the observed in δ range increase frontal and central area is a known correlate of emotional regulation: it could reflect the inhibition exerted by the prefrontal cortex and anterior cingulate cortex over emotionally related areas [9]. This tends to confirm a cross-cultural positive effect of touching care on emotional regulation, despite potential differences in cultural representations about body contact and intimacy.

Between the two populations, we can observe differences in the neural correlates of fear emotional regulation:

- In the Japanese population, no significant difference is found in specific areas and frequency ranges when comparing touch vs. non touch cognition. In the French population, several areas presented significant changes between those conditions.
- In the French population only, parietal α activity was anti-correlated with subjective reports of fear. Note that parietal α is associated with the activity of the default mode network, which increases in relaxed state [10].

These differences could be attributed to cultural specificities in emotional regulation strategies. Indeed, previous studies have shown that Japanese subjects experience less intense fear reactions than French subjects [11]. Note that there is also a slight difference in the way the touching care stimulus was applied, which may bias these results. The French subjects had 2 female participants, not the Japanese subjects, and the age span was slightly larger; which could also have introduced some bias.

ACKNOWLEDGMENT

This research project was funded by a KDDI grant.

REFERENCES

[1] A. Debrot, D. Schoebi, M. Perrez, and A. B. Horn. "Touch as an interpersonal emotion regulation process in couples' daily lives: The mediating role of psychological intimacy," Personality and Social Psychology Bulletin. 39(10), 1373-1385.J. Clerk Maxwell, A Treatise on Electricity and Magnetism, 3rd ed., vol. 2. Oxford: Clarendon, 2013, pp. 68–73, 1892,

[2] A. Weller and R. Feldman, "Emotion regulation and touch in infants: the role of cholecystokinin and opioids," Peptides, vol. 24(5), pp. 779-788. 2003.

[3] S. G. Shamay-Tsoory and N. I. Eisenberger. "Getting in touch: A neural model of comforting touch." Neuroscience & Biobehavioral Reviews, vol. 130, pp. 263-273, 2001.4

[4] A. Korisky, N. I. Eisenberger, M. Nevat, I. Weissman-Fogel, and S. G. Shamay-Tsoory, "A dual-brain approach for understanding the neuralmechanisms that underlie the comforting effects of social touch," Cortex, vol. 127, pp. 333-346, 2020.

[5] The RooM : VR 360° horror, https://www.youtube.com/watch?v=9vgBDiDpLmU

[6] a roller coaster perspective movie, https://www.youtube.com/watch?v=injtBhJCNdA

[7] a natural water fall movie for the control condition, https://www.youtube.com/watch?v=zURLuAH

[8] H. Y. Huang and P. C. Lo, "EEG dynamics of experienced Zen meditation practitioners probed by complexity index and spectral measure," Journal of medical engineering & technology, vol. 33(4), pp. 314-321, 2009.

[9] G. Lapomarda, S. Valer, R. Job, and A. Grecucci, "Built to last: Theta and delta changes in resting-state EEG activity after regulating emotions," Brain and Behavior, vol. 12(6), e2597, 2022.

[10] J. A. Micoulaud-Franchi, J. M. Batail, T. Fovet, P. Philip, M. Cermolacce, A. Jaumard-Hakoun, and F. Vialatte, "Towards a pragmatic approach to a psychophysiological unit of analysis for mental and brain disorders: an EEG-copeia for neurofeedback,". Applied psychophysiology and biofeedback, vol. 44, pp. 151-172, 2019.

[11] K. R. Scherer, D. Matsumoto, H. G. Wallbott, and T. Kudoh, "Emotional experience in cultural context: A comparison between Europe, Japan, and the United States1," In Facets of Emotion (pp. 5-30), Psychology Press, 925 2013.

NN2EQCDT: Equivalent Transformation of Feed-Forward Neural Networks as DRL Policies into Compressed Decision Trees

Torben Logemann
Carl von Ossietzky University Oldenburg
Research Group Adversarial Resilience Learning
Oldenburg, Germany
Email: torben.logemann@uol.de

Eric MSP Veith
Carl von Ossietzky University Oldenburg
Research Group Adversarial Resilience Learning
Oldenburg, Germany
Email: eric.veith@uol.de

***Abstract*—Learning systems have achieved remarkable success. Agents trained using Deep Reinforcement Learning (RL) (DRL) methods, e.g., promise real resilience. However, no guarantees can yet be provided for the learned black-box models. For operators of Critical National Infrastructures (CNIs), this is a necessity as no responsibility can be assumed for an unknown and unvalidatable control system. Intrinsically secure learning algorithms and approximate, post-hoc interpretable models exist, but they lack either learning performance or explainability. To optimize this trade-off, this paper presents the NN2EQCDT algorithm, which equivalently transforms a Feed-Forward Deep Neural Network (DNN) (FF-DNN)-based policy into a compressed Decision Tree (DT). The compression is achieved by dynamically checking the satisfiability of the paths during construction, removing checks that are not needed further, and considering invariants. For a small policy model, NN2EQCDT was observed to drastically compress the DT, making it possible to accurately trace action regions to their observation regions in a plotted DT and visualization.**

***Keywords*—*reinforcement learning*; *explainable AI*; *equivalent transformation*; *neural network*; *decision tree*; *compression*.**

I. Introduction

Learning systems have achieved remarkable successes. DRL is at the core of many remarkable successes, beginning with its breakthrough in 2013 by end-to-end learning of Atari games [1] and Double Q-learning [2]. Further successes were made with AlphaGo (Zero), AlphaZero [3] and MuZero [4]. DRL involves learning agents with sensors and actuators to achieve specific goals through trial and error, using algorithms, such as Twin-Delayed Deep Deterministic Policy Gradient (DDPG) (TD3) [5], Proximal Policy Gradient (PPO) [6], and Soft Actor Critic (SAC) [7] have proven that they are capable of handling complex tasks. Due to its success, learning system are applied in various fields, such as the following.

- In healthcare, RL is preferred over traditional DNN methods to determine the best treatment policy [8].
- In robotics, RL agents can learn tasks, such as pouring water, reaching through a human teacher, grasping, balancing balls, and more [8].
- DRL is used in autonomous driving because of its strong interaction with the environment [9].
- In cybersecurity, DRL is used for automatic intrusion detection techniques and defense strategies [10].
- To be able to keep the power grid stable, DRL is used to train defender agents with the Adversarial Resilience Learning (ARL) framework to recover deviations from the healthy state by deploying attacker agents in an autocurriculum setting [11].

DRL agents promise true resilience by learning to counter the unknown unknowns. However, unlike intrinsically interpretable DRL models [12], no guarantees can yet be made about the behavior of DRL agents learned with black-box models. This is, however, a necessity for operators, since no responsibility can be taken for an unknown control system that cannot be validated, especially when it is used in such critical or very critical areas as CNIs.

If agents with learned black-box models are to be deployed in CNI, it is of absolute necessity to be able to provide guarantees for them, as they have the potential to significantly threaten the safety the overall system. Without guarantees, operators cannot take responsibility for such an unknown and unverifiable control system. An architecture, designed to provide such guarantees, is presented in [13], which is suitable for usage in CNIs, such as the power grid.

Agents deployed in complex environments, such as complex interconnected systems, potentially face many different situations and learn complex behaviors to cope with them according to their goals. To understand how agents achieve their goals, the effects of their strategies are studied in terms of rewards or impact on the environment. One such example is in [11], which ARL attack agents are deployed with the goal of causing voltage band violations in a power grid. They achieve this goal by exploiting a vulnerability in the deployment of voltage controllers in the used network. How the actual exploit works, is analyzed by examining the impact of the attacker actions on the victim buses. This is sufficient for commonly observed behaviors, but it is not deeply interpreted and there is no guarantee that the extracted strategy explained by the investigations is used for all situations, i.e., for all observations from the environment. This is especially important when dealing with control agents, who are expected to achieve a goal in all possible situations, e.g., defender agents, for whom the even greater problem of coping with an infinite horizon exists in the explanation.

Thus, the need arises to provide transparency to the learned strategies of agents, i.e., to approximate their behavioral model as well as possible by a more comprehensible model. This leads to the conflict of goals of wanting to construct powerful learning systems on the one hand, i.e., to rely on DRL, but on the other hand to be able to explain them afterwards with more comprehensible models, such as DTs.

DTs can be trained directly, which immediately leads to an interpretable model. On the other hand, DNNs are better regularized, which increases trainability [14]. This is particularly relevant when sampling efficiency is required, as in the training of DRL models where there may be long trajectories that need to be calculated by computationally intensive simulations. Thus, the goal is to achieve high trainability with high interpretability of the resulting model.

The main contribution to this problem of explainability of efficiently learned policies is that, in terms of input-output behavior, the presented approach transforms efficient-learnable FF-DNNs into compressed DTs to improve explainability, interpretability, and verifiability. The presented algorithm NN2EQCDT relies heavily on the equivalence description of DNNs and DTs in [15], but there are still research gaps to better use it for explainability, which will be addressed with the following contributions:

- The equivalence description of DNNs and DTs from Aytekin [15] is not so easy to implement, so this paper proposes a transformation to directly use models learned with the widely used Deep Learning (DL) framework PyTorch
- Using the equivalence transformation, the DT grows exponentially with branching. This problem is addressed by lossless compression for smaller but equivalent models, which enhances human interpretability.
- The dynamic compression method reduces the computation time significantly and may reduce the inference time of the DT.
- There may be constraints inherent in the system that affect the model but are not considered in the transformation. Therefore, these are included as invariants in the satisfiability check to further compress the DT.
- Finally, we provide an implementation [16] for the transformation of FF-DNN into equivalent, compressed DTs and the generation of visualizations from DTs.

This paper fits the conference because it aims to understand hidden knowledge of machine-learned DNNs cognitively through DTs. For the essential compression, satisfiability and other constraints are used to achieve an equivalent transformation instead of an approximation with uncertainty.

The rest of this paper is organized as follows: First, related work is presented in Section II. The construction of the equivalent compressed DT from a FF-DNN is described in general terms in Section III. All necessary components and details and their meaning are explained in later sections. In Section IV, the derivation for a right-handed linear transformation is described to be able to use PyTorch models. Dynamic path checking when adding subtrees to dynamic compression is described in Section V and further compression is described in Section VI. Furthermore, the application of the NN2EQCDT algorithm to a simple model is presented in Section VII. Finally, the presented approach is discussed in Section VIII as well as a conclusion is drawn and possible future work is described in Section IX.

II. Related Work

In general, there is a tradeoff between model readability and performance [12]. Tree-based models are, e.g., more readable than DNNs, but their performance is worse. Not only performance, but also explainability is crucial for the use of a system. If a system is not trustworthy, especially in critical environments, it will not be used. In the case of DRL, there may be concerns about correctness, or at least doubts that the black box system in question does not always behave as it should to achieve a particular goal.

There are different types of interpretability in terms of the scope and timing of information extraction [12]. Interpretable models are either global or local and either intrinsic or post-hoc. Here, scope refers to the explained domain of the model in question and the timing of information acquisition. An intrinsic model is directly interpretable by itself at creation time, like a DT. Post-hoc interpretable models are models that become interpetable only after creation, e.g., by a transformation or distillation of a black-box DNN model into an interpretable model.

DTs have a simple, understandable structure and are therefore easy to interpret [17], so they are intrinsic models. But they are not suitable to be used directly as policy representation of RL agents. Only DNN-based strategies can be efficiently obtained using existing DRL methods. One approach to optimize the tradeoff between predictive accuracy and interpretability is to train DTs from DNN-based policies or to use a more direct transformation for given states [18].

In [19], it is described that DTs can be trained from samples of pre-trained DNN policies with the (Q-)DAGGER and VIPER algorithms. Such imitation learning have the problem that much larger DTs than necessary are learned and the performance can be lower compared to the original DNN.

This approach uses efficient FF-DNN policies, but approximates the DT, which can then also become large, which in turn reduces the explainability. It is therefore less suitable for the use of the explainability of learned FF-DNN policies as agent controllers in CNIs.

III. Decision tree construction

FF-DNNs can equivalently be transformed into compressed DTs using the NN2EQCDT construction algorithm shown in Figure 1. The algorithm generates DTs by iterative computing and connecting subtrees with effective layer-wise filters from weight and bias matrices of neural networks. It shows accessing the final effective filters and computing the activation vector from the paths of the subtrees, as well as converting the final rules into expressions and compressing the whole tree. Here the algorithm is described in general and how it can be used. The individual components are explained in more detail in later sections.

$\hat{\boldsymbol{W}} = \boldsymbol{W}_0$
$\hat{\boldsymbol{B}} = \boldsymbol{B}_0^\top$
$rules$ = calc_rule_terms($\hat{\boldsymbol{W}}, \hat{\boldsymbol{B}}$)
T, new_SAT_leaves = create_initial_subtree($rules$)
set_hat_on_SAT_nodes(T, new_SAT_leaves, $\hat{\boldsymbol{W}}, \hat{\boldsymbol{B}}$)
for $i = 1, \dots, n-1$ **do**
    SAT_paths = get_SAT_paths(T)
    for SAT_path in SAT_paths **do**
        $\boldsymbol{a}$ = compute_a_along(SAT_path)
        SAT_leave = SAT_path[−1]
        $\hat{\boldsymbol{W}}, \hat{\boldsymbol{B}}$ = get_last_hat_of_leave(T, SAT_leave)
        $\hat{\boldsymbol{W}} = (\boldsymbol{W}_i \odot [(\boldsymbol{a}^\top)_{\times k}])\hat{\boldsymbol{W}}$
        $\hat{\boldsymbol{B}} = (\boldsymbol{W}_i \odot [(\boldsymbol{a}^\top)_{\times k}])\hat{\boldsymbol{B}} + \boldsymbol{B}_i^\top$
        $rules$ = calc_rule_terms($\hat{\boldsymbol{W}}, \hat{\boldsymbol{B}}$)
        new_SAT_leaves = add_subtree(T, SAT_leave, $rules$, $invariants$)
        set_hat_on_SAT_nodes(T, new_SAT_leaves, $\hat{\boldsymbol{W}}, \hat{\boldsymbol{B}}$)
convert_final_rule_to_expr(T)
compress_tree(T)

Figure 1. NN2EQCDT algorithm

The weight and bias matrices $\boldsymbol{W}_i$ and $\boldsymbol{B}_i$ from the FF-DNN model are processed layer by layer. These are used to compute rules that are used to add subtrees to the overall DT. This allows the DT to be built dynamically as the model is iterated layer by layer. From the second layer, when multiplying the weight and bias matrices, it is necessary to take into account the position of the node to which the generated subtree will be attached. This is done by applying the slope vector $\boldsymbol{a}$ to the current weight matrices. It represents the node position of the connection, since it is the vector of choices according to the ReLU activation function along the path from the root to the connection node.

When adding a node of a newly created subtree to the overall tree, each path from the root to the node in question is checked for satisfiability. If there can be no input so that its evaluation of the DT that takes this path, the node in question and thus further subtrees are not added to keep the size of the DT dynamically small. Finally, the last checks are converted into expressions, and the DT can be further compressed by removing unnecessary checks, since they are evaluated the same for all possible inputs.

IV. Derivation of the Representation with Right-Handed Linear Transformation

DTs can be constructed from the effective weight matrices $\hat{\boldsymbol{W}}$ computed by spanning and connecting subtrees through them. The algorithm for this is shown in Figure 2. It is first motivated and then explained with its construction.

$\hat{\boldsymbol{W}} = \boldsymbol{W}_0$
$\hat{\boldsymbol{B}} = \boldsymbol{B}_0^\top$
for $i = 0, \dots, n-2$ **do**
    $\boldsymbol{a} = [\,]$
    for $j = 0, \dots, m_i - 1$ **do**
        if $(\hat{\boldsymbol{W}}_j \boldsymbol{x}_0^\top + \boldsymbol{B}_j^\top)^\top > 0$ **then**
            $\boldsymbol{a}$.append(1)
        else
            $\boldsymbol{a}$.append(0)
    $\boldsymbol{W}_{i+1} \in \mathbb{R}^{m_i \times k}, \boldsymbol{a} \in \mathbb{Z}_2^{m_i}$
    $\hat{\boldsymbol{W}} = (\boldsymbol{W}_{i+1} \odot [(\boldsymbol{a}^\top)_{\times k}])\hat{\boldsymbol{W}}$
    $\hat{\boldsymbol{B}} = (\boldsymbol{W}_{i+1} \odot [(\boldsymbol{a}^\top)_{\times k}])\hat{\boldsymbol{B}} + \boldsymbol{B}_{i+1}^\top$
return $(\hat{\boldsymbol{W}}\boldsymbol{x}_0^\top + \hat{\boldsymbol{B}})^\top$

Figure 2. Algorithm for calculation of effective weight matrices with right-handed linear transformation and bias for ReLU activation function, based on [15]

In the basis of the NN2EQCDT algorithm, the linear transformation is performed with a left multiplication of the weight matrix in [15], but there is no implementation given. For an implementation there was raised the requirement, that an algorithm must be able to use FF-DNN models in the format of the widely used DL framework PyTorch to be able to effienctly reuse existing models in a quasi standard format. But unfortunately, PyTorch uses a right instead of a left side multiplication of the weight matrices [20] as follows:

$$Y_l = \boldsymbol{W}_l^\top \boldsymbol{X} + \boldsymbol{B} \qquad Y_r = \boldsymbol{X}\boldsymbol{W}_r^\top + \boldsymbol{B}$$

To construct a DT from a Pytorch model consisting of linear layers with bias and applying the activation function $\sigma = \mathrm{ReLU}$ between them, the layer-wise effective weight matrices $\hat{\boldsymbol{W}}_i$ must be computed using the right-handed linear transformation with bias as shown in Eq. (1) based on [15]. Here, the activation function is performed by multiplying the activation slopes element-wise by the weight matrices. The activation vector $\boldsymbol{a}$ must be repeated k times for the multiplication to match the size of the matrices to which it is applied. In the following equations, however, it is written simply as $\boldsymbol{a}$ when repeated to be analogous to [15].

$$\begin{aligned}
\hat{\boldsymbol{W}}_i^\top &= \sigma(\boldsymbol{x}_{i-1}\boldsymbol{W}_{i-1}^\top + \boldsymbol{B}_{i-1})\boldsymbol{W}_i^\top + \boldsymbol{B}_i \\
&= \sigma((\boldsymbol{W}_{i-1}\boldsymbol{x}_{i-1}^\top + \boldsymbol{B}_{i-1}^\top)^\top)\boldsymbol{W}_i^\top + \boldsymbol{B}_i \\
&= (\boldsymbol{a}_{i-1} \odot (\boldsymbol{W}_{i-1}\boldsymbol{x}_{i-1}^\top + \boldsymbol{B}_{i-1}^\top)^\top)\boldsymbol{W}_i^\top + \boldsymbol{B}_i \\
&= ((\boldsymbol{a}_{i-1}^\top \odot (\boldsymbol{W}_{i-1}\boldsymbol{x}_{i-1}^\top + \boldsymbol{B}_{i-1}^\top))^\top)\boldsymbol{W}_i^\top + \boldsymbol{B}_i \\
&= (\boldsymbol{W}_i(\boldsymbol{a}_{i-1}^\top \odot (\boldsymbol{W}_{i-1}\boldsymbol{x}_{i-1}^\top + \boldsymbol{B}_{i-1}^\top)))^\top + \boldsymbol{B}_i \\
&= ((\boldsymbol{W}_i^\top \odot \boldsymbol{a}_{i-1}^\top)^\top(\boldsymbol{W}_{i-1}\boldsymbol{x}_{i-1}^\top + \boldsymbol{B}_{i-1}^\top))^\top + \boldsymbol{B}_i \\
&= ((\boldsymbol{W}_i \odot \boldsymbol{a}_{i-1})(\boldsymbol{W}_{i-1}\boldsymbol{x}_{i-1}^\top + \boldsymbol{B}_{i-1}^\top))^\top + \boldsymbol{B}_i \\
&= (((\boldsymbol{W}_i \odot \boldsymbol{a}_{i-1})(\boldsymbol{W}_{i-1}\boldsymbol{x}_{i-1}^\top + \boldsymbol{B}_{i-1}^\top)) + \boldsymbol{B}_i^\top)^\top \qquad (1)
\end{aligned}$$

The recursive form in Eq. (1) can be used to formulate a general closed of as shown in Eq. (2) based on [15]. It is equivalent to the right-handed linear transformation with bias and ReLU activation function.

$$
\begin{aligned}
\mathrm{NN}(\boldsymbol{x}_0) &= (\ldots((\boldsymbol{W}_1 \odot \boldsymbol{a}_0)(\boldsymbol{W}_0\boldsymbol{x}_0^\top + \boldsymbol{B}_0^\top) + \boldsymbol{B}_1^\top)\ldots)^\top \\
&= (\ldots(\underbrace{(\boldsymbol{W}_1 \odot \boldsymbol{a}_0)\boldsymbol{W}_0}_{\hat{\boldsymbol{W}}_{1,a_0}}\boldsymbol{x}_0^\top + \underbrace{(\boldsymbol{W}_1 \odot \boldsymbol{a}_0)\boldsymbol{B}_0^\top + \boldsymbol{B}_1^\top}_{\hat{\boldsymbol{B}}_{1,a_0}})\ldots)^\top
\end{aligned}
\tag{2}
$$

The corresponding algorithm for a simple FF-DNN with linear transformation, bias, and ReLU activation function is shown in Figure 2. The subscript j of $\hat{\boldsymbol{W}}_j \in \mathbb{R}^{1\times fs}$ with $\boldsymbol{x}_0 \in \mathbb{R}^{bs\times fs}$ and a batch size of $bs \geq 1$ and a feature size of $fs \geq 1$ refers to the j-th row of the current $\hat{\boldsymbol{W}} \in \mathbb{R}^{k\times fs}$, but the subscript $i+1$ of $\boldsymbol{W}_{i+1}$ refers to the weight matrix of the $i+1$-th layer and not to a row. The same is true for the bias matrix. $[(\boldsymbol{a}^\top)_{\times k}]$ means that the transposed vector $\boldsymbol{a}^\top \in \mathbb{R}^{m_i\times 1}$ is repeated line by line k times.

To better understand the application of the algorithm in Figure 2, a simple example of converting the XOR function into a DT is given in Figure 3. The XOR function is represented by the following weight matrices of linear layers without bias as in the example for the EC-DT algorithm of [21]:

$$
\boldsymbol{W}_0 = \begin{bmatrix} 1 & -1 \\ -1 & 1 \end{bmatrix} \qquad \boldsymbol{W}_1 = \begin{bmatrix} 1 & 1 \end{bmatrix}
$$

Each coefficient of a row of $\hat{\boldsymbol{W}}_i$ is linearly expanded and used as a split point rule with ReLU activation function. After a layer, only the $\hat{\boldsymbol{W}}_{i+1,\boldsymbol{a}}$ with the respective previous activations $\boldsymbol{a}$ are used for branching.

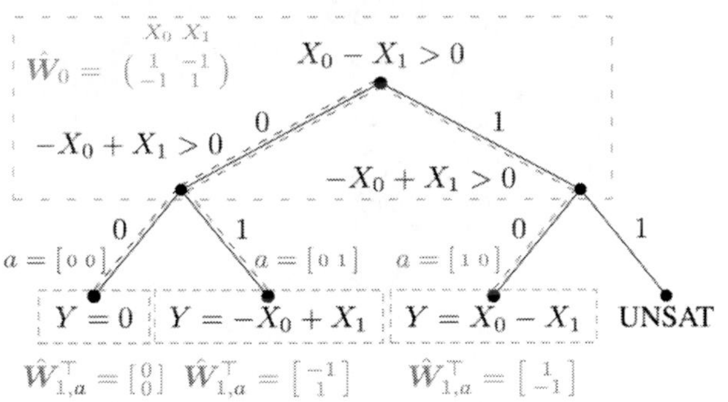

Figure 3. Simple example of an DT representing an XOR function constructed using the algorithm of Figure 2 without bias based on an example of the EC-DT algorithm [21]

In the algorithm in Figure 2, the calculation of $\hat{\boldsymbol{W}}$ requires the next weight or bias matrix. The iteration index can be equivalently converted from $i+1$ to i by iterating with **for** $i = 1, \ldots, n-1$ **do**. Thus, the last effective weight or bias matrix is required for the calculation of the current weight or bias matrix and of the next subtree to be attached. This is used in the NN2EQCDT algorithm in Figure 1 to be able to use the last instead of the next effective weight and bias matrices. To access them in the current iteration, they are stored in the iteration before by appending them to all SAT nodes of the subtrees they span.

In addition to the last effective and current weight or bias matrix, the activation vector $\boldsymbol{a}$ is also needed for the calculation of the new effective weight or bias matrix. In the concept algorithm in Figure 2, it is computed by using the input to branch to different activations. When converting the concept into an implementation of a dynamic design in Figure 1, the activation vector is required for each temporary SAT node for which the next effective weight and bias matrices are computed and attached as a subtree. Since the activation vector corresponds to the branches of a path, it is computed along it in the DT as seen in Figure 3.

V. Dynamic Path Checking when Adding Subtrees

In a DT spanned by the algorithm in Figure 2, there may be regions that are invalid due to conflicting categorizations. For example, the split point rule $x > 0$ and its inverse $x \leq 0$ contradict each other, so they are not jointly satisfiable. If such jointly unsatisfiable split point rules occur along a path in a tree, the path is invalid from that point on.

When a subtree is added to the entire DT, the joint satisfiability of all path rules is checked to avoid unnecessary calculation of additional paths that cannot be satisfied. If a path is not satisfiable from a certain node, there is no input where the evaluation of the DT follows the path from the node in question. The path is then terminated with an UNSAT node, as seen in Figure 3. Since the path cannot be followed any further, further checks and associated nodes and subtrees are not required. As a result, node concatenation and subtree computation can be stopped from this node. In this way, the DT is dynamically compressed in the design phase, but is still equivalent to the input FF-DNN, since only unreachable checks are omitted.

In addition to path rules, other constraints, such as input ranges or output checks for input ranges can also be used as invariants by expressing them as assertions. This allows the DT to be further compressed while maintaining equivalence, since further potentially unnecessary nodes can be omitted due to the invariants. All related assertions, such as path assertions and general input domain assertions can be written in the Satisfiability Modulo Theories (SMT) format and are checked for satisfiability together with the SMT solver Z3 [22].

Since path generation can be dynamically stopped at certain nodes, entire subtrees may not be computed. This can compress an DT and increase the overall computation time while maintaining an equivalent representation.

VI. Further Tree Compression

In addition to pruning the DT when it is created, it can be further compressed by deleting checks in it that are evaluated the same for their entire direct input space and are therefore not needed to distinguish inputs from each other. If an DT is created while its paths are dynamically checked for satisfiability, it can have UNSAT nodes as leaves, as seen in Figure 3. This example can be compressed, as seen in Figure 4, by removing the right-hand check $-X_0 + X_1 > 0$, which evaluates to false for all inputs, since the root check $X_0 - X_1 > 0$ evaluates to true in this branch.

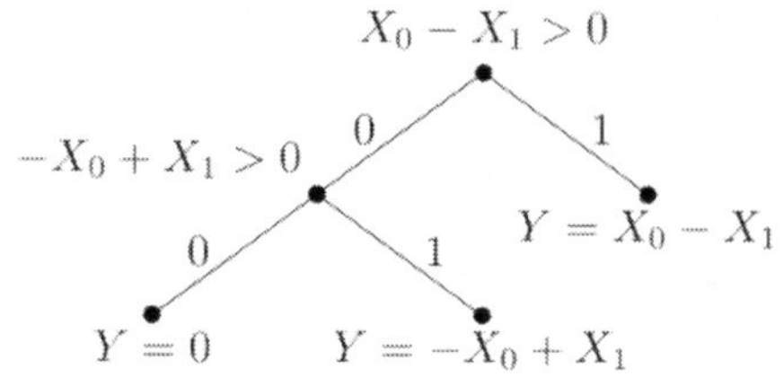

Figure 4. Simple compression example using DT from Figure 3

In any case, the rule of a parent node to an UNSAT node is evaluated on the further path of the non-UNSAT node, since the rules and their evaluations of the nodes preceding it in the path cuts the input space to this evaluation region. Since there is otherwise no input to evaluate, the rule check of a parent node to an UNSAT node can be omitted. Therefore, the entire parent node of an UNSAT node can be replaced by the non-UNSAT child node and its associated subtree, without the DT losing accuracy compared to the neural network model. This operation is therefore consistent with the goal of equivalent transformation of a neural network into a DT.

VII. Application to Simple Model

A simple controller model was trained using the DDPG algorithm for MountainCarContinuous-v0 environment (MCC) [23], [24]. Originally an actor model shown in Figure 5 was trained with larger hidden size of *hid* = 64. Since it is not necessary and more difficult to further analyse a model of that size a student model with *hid* = 8 and MSE-loss was destilled from the larger one only in the relevant region of $x \in [-1.2, 0.6]$ and $y \in [-0.7, 0.07]$ and stepsize of 0.1. It was visually found to perform about the same as the larger model [16].

```
nn.Sequential(
    nn.Linear(2,   hid, bias=True), nn.ReLU(),
    nn.Linear(hid, hid, bias=True), nn.ReLU(),
    nn.Linear(hid,   1, bias=True)
)
```

Figure 5. Actor model in PyTorch with variable hidden size

The smaller student model was then converted to an equivalent compressed DT using the algorithm from Figure 1. DTs are represented by networkx graphs that can be plotted with pyvis, as shown for the simple control example in Figure 6. The rules and expressions are node labels that are not visible at this zoom factor. Both models have the same output ($\delta = 1e{-}4$) for a sampled grid, strongly confirming the correctness of the implementation. The relevant input range was specified as an invariant for further compression.

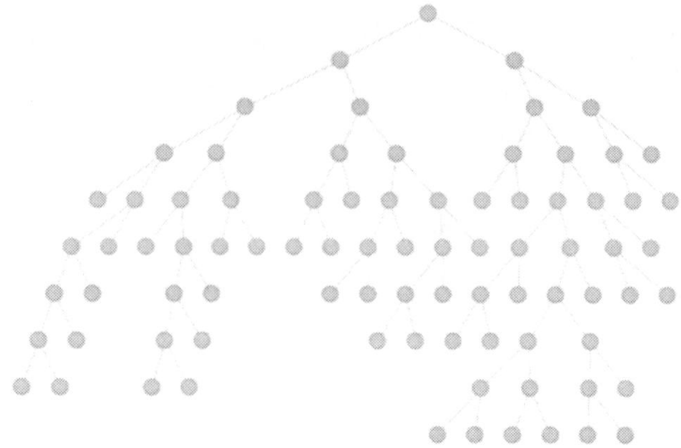

Figure 6. Compressed DT equivalent to the FF-DNN of a MCC controller

The different regions of a DT can be easily separated for 2D inputs. If the expressions for each input are to be visualized, they can be evaluated for the corresponding decision region and plotted as a third dimension, as shown in Figure 7. The points for the 2D regions (x and y) are obtained by implicitly plotting with sympy. The values for the z dimension are evaluated for each x and y point by the final expression and then drawn as a scatter plot using plotly. The gaps between the planes are due to a plotting problem, the input space is actually completely covered.

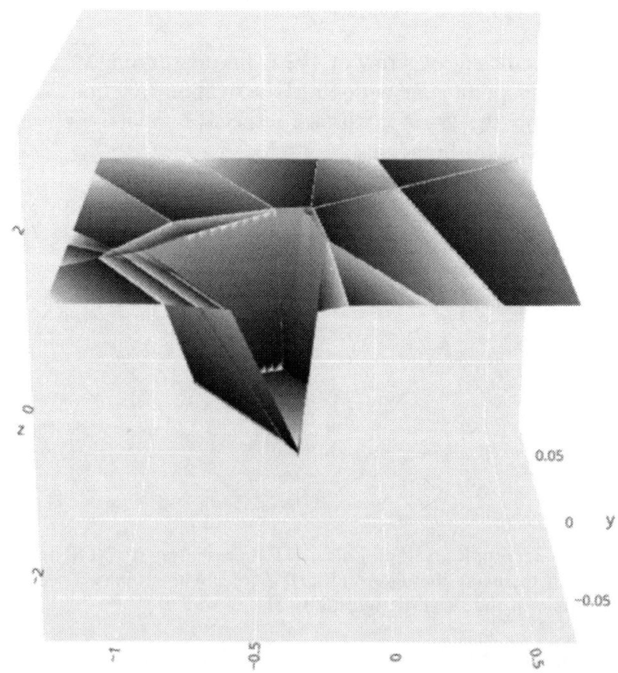

Figure 7. 3D visualization of DT regions for the MCC example

The compressed DT from the example in Figure 6 contains 83 nodes. It was computed with a median computation time of 9.75s as seen in Figure 8.

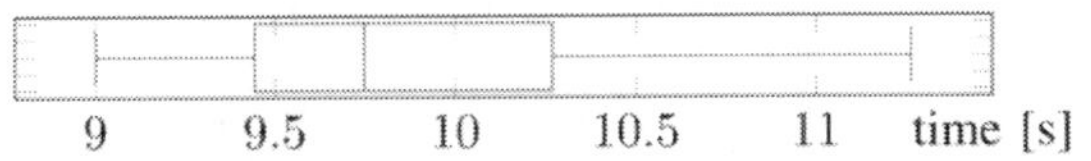

Figure 8. Boxplot ($n = 30$) for the computation time of the NN2EQCDT algorithm for the simple model

The amount of nodes of a DT according to the equivalence description of [15] without compression can be calculated with the following formula. It depends on the depth of each layer $d = \sum_{i=0}^{n-2} m_i$ with the number of filters in each layer m_i.

$$\#_{\text{nodes}} = \sum_{i=0}^{d-1} 2^i$$

This formula was tested by computing the DT with the equivalence description but without compression and summing the number of nodes for different Linear-ReLU FF-DNN architectures and hidden sizes. For an architecture as in Figure 5, it can be calculated as $d = 2 + 2hid$. Thus, for $hid = 8$, such a DT already consists of $\sum_{i=0}^{18-1} 2^i = 262143$ nodes, which corresponds to a compression ratio of 99.97% with respect to the number of nodes. At this size, the computation was aborted after a computation time of 1.5h. However, for other small sizes of *hid*, it was also observed that the computation time without compression starts to explode compared to the computation with compression.

VIII. Discussion

The principle of equivalence description of Aytekin [15] could be verified by implementation, testing and application to a simple model. The presented compression method seems to be a useful tool in transformation to increase the explainability of FF-DNN-based DRL policies, since the transformed, relatively small DT model and visualization can be used to trace actions back to observations. But in this form it is not meaningful enough to intuitively recognize a learned strategy. Probably, for this, the environment with its dynamics must be included in order to explain the agent's reactions and their effects on the next observations.

The transformation was successfully tested on a learned DRL model in a benchmarking environment. The results are summarized in Table I. However, the calculated compression ratio of 99.97% cannot be assumed to be representative without further evaluations. Also, a general statement about the performance of this approach for more complex environments and larger models cannot be made yet.

The NN2EQCDT algorithm can in principle transform arbitrary Linear-ReLU FF-DNN with any size for the input and output dimensions. The number of coefficients and variables in the transformed DT would then correspond to the size of the input dimension and the number of output values would then correspond to the size of the output dimension, but this has not yet been implemented due to implementation difficulties. Also, only three dimensions can be easily visualized together, more dimensions require more work and possibly information splitting or reduction.

Table I. Comparison of results or calculations for the construction of a DT from the simple model without and with compression of the NN2EQCDT algorithm

Compression	$\#_{\text{nodes}}$	Computation time
☐	262143	> 1.5h
☑	83	9.75s

IX. Conclusion and Future Work

In this paper, an algorithm capable of equivalently transforming a FF-DNN into a compressed DT was presented. Using a simple model, it was shown that a compressed DT may be significantly smaller than one without compression.

This approach can be used to trace the output regions exactly to the input regions. It can furthermore be a useful tool to accurately analyze the behavior of black-box models of FF-DNN. Furthermore, if a FF-DNN was learned as a DRL policy for an agent in a CNI, this approach has the potential to fundamentally strengthen the explainability, operator confidence, and hopefully the safety of the system.

For future work, better benchmarking of the algorithm in terms of computation time and compression ratio could be interesting. To better counteract unkown-unkowns in explaining FF-DNN models as DRL policies, the learned policies should be better analyzed with such an equivalently transformation approach. Therefore, we will attempt to combine the agent model with a learned world model and identify useful metrics based solely on the agent model and its traceability of output to input DT regions to indicate specific behaviors.

In particular, we will try to explain the learned strategy of ARL attack agents without unknown-unkowns using this approach. In addition, for visualization of more than three dimensions together, multiple combinations of three dimensions or other reduction methods, such as Principle Component Analysis (PCA) may be of interest. The implementation of the transformation could further be generalized to arbitrary sizes of input and output dimensions. And furthermore, for other use cases, it could also be interesting to use other layers for exact transformations.

Acknowledgements

This work was funded by the German Federal Ministry for Education and Research (BMBF) under Grant No. 01IS22071.

References

[1] V. Mnih *et al.*, "Playing atari with deep reinforcement learning," *CoRR*, vol. abs/1312.5602, pp. 1–9, 2013, [retrieved: 05, 2023]. arXiv: 1312.5602. [Online]. Available: http://arxiv.org/abs/1312.5602.

[2] H. Van Hasselt, A. Guez, and D. Silver, "Deep reinforcement learning with double q-learning," in *Proceedings of the Thirtieth AAAI Conference on Artificial Intelligence, February 12-17, 2016, Phoenix, Arizona, USA*, vol. 30, AAAI Press, 2016, pp. 2094–2100.

[3] D. Silver *et al.*, "A general reinforcement learning algorithm that masters chess, shogi, and go through self-play," *Science*, vol. 362, no. 6419, pp. 1140–1144, 2018.

[4] J. Schrittwieser *et al.*, "Mastering atari, go, chess and shogi by planning with a learned model," *Nature*, vol. 588, no. 7839, pp. 604–609, 2020.

[5] S. Fujimoto, H. Hoof, and D. Meger, "Addressing function approximation error in actor-critic methods," in *Proceedings of the 35th International Conference on Machine Learning, ICML 2018, Stockholmsmässan, Stockholm, Sweden, July 10-15, 2018*, ser. Proceedings of Machine Learning Research, PMLR, vol. 80, 2018, pp. 1587–1596.

[6] J. Schulman, F. Wolski, P. Dhariwal, A. Radford, and O. Klimov, "Proximal policy optimization algorithms," *CoRR*, vol. abs/1707.06347, Jul. 19, 2017, [retrieved: 05, 2023]. arXiv: 1707.06347. [Online]. Available: http://arxiv.org/abs/1707.06347.

[7] T. Haarnoja, A. Zhou, P. Abbeel, and S. Levine, "Soft actor-critic: Off-policy maximum entropy deep reinforcement learning with a stochastic actor," *CoRR*, vol. abs/1801.01290, 2018, [retrieved: 05, 2023]. arXiv: 1801.01290. [Online]. Available: http://arxiv.org/abs/1801.01290.

[8] M. Naeem, S. T. H. Rizvi, and A. Coronato, "A gentle introduction to reinforcement learning and its application in different fields," *IEEE access*, vol. 8, pp. 209 320–209 344, 2020.

[9] A. E. Sallab, M. Abdou, E. Perot, and S. Yogamani, "Deep reinforcement learning framework for autonomous driving," *Electronic Imaging*, vol. 29, no. 19, pp. 70–76, Jan. 2017, [retrieved: 05, 2023]. DOI: 10.2352/issn.2470-1173.2017.19.avm-023. [Online]. Available: https://library.imaging.org/ei/articles/29/19/art00012.

[10] T. T. Nguyen and V. J. Reddi, "Deep reinforcement learning for cyber security," *IEEE Transactions on Neural Networks and Learning Systems*, pp. 1–17, 2021. DOI: 10.1109/TNNLS.2021.3121870.

[11] E. M. S. P. Veith, A. Wellßow, and M. Uslar, "Learning new attack vectors from misuse cases with deep reinforcement learning," *Frontiers in Energy Research*, vol. 11, pp. 01–23, 2023, [retrieved: 05, 2023], ISSN: 2296-598X. DOI: 10.3389/fenrg.2023.1138446. [Online]. Available: https://www.frontiersin.org/articles/10.3389/fenrg.2023.1138446.

[12] E. Puiutta and E. M. S. P. Veith, "Explainable reinforcement learning: A survey," in *Machine Learning and Knowledge Extraction. CD-MAKE 2020*, vol. 12279, Dublin, Ireland: Springer, Cham, 2020, pp. 77–95. DOI: 10.1007/978-3-030-57321-8_5.

[13] E. M. Veith, "An architecture for reliable learning agents in power grids," *ENERGY 2023 : The Thirteenth International Conference on Smart Grids, Green Communications and IT Energy-aware Technologies*, pp. 13–16, 2023, [retrieved: 05, 2023], ISSN: 2308-412X. [Online]. Available: https://www.thinkmind.org/articles/energy_2023_1_30_30028.pdf.

[14] J. Ba and R. Caruana, "Do deep nets really need to be deep?" *Advances in Neural Information Processing Systems*, vol. 27, pp. 2654–2662, 2014.

[15] Ç. Aytekin, "Neural networks are decision trees," *CoRR*, vol. abs/2210.05189, pp. 1–8, 2022, [retrieved: 05, 2023]. arXiv: 2210.05189. [Online]. Available: https://arxiv.org/abs/2210.05189.

[16] T. Logemann, *Nn2eqcdt implementation*, [retrieved: 05, 2023], 2023. [Online]. Available: https://gitlab.com/arl-experiments/nn2eqcdt.

[17] M. Du, N. Liu, and X. Hu, "Techniques for interpretable machine learning," *Communications of the ACM*, vol. 63, no. 1, pp. 68–77, 2019.

[18] Y. Qing, S. Liu, J. Song, and M. Song, "A survey on explainable reinforcement learning: Concepts, algorithms, challenges," *CoRR*, vol. abs/2211.06665, pp. 1–25, 2022, [retrieved: 05, 2023]. arXiv: 2211.06665. [Online]. Available: https://arxiv.org/abs/2211.06665.

[19] O. Bastani, Y. Pu, and A. Solar-Lezama, "Verifiable reinforcement learning via policy extraction," *Advances in neural information processing systems*, vol. 31, pp. 2499–2509, 2018.

[20] PyTorch Foundation, *Pytorch linear*, [retrieved: 05, 2023], 2023. [Online]. Available: https://pytorch.org/docs/stable/generated/torch.nn.Linear.html.

[21] D. T. Nguyen, K. E. Kasmarik, and H. A. Abbass, "Towards interpretable deep neural networks: An exact transformation to multi-class multivariate decision trees," *CoRR*, vol. abs/2003.04675, pp. 1–57, 2020, [retrieved: 05, 2023]. arXiv: 2003.04675. [Online]. Available: https://arxiv.org/abs/2003.04675.

[22] L. De Moura and N. Bjørner, "Z3: An efficient smt solver," in *Tools and Algorithms for the Construction and Analysis of Systems: 14th International Conference, TACAS 2008, Held as Part of the Joint European Conferences on Theory and Practice of Software, ETAPS 2008, Budapest, Hungary. Proceedings 14*, Springer, vol. 4963, 2008, pp. 337–340.

[23] A. W. Moore, "Efficient memory-based learning for robot control," University of Cambridge, Computer Laboratory, Tech. Rep. UCAM-CL-TR-209, 1990, [retrieved: 05, 2023], pp. 1–248. DOI: 10.48456/tr-209. [Online]. Available: https://www.cl.cam.ac.uk/techreports/UCAM-CL-TR-209.pdf.

[24] Farama Foundation, *Mountain car continuous*, Gymnasium Documentation, [retrived: 05, 2023], 2023. [Online]. Available: https://gymnasium.farama.org/environments/classic_control/mountain_car_continuous/.

International Academy, Research,
and Industry Association (IARIA)
412 Derby Way
Wilmington, DE 19810

ISBN 978-1-7138-8094-3

9 781713 880943

CURRAN ASSOCIATES INC.
proceedings.com

Ninth International Conferences on Advances in Multimedia (MMEDIA 2017)

Held at NexComm 2017

Venice, Italy
23 - 27 April 2017